A Rare Woman's Club
The First Hundred Years of the Westport Woman's Club
1907–2007

A Rare Woman's Club

The First Hundred Years of the
Westport Woman's Club
1907–2007

Dustjacket painting by Jacquie Coleman

The Westport Woman's Club
44 Imperial Avenue
Westport, Connecticut 06880

(203) 227-4240 tel.
(203) 227-0367 fax

e-mail: westportwomansclub@sbglobal.net

WWW.WESTPORTWOMANSCLUB.ORG

ISBN-13: 978-0-615-13957-9

34 Main Street #9
Amherst, Massachusetts 01002
www.modernmemoirs.com
413-253-2353

Publication of this book was made possible by
the kindness and generosity of
Marian Mabee Harding,
friend of the Westport Woman's Club.

Collect

Keep us, oh God, from pettiness.

Let us be large in thought, in word, in deed.

Let us be done with fault-finding and leave off self-seeking.

May we put away all pretense and meet each other face to face, without self-pity and without prejudice.

May we never be hasty in judgment and always be generous.

Let us take time for all things.

Make us to grow calm, serene, gentle.

Teach us to put into action our better impulses, straightforward and unafraid.

Grant that we may realize it is the little things that create differences.

That in the big things of life we are as one.

And may we strive to touch and to know the great common human heart of us all.

And, oh Lord God, let us not forget to be kind.

—Mary Stewart, 1904

Table of Contents

Collect 7

Preface 11

Acknowledgements 13

Introductory 15

The Beginning 17

The Founding Years, 1907–1908 19

The Formative Years, 1909–1916 26

The War Years, 1917–1919 29

Years of Diversification and Growth, 1919–1925 32

From WTIA to WWC, 1926–1940 43

The War Years and After, 1941–1950 55

After the War—Back to Business 67

Achievements, National Recognition, Emerging Problems, 1950–1960 79

WWC's Historic Role in Establishing the Town's Public Health Services 90

The Golden Anniversary—1957—A Celebrated Milestone 98

The Years of Consolidation, 1960–1972 101

The Greening of the Post Road Begins, 1972–1982 112

Proclamation of 1982 119

Momentum Regained, 1982–1990 121

A Shift from Leadership to Participation and Celebration, 1991–2000 .... *130*

The End of the First Centennial, 2001–2007 .... *138*

The First 100 Years—Who Were These Women? *144*

"How to Be a Clubwoman in One Easy Lesson"—Ina Bradley *148*

The Community Joins in to Celebrate the First 100 Years *152*

Proclamation of 2007 .... *154*

Now, for the Next 100 Years! *155*

APPENDIX A—Officers and Boards of Directors Over the Years *157*

INDEX *179*

Preface

It is very easy for me to say that the town of Westport, Connecticut would not be what it is today without the influence of the Westport Woman's Club (WWC). What began in 1907, with twenty women on a mission to make Westport a better place, developed into a thriving organization that I believe far exceeded their wildest dreams. The Club grew to include over 300 members and has consistently provided essential social services to the community.

In addition to all the WWC women who have worked so tirelessly through the decades, there has been a host of men who not only gave emotional support to their wives, but also gave of their time and labor in assisting their wives in the Club's mission. These men provided strong backs, cooking skills, and skillfully manned the beer booth at the Yankee Doodle Fair. Husbands have helped by moving the Steinway piano from one side of the stage to the other for fund-raisers. Men (including my husband, Hal) have volunteered technical and computer help whenever needed.

In creating this book, Peter and Eileen Petropoulos have given an invaluable contribution to the Westport Woman's Club. They worked for years, spending endless hours researching old records, newspaper clippings, and "The Minutes" to compile a text that overflows with rich history, lore, and goodwill. Unfortunately, Peter's untimely death prevented him from seeing the book in its completed form. I know he would have been as proud as we are to have this book—a true legacy for all to enjoy.

Faith in the WWC has been also expressed through grants from foundations, contributions from service organizations, and personal contributions. Marian M. Harding, a long-time Westport resident and community activist, was not a member of the Club, but she thought so highly of its accomplishments that in her last will and testament, she bequeathed a sum of money to the Westport Woman's Club. It is through her admiration of the Club and her generosity that it became possible to publish this book, and I am honored to keep her memory alive in this manner.

In addition, Mary Cina, Westport resident and friend, contributed her meticulous skills in creating the index for this book.

Serving the Westport Woman's Club as president for the past two years has given me the opportunity to continue a legacy that began with an indomitable group of twenty women who gathered together one warm summer evening in 1907. They worked diligently to make Westport a better place to live. My hope now is that the women of the Club and of Westport will continue, with the same spirit and wisdom, the work that was begun a hundred years ago.

Barbara Levy, WWC President
May 2007

Acknowledgements

This history of the first hundred years of the Westport Woman's Club would have been impossible without Carol Panish's outstanding document, *History of the Woman's Club,* which eloquently covered the Club's achievements from 1907 to 1972.

We also want to acknowledge the resources we used in expanding on Carol's work and in extending the Club's history to the current period:

Woody Klein's book *Westport, Connecticut* provided valuable insight and coverage of activities affecting the community. *Westport... A Special Place,* written and beautifully compiled by Eve Potts and designed by Howard Munce, who provided several photographs. Tom Ghianuly, owner of Compo Center Barber Shop, loaned us some of his many photographs of historic Westport. The Westport Weston Health District's archives and their staff helped to expand the history of the development of the town's health services and its evolution into Connecticut's first health district. *The New York Times* and *Life* magazine archives turned up a variety of previously unreported commentary on several episodes of the Club's early history. Local newspaper coverage of special WWC events helped provide a community's perspective on many of these events. *The Westport Town Crier & Herald's* special supplement on February 28, 1957 provided valuable coverage of the events the Westport Woman's Club's Golden Anniversary celebrated. *The Westport News'* special supplement on April 2, 1982 did the same with the Westport Woman's Club's 75th Anniversary.

Club members Susan Mahar and Gerry Munce found, researched, and catalogued countless noteworthy clippings and photographs. Past presidents Nat Sylander, Winnie Martinek, and Barbara Culp helped research and edit events covered.

Most of this material was not used in its original form. Many of the original sources are not clearly identified and their individual contributions cannot be adequately shown. Our task was to find and edit existing documents, sort out their relevance to significant events, create a larger context for them, and integrate them into a chronicle of the Westport Woman's Club's first 100 years. And we have added information and illustrations that may provide further insights and historic perspective to what took place.

It was an honor and a privilege to play this role in documenting the history of *A Rare Woman's Club.*

Eileen Petropoulos, WWC Historian
May 2007

Introductory

I n the first decade of the twentieth century, the town of Westport, Connecticut was a typical New England community some 4,200 strong. It was not yet discovered by the artists, the writers and the commuters who later were to give it the unique essence of urban sophistication combined with the small town flavor it has today.

Main Street, Westport, Conn.

At that time, there wasn't a paved road in town. With the coming of the automobile, much talk was heard about the costs and merits of oil-spraying roads versus water-spraying to alleviate the threat of the dirt roads being blown away in clouds of dust. The State Street trolley, converted from horse-drawn to electrically operated in 1936, was still the principal means of transportation. It was quite the news in town one day when the trolley lost its brakes and careened madly down the State Street hill at 25 miles an hour, to the consternation of passengers and spectators alike.

There was no radio to beguile the long winter evenings. Nor were there motion-picture theaters (cinemas) to entice people to go out. Families were home-oriented, and a social evening might involve some rounds of whist or a songfest at the piano. Community life centered around the church. Other interests manifest in the town were the Westport Dramatic Club, the Current Events Club, the Musical Society, and the Historical Society.

This, then, was a period of community consciousness and a period of joining together to pursue common interests.

In 1907, in Westport, Connecticut, a small group of women organized for the purpose of cleaning the town streets, caring for and planting trees, and laying sidewalks. They called themselves the *Woman's Town Improvement Association* (WTIA).

The WTIA was one of the most potent civic groups ever to flourish in Westport. Government did not do then what it does now. Nor were there all the social service organizations that are commonplace today. The WTIA, the forerunner of the Westport Woman's Club, concerned

itself with issues such as improving the beach, putting in sidewalks, the incineration of garbage—whatever was needed to make Westport a better place. The needs of less fortunate citizens were seen to through club scholarships and the gradual initiation of an array of services, especially during the Great Depression years.

The programs the Westport Woman's Club has since initiated for the town are numerous. The "Greening of the Post Road" and Canal Green are but two firsts. The Visiting Nurse Service was started by the Club in 1925 and turned over to the town in 1960. Free dental clinics, vaccination clinics, well-child clinics, tuberculosis campaigns, free milk distribution, polio saliva tests, a lending service of sickroom equipment—all these were inaugurated by the Club.

The Club pioneered classes for developmentally challenged school children by conducting experimental classes with a trained teacher and volunteers for three years until the program was integrated into the local schools. The Club has worked closely with the schools on many projects from the earliest years and it currently awards academic scholarships to deserving students.

It was the Club that introduced the idea of a "visiting teacher" to consult with parents—the counterpart of today's guidance counselor. It also gave Westport its first school nurse, dental hygienist, and district nurse.

The now-independent Visiting Homemaker Service was maintained by the Club from 1960 to 1965. Later, the Club actively supported organizations that worked to combat the drug problem and assist in rehabilitation programs. In 1975, the Club started an Emergency Food Distribution Program for the local needy under the leadership of Volunteer Services. In 1976, this program was extended to include an Emergency Fund. The program continues to this day.

The WTIA was concerned as well with the history and traditions of the community and the honoring of patriotic anniversaries. Thus, in 1921, it sponsored the historical pageant in which artists and other citizens celebrated the Fourth of July. Such entertainments were true community events, a magnet for people from all the strata of Westport. Nationally renowned artist Ossip Linde's daughter remembers the summer festivals in which fellow artists participated.

Howard Munce

Howard Munce, a leader in preserving the town's artistic heritage, recalls later Yankee Doodle Fairs, when the age of illustration was still golden. There, lined up during afternoons and evenings, would be a battery of prominent illustrators doing portraits of fellow townspeople for a dollar apiece, the money, of course, going to charity. Howard Munce—artist, designer, teacher—has been part of the Westport art scene since the 1930s. In 1963, after a sixteen-year career as an advertising agency art director, he turned to freelance graphic design, illustration, writing, and teaching.

Munce, curator for the "Westport Artists and Their Models" exhibit at the Historical Society, is an illustrator and a painter. He has many anecdotes about artists who made up Westport's large community of mid-twentieth century illustrators, such as Steven Dohanos, who illustrated 139 covers for the *Saturday Evening Post*.

In the cultural arena, the Club has given the community countless art shows, musical events, handicraft programs and drama productions.

In sum, the Westport Woman's Club has a successful history of answering calls for "help where needed" and in recognizing areas of need before calls for help go out.

Star Pitcher
Steven Dohanos

The early years of the twentieth century saw the creation of an organization unique for the times, an association dedicated to the social and material betterment of the town. This organization was to evolve into the Westport Woman's Club of today.

Mrs. William G. Staples, founder of Westport WTIA

Westport was still a country town in those days—an old one, to be sure, with its rural complacency unruffled by forebodings of an evolution toward suburbanism. And in Westport, during that summer of 1907, Mrs. William G. (Mary Coley) Staples, whose name was by no means unfamiliar to the townspeople, decided that the time had come, now that her children were grown, to get underway with a long-cherished plan.

Mrs. Staples had no special interest in women's suffrage. She had no desire to get out and haggle with politicians, though she did plenty of that before she was through. She merely wanted to clean up Westport—to clean it up just as she might clean up her attic, her cellar, or her own backyard. And she wasn't particularly concerned with obtaining a Constitutional amendment in order to do it.

The materialization of this plan was the formation of the Woman's Town Improvement Association.

For some months, Mrs. Staples had been laying groundwork for her project. When she attended meetings of the Compo Reading Club, she chatted with other members about her idea. When she went to the Current Events Club, she did the same. "If I can get them all enthusiastic," she said, "then we'll have a big crowd at our first meeting." And she succeeded. Upwards of 75 women attended the August 12, 1907 meeting, where the purpose of the organization was stated and approved; i.e., "...cleaning of town streets, caring for and planting trees on outskirts of town, laying sidewalks that were needed, etc."

First to sign her name to the roster of members was Mrs. John F. Godillot, a future Secretary, and later Mrs. Staples' successor as President of the organization. Others who signed up that day or shortly thereafter were Mrs. Channing Harris, Mrs. Isaac Wakeman, Miss L.V.M. Thomas, Miss Edith Wheeler, Mrs. Arnold Schlaet, Mrs. Wm. H. Smith, Mrs. F. M. Salmon, Mrs. W. S. Adams, and Mrs. D. B. Bradley.

Within a week, a constitution was adopted and the membership fee set at a dollar. In the short space of five weeks, the 20 members of this infant organization had put their shoulders to the wheel and completed arrangements for their first money-raising affair, "A Woodland Festival."

At the August 12, 1907 meeting, the WTIA was founded by a group of over 20 women who gathered in the Westport Reading Room (a room in the "brick block" on State Street, which was the precursor of the Westport Public Library). The minutes of this meeting were short and to the point:

> *In spite of the fact that Monday was a very warm day, there were over twenty women present at the meeting called for the purpose of organizing a town Improvement Society.*
>
> *Mrs. Channing Harris was made Chairman and a Secretary appointed to serve until officers are duly elected.*
>
> *The motion was made and carried that the Society be known as the Woman's Town Improvement Association. A committee consisting of Mrs. Landers, Mrs. Coley and Mrs. Staples was chosen to draw up a Constitution.*
>
> *A nominating committee was named consisting of Mrs. Staples, Mrs. F. M. Salmon and Mrs. Chas. Mulkley. The annual membership fee will be one dollar.*
>
> *Next meeting will be held at Toquet Hall on Monday after, August 19th at four o'clock.*
>
> *—Mrs. J. F. Godillot, Sec. pro-tem.*

At the next meeting of the Association, attended by about 40 women, Mrs. William G. Staples was elected president, an office that she retained practically continuously for ten years. Also elected were an Advisory Board of 15 members, a secretary and a treasurer and a panel of ten vice presidents—each of whom represented one of the school districts then in Westport.

For fifteen years, these women held office with scattered exceptions. After the consolidation of the schools, the number of districts was reduced to three.

GOALS ESTABLISHED

The newly elected President then took the chair. She thanked the ladies for the honor conferred upon her and spoke of the goals toward which this Association has pledged its work—namely, cleaning of town streets, caring for and planting of trees on outskirts of town, laying of sidewalks where needed, etc.

Thus the aims and objectives of the Association were initially directed towards the improvement and development of the physical facilities of the town, a policy that continued in force until World War I when the emphasis was redirected to providing social services. This policy is still in effect. In its work, the Association initiated many services that were later recognized as public responsibilities and taken over by the town.

The WTIA established its routine at its second meeting. The third Monday of each month was designated for regular meetings. The annual meeting and election of officers was to be in September. Bylaws were adopted in August 1907, then printed and distributed in September. At about this time, the question arose as to whether or not men should be permitted to join the organization as auxiliary members, but this was defeated by a resounding vote of 28 to 1.

The Jesup Library

During the latter part of 1907, meetings were held first in the study of Trinity Church, then later in private homes. After the Jesup (Westport Public) Library was formally opened to the public on May 11, 1908, the meeting place was changed to the library auditorium beginning with the second annual meeting in August 1908. In lieu of rent, the Association donated $50 per year to the library over a period of several years, starting in 1911.

PONIES, FERRIS WHEELS, AND COMMUNITY SERVICE ANNUAL EVENTS

Every year, as summer approaches, a large well-kept white house on Imperial Avenue suddenly sprouts all the carnival trappings of a street fair. There are rides, games of chance, baked goods, books, plants and a giant attic sale, not to mention things to eat. This is the traditional Yankee Doodle Fair of the Westport Woman's Club.

National Hall, early 1900s

Although neither the fair nor the Westport Woman's Club were originally known as such, it was in 1907 that this energetic organization of Westport women held its first such fund-raising event. Mrs. Staples, Mrs. Salmon and the others who had organized as the Woman's Town Improvement Association in August of that year lost no time in planning a Woodland Festival for the following month. It was held in National Hall, a large gathering place on the second floor of the building at the west end of the bridge that was referred to as the old Fairfield Furniture store and is now part of the luxurious Inn at National Hall.

The first fair was christened a Festival of Nations, but program changes dictated its re-designation as a Woodland Festival. It was held on two evenings, September 18 and 19, 1907, at National Hall. A "woodland" touch was provided by several cartloads of tree branches and other greenery, chosen because they made a big splash of decoration with little effort. The expenses of the whole affair were negligible. The Advisory Board voted a general admission charge to the fair of 10 cents, and the price of supper 35 cents.

In addition to general entertainment by a band and singing groups, there were booths for the sale of cake and preserves, candy, artwork—including china and baskets, fancy work, dolls, bags and aprons—and finally "mysteries." In addition, a lottery was held. Following this event, the Treasurer announced that the net receipts were $920.15.

A similar Country Fair was held the following year, on September 9 and 10, 1908, at the Old Methodist Church. Net proceeds were $936.16. The allocation of these funds set the pattern of Association activity for several years to come. The first annual report of the Recording Secretary, Florence A. Wakeman, in September 1908, noted that the Association had 81 members and that:

> The work accomplished by the Association during the year has been the placing of rubbish cans in various parts of the town, marking of the street corners with neat name boards and the erection of a drinking fountain at Saugatuck.
>
> In June, prizes were awarded to the various schools for exterior and interior improvements.
>
> $600 of the funds of the Association was appropriated for the building of sidewalks, a work which we hope soon to see completed.

In following years, the fair was often held at Jesup Green or on the King's Highway School field. The fairs had a variety of themes.

At the 1925 fair, a large booklet, *The Town Crier of Westport*, was sold. It included contributions of drawings, poems, and bits of Westport history that the women had gathered from local artists and writers. This delightful publication reflected Westport's spirited artistic community of that time. The purpose was to help raise money to start a scholarship for Staples graduates.

By 1946, the fair had taken on the name Yankee Doodle Fair, which board member Suzanne Conn had suggested several years earlier. At that fair, Francesca Lodge had volunteered to run the pony cart rides. All went well until a balloon popped in front of a pony's nose. He bolted, and when Mrs. Lodge attempted to stop him, she was thrown beneath the wheels of the cart. Fortunately, she was not badly hurt, though shaken up. But the pony had made his escape. Pony and cart headed for the center of town and successfully snarled early evening traffic before they were finally caught and escorted back to the fair.

The Woman's Town Improvement Association quickly embarked on their most ambitious project—the town's need for sidewalks. After a year of lobbying, the prospects for the sidewalk construction work proposed by the women was slowly materializing. The proposal was that the costs for 6-foot wide concrete walks were to be allocated one-half to the property owner, one-quarter to the town, and one-quarter to the WTIA. Most of the property owners contacted were receptive to the idea, but the town selectmen were slow to accede. An eminently reasonable proposal, thought the town improvers, but not so the selectmen. It was their first official encounter with the feminine element and they balked and balked hard. To quote Mrs. Staples:

> *The Selectmen were loath to give their consent. They said people would slip and fall on such smooth walks and if we built them they must be level—no grades. I asked, if we started at the top of Wright Street and kept on the level, how was I to get down? It was nearly a year before we got the (town) permit and money to build the first walk. We knew nothing about cement, but Mrs. Salmon sent for books on cement work and we studied the matter and were fortunate in securing the services of a man willing to let us direct him.*

Another stalwart gentleman announced that he wouldn't walk on such sidewalks. He'd be darned if he was going to stand for Westport being turned into a skirt-ridden town. True to his word, he could be seen many years later striding protestingly down the middle of the street.

After many months of struggle, however, the battle was finally won, and Mrs. Staples, with her committee comprising Mrs. Salmon and Miss Lizzie Thomas, proceeded to lay the first walk. They didn't actually mix the cement, we're told, but they delved into books and asked questions until they had become virtual authorities on the subject. And in true housewifely fashion, they stood over the men and saw that the job was done properly, while their amused families chided them about the amount of time spent with their newfound gentlemen friends.

The first sidewalk project to be undertaken was variously described as "from the new grounds of the town to what is known as Dead Man's Brook" and "from the town property to the road that leads to John F. Godillot's place"; i.e., on the south side of State Street (now Post Road East) from the Old Town Hall to Imperial Avenue. Work was started in August 1908, with Thomas Glynn as contractor. The cost was 12 cents per square foot. The first sidewalk was laid "on the east side of the bridge and a crosswalk on the west side." After the work was completed, Mr. C. B. Kemper complained that the walk in front of his house was too high but the contractor had a paper signed by him agreeing to what had been done.

The sidewalk work continued apace until, in the annual report for 1912, it was stated that a total of 11,229 lineal feet of sidewalk had been laid for 70 property owners over the past five years. Although another 2,000 feet were laid the following year, mostly on Riverside Avenue, the work of future years continued at a somewhat slower pace until the town assumed the responsibility in 1926. This established a pattern that was to be repeated time and again: A project begun by the WTIA, once it became self-sufficient, would be turned over to the town or other interested agencies. In its August 11, 1947 issue, *Life* magazine included an article on the Westport Woman's Club, highlighting a picture with the caption: "Children of Club members play on a sidewalk that was resulted from the women's campaign."

SETTING A PRECEDENT FOR THE P.T.A.

Kings Highway North School District

In respect to education, the WTIA pioneered several activities that foreshadowed the P.T.A. (Parent Teacher Association). At this time, the schools were not a consolidated unit as they now are, and it was the WTIA's idea to draw together the somewhat diverse interests of the different school districts by working toward the same end through one channel—hence the appointment of ten vice presidents, each responsible for one school district. Each year, prizes were offered to the school that showed the greatest improvement in school grounds and interiors, and while these prizes were small ($2 to $10) they had the effect of establishing communication and competition among the schools. This promoted a unifying influence that culminated in 1914 in the consolidation of the school districts under the town Board of Education. Competitions of this type were conducted each year by the WTIA for many years thereafter.

However, all of the schoolwork wasn't accomplished in an aura of appreciation. The *Westporter-Herald* issue of June 12, 1908 reported that Selectman Kemper personally descended on the grounds of Cross Highway School to stop the grading and planting that were then in progress, to the utter indignation of the members of the WTIA. Nor was all the work at the schools aimed at beautification, as seen in one item of expense in the Secretary's report for 1915–1916: "$10.00 for rat virus to be used at public schools."

IMPROVING THE LANDSCAPE

The project for placing street signs was also extended over a period of several years. Some streets, as yet unnamed, had to be given names. By the end of 1908 there had been made "163 street signs at a cost of $24.45, placed free of charge by the Selectmen." By 1913 an additional 200 street signs had been placed, some of these being replacements due to vandalism.

The WTIA also planted trees in various localities in town and graded and seeded the small triangular area at the junction of State Street and Myrtle Avenue. Other vest-pocket parks and several cemeteries were tidied up in various localities and were maintained each year by the WTIA until this work was taken over by the town in 1926.

U ntil World War I in 1914, the WTIA continued under the aegis of Mrs. Staples as president and Mrs. Wakeman as secretary. By August 1909, the membership had grown to 103. Meetings continued to be held in the "auditorium" of the public library. In September 1909, the WTIA was accepted for membership in the Connecticut State Federation of Women's Clubs, an organization made up (in 1911) of 63 clubs with 3500 members, of which 1200 were in Fairfield County.

DE-PRIVATIZING COMPO BEACH

Interest in Compo Beach was shown early during the existence of the Association. At this time the beach was occupied by privately owned "beach houses" that were built on town land and were occupied without payment to the town. As early as September 1908, the WTIA voted: *"...that a paper be drawn up and presented for action at the Annual town meeting calling attention to the unpleasant conditions at Compo Beach and suggesting various improvements, asking that a tax be laid upon holders of bath houses, that there may be sufficient money to keep the beach in a fairly decent and safe condition."*

On May 5th, 1909, the selectmen issued a public notice that all owners of bathhouses at Compo Beach must remove them by May 25 or suffer their removal by the town. Finally, on the night of August 2, Selectmen Lewis B. Wakeman, Robert H. Coley, and Merrick H. Coley issued an order to tear down every bathhouse standing on Compo Beach, thus dedicating the area to full public use. It was estimated that at least $2,000 worth of property was destroyed. On June 8, 1909, the WTIA held a whist party at the Town Hall that realized $650.39 from fees and subscriptions toward the construction of a public bathing pavilion at the beach.

In subsequent years, the Association continued to evince interest in the beach activities, helping to purchase life-saving equipment, installing a shower in the Beach Pavilion (1914), and furnishing money toward the purchase of a lifeboat. In 1915 a contribution was made toward the maintenance of lifeguards and to the purchase of a pulmotor (artificial breathing apparatus.) In the same year, the WTIA contributed toward the construction of a coping wall around the cannon at Compo Beach.

In 1909 arrangements were made with the New York, New Haven and Hartford Railroad management to effect both grading and landscaping at the Saugatuck railroad station. The minutes of the May meeting of that year reveal that "twenty loads of loam and six or eight of crushed stone with labor required for spreading have been furnished by the Company. Grass seed has been sown and evergreens, maples and shrubs planted." In 1912, funds were similarly allocated for improvements at the Greens Farms railroad station. Yearly maintenance was thereafter provided by the WTIA.

The traditional annual fair was continued as a fund-raiser during this period. A "Lawn Fete" was held September 1 and 2, 1909, on the grounds of Mrs. Charles Buck on State Street, the net proceeds of which were $883. The following year a "Grand Kermiss" was held in the Town Hall on July 21 and 22, with net receipts of $1,456. On April 24, 1911, it was voted that "the time of the July moon be established as the regular date for the yearly fair." Consequently the 1911 fair was held in the Town Hall on July 12 and 13, accommodating "five booths, with supper in the basement and ice-cream on the main floor" netting $1,145.36 to the Association treasury.

In 1912, 1913, and 1914, a "Flower Carnival", a "Seventh Annual Fair", and a "Rainbow Carnival" were held, netting the Association $1,295, $875, and $684 respectively. The 1915 fair was christened an "Alphabet Fair", bringing to the WTIA $1,151.51. And on July 14 and 15, 1916, there was held in the Town Hall a "Shops of New York Fair" that cleared $1,059.31.

AN EARLY COMMITMENT TO TOWN IMPROVEMENTS

Virtually the entire balance sheet during the founding years was dedicated to listing the revenues raised and disbursements for town improvements. They ranged from landscape improvements in local cemeteries to keeping school toilets clean and neat. In 1910–1911, a small group of members contributed $78.00 in membership dues and raised another $5,540.89 to finance $4,312.30 in public improvements. In connection with planned future fair activities, the July 1912 meeting of the Association considered "the advisability of erecting a building on the town grounds in which the fair paraphernalia and other possessions of the Association" could be housed. After town permission was received in December, a stucco building was erected at a cost of $800, the work being done by Mr. Maddock. Some years later (1924), this building was used by the Woman's Club for art classes.

The beginnings of the Garden Department were foreshadowed on April 8, 1910, at a social tea given for the schoolteachers of Westport when President Staples announced a competition to be held among the school children for the best flower and vegetable gardens. On September 9, 1910, prizes in an amount of $35 were awarded to the children at Town Hall and "ice-cream and cake was served to all present." An annual Children's Flower Show and Garden Contest was held each September for several years thereafter.

Tree planting was continued through these years, as well as cemetery improvements (Green's Farms and King Street cemeteries in 1911 and "Old Cemetery" in 1913). Annual allocations were made for their maintenance.

In October 1913, a plan was discussed for the collection and disposal of garbage and ashes under the auspices of the WTIA. On November 17, the Association entered into a contract with Mr. Dykeman for such collection at the rate of 10 cents for each barrel or box collected in the "West-Side from Burr Avenue to State Street Bridge" on Tuesday and Friday each week. However, after this work had been conducted for about a year, it was discontinued because not as many people as had been expected availed themselves of this service.

In 1914 a large boulder was placed by the WTIA "at the head of Compo Road" on which the Sons of the American Revolution placed a bronze tablet "marking the spot upon which occurred the first engagement with the British in 1776." This was dedicated on June 27, 1914.

In an unusual demonstration of foresight, Mrs. Staples at the 1915 annual meeting "spoke at some length regarding the purchase of Gorham's Island, which can now be bought for $1,000" and which could serve admirably as a public recreation area. It was stipulated that if the town were to purchase the property, the WTIA would provide $1,000 over a period of five years to aid in its development. Unhappily, it was found that the public access to the island was a strip only five feet wide, and that a considerable additional expense would be entailed to obtain an adequate right-of-way. The project was therefore abandoned.

"BY THEIR WORKS SHALL YE KNOW THEM"—GAINING NATIONAL RECOGNITION

In May 1916, the bylaws were amended to provide that: "This shall be a non-partisan Society at which no discussion of a political or sectarian nature shall be brought before a meeting." Four months later a Press Committee was appointed. In 1913 it was proposed that the Association adopt as its motto: "By their works shall ye know them."

Among its other civic betterment programs the WTIA voted in November 1915 to pay for planting a Norway spruce in the triangle at East Church Street and Myrtle Avenue, to be used as a community Christmas tree.

The work of the Association was given national exposure in a short article that appeared in the March 1913 issue of the *Ladies Home Journal*. As a result, letters of inquiry were received from eight states. In 1916, a pamphlet was prepared by Miss C. E. Thomas that outlined the work of the Association. A thousand copies were printed and distributed. "It was intended that these pamphlets be sent to each member of the Association, to the State Federation and other Civic Societies and that they be distributed at the (1916) Fair."

C ommunity service on a large scale marked WTIA activity during World War I. It was announced that "the WTIA has decided to devote its energies to patriotic measures for the duration of the war."

And indeed it did. As noted in the 50th anniversary issue of the *Westport Town Crier & Herald*:

> *It formed a Food Conservation Committee that conducted an exhibit in the Library and demonstrated means to use substitutes for vital foodstuffs. It organized a Home Economics Committee that managed to send a record 188 gallons of jelly to Westport soldiers. And it promoted Children's War Gardens encouraging youngsters to grow their own food.*

The Children's War Garden project was initiated on a statewide basis when the Governor's Committee on Food Supply issued a proclamation in April 1917 that "all must serve either in an army to fight the enemy or in an army to produce food." In Westport, an Agricultural Preparedness Program for children from 10 to 14 years of age was organized by the WTIA, in cooperation with the Westport Superintendent of Schools. Each child was to cultivate a 100-square foot plot of ground under the general supervision of Mr. Coley, a graduate of the Massachusetts Agricultural College, who was retained by the WTIA at a cost of $350 for the season. The Association also financed all seed costs, subject to reimbursement by the children out of their proceeds. Several tracts of land were offered: one of nine acres by Mr. E. C. Nash, another of two acres by Mr. Karl Anderson, and two smaller plots by Mrs. Alger and Miss Wilcox. By the end of the summer, a total of eight acres had been placed under cultivation and the resulting produce was sold for slightly over $1,000. The WTIA gave prizes for excellence in this work, having "$567 expended, of which $107.97 was received from the children for seeds."

A NEW CHALLENGE—WARTIME ACTIVITIES

Because of the war, the Association decided to dispense with its regular annual fair in 1917. Instead, it joined with other local groups to hold a "Fairfield County War Benefit Lawn Fete", with the proceeds to be donated in equal amounts to the American Red Cross, the U.S. Navy League, the Aero Club of America (for a spotting plane), and the American Field Ambulance unit of Fairfield County. The WTIA organized a "Chinese Booth", where tea was served and where various donated items were sold. The affair was held on June 30, 1917, at the F. E. Lewis estate in Saugatuck. Mr. Harry Houdini, the colorful escape artist and magician, was the star performer and nearly $10,000 was realized from the event.

Other wartime activities of the Association included donations of $100 each to the American Red Cross and the Westport War Relief Committee, and the presentation of a flag to the Home Guard—all in 1917. Two trainees were sent to the Connecticut Agricultural College to study canning and preserving, and "to teach canning in Westport." In February 1918, the WTIA conducted a "Food Pledge Card Campaign" as Westport's contribution to a national effort to conserve food by canning and by the use of wheat, sugar, and fat substitutes. Over 500 signatures were obtained on pledge cards, and 2,500 informational circulars were distributed. The WTIA also acted as local agent in reporting weekly to Washington on food prices in town.

WAR AND ALL—TOWN IMPROVEMENT PROJECTS GO ON

For all its war-support activities, the Association found time in 1917 to continue with several town improvement projects. Large road signs were erected on the four principal approaches to Westport. Prizes for improvements, aggregating $72, were awarded to schools. About 600 feet of sidewalk was constructed at the Gault property on Compo Road, and another 1,000 feet on Main Street at the Willow Brook Cemetery. At the September 1917 meeting, the Association went on record as being "in favor of a No-License town", but the minutes fail to amplify further. In June 1918, it hired a man for $10 a month to pick up waste paper and to cut the grass at the Saugatuck Railroad Station, but the Greens Farms Station Committee got a man to perform the same work for $6.

In November 1918, the Association inaugurated a program to serve hot cocoa to pupils at the Bridge Street School during the winter months, thus becoming a "first" in the school lunch program. This program was further developed in December 1922, when a full-fledged hot lunch service went into effect at the Bridge Street School in cooperation with the P.T.A. By 1924, hot lunches were also being served at Saugatuck Elementary School and Staples High School. The chairman of the Hot Lunch in School Committee reported that "the children were greatly pleased, and were all showing increase in weight." Another school effort involved the establishment of a branch library at the Bridge Street School in January 1922, with annual donations provided over a period of years thereafter.

In April 1918, the Association joined with the Connecticut Council of National Defense in endorsing a resolution to be sent to President Wilson and to the Secretaries of War and Navy asking that "military rank be conferred upon the Red Cross at the front to put the Red Cross nursing service on a par with the Canadian and English service whose efficiency is due to its military status."

During the war period, Mrs. Staples retired as president of the Association, having served continuously since its founding, except for 1914–1916, when Mrs. John F. Godillot served instead. On her retirement, Mrs. Staples was unanimously elected Honorary President. She was succeeded by Miss Edith Wheeler, who served from 1917 until 1919. At this time the membership numbered 86.

The post-war period witnessed the addition of a new dimension to the activities of the WTIA. Under the leadership of Mrs. John Crawford (1919–1924), civic services and social activity were keynoted, although physical improvement of the town was not abandoned. It was announced by Mrs. Crawford, on her assumption of office, that "the WTIA would broaden its scope without sacrificing the actual beautifying of the town which has hitherto been its particular mission. The Association will endeavor to use the united interest of all the social groups of the town in civic work that will truly be town improvement with a little different emphasis."

A Program Committee was appointed in November 1919 "whose duty it shall be to arrange interesting programs to follow the business of each meeting and also to arrange for interesting lectures that will be an intellectual stimulus to the whole town." The first such program, a lecture by Miss Ritar on "Family Social Work", took place on March 15, 1920. Many subsequent lectures occurred, related to public health, civil government, landscaping and gardening, and education.

A Membership Committee was first appointed in September 1919, "to divide the Fair lists into sections, each district to be solicited by some member of the Advisory Board." The membership drive paid off handsomely. In September 1919, although the town had grown to about 5,000 population, the paid-up membership of the Association was only 80. However, by January 1920, this figure rose to 193. Through aggressive recruitment, the membership continued to rise—to 412 in 1922–1923 and to a peak of 584 in the following year. Annual membership dues were maintained at the original $1, with a life membership available at $25.

In October 1919 the bylaws were updated, and 300 copies were printed and distributed to the membership. One change in the bylaws involved combining the two offices of Recording Secretary and Corresponding Secretary into a single position, but because of the workload, a Secretary and an Assistant Secretary continued to be elected until 1928. In August 1923, the School District work formerly performed by ten vice presidents was relegated to a committee, and the number of vice presidents was reduced to three—having primary responsibility for educational, civic, and social activities, respectively. At about the same time, three classes of membership were created: Resident, Non-resident, and Junior. The latter consisted of girls from 12 to 18 years of age who paid annual dues of 50 cents. By the end of 1924, the junior membership numbered fourteen.

BECOMING A FACTOR IN COMMUNITY ISSUES

In January 1920, as an outgrowth of its activities in promoting public health service in the schools, the WTIA became a corporate member of the National Organization for Public Health Nursing. Then followed a series of public health projects. In May 1922, under threat of a smallpox epidemic, free clinics jointly sponsored by the WTIA and the selectmen gave vaccinations to 74 persons. In December 1922, $300 was allotted toward the establishment of a school dental clinic in cooperation with the Red Cross and the P.T.A. Contributions were also made at a later date to the Saugatuck clinic.

In 1920–1921 the Association joined the Connecticut Chamber of Commerce, the Connecticut League of Women Voters, and the Consumer League of Connecticut.

In the fall of 1919, President Crawford appointed a Civic Committee, whose function was to arrange social activities. Under its auspices, several Community Dances were held as well as a number of bridge parties and afternoon teas, and a series of Sewing Bees to include "the making of men's shirts." However, almost at the outset of its existence, this committee found more significant work to be done.

The Bedford House—A Community Recreation facility—Our New Home

Westport Hotel

In September 1919, the Westport philanthropist, E. T. Bedford, purchased the old Westport Hotel on the corner of Main and State streets, with a view to erecting a YMCA building that became one of Westport's most attractive landmarks. Allen Raymond, the town historian, speculated that the reason Bedford did so was because he liked to play pool and, as a boy, he would stand outside of the Westport Hotel where he couldn't get a chance to play because kids weren't allowed into a saloon. So he bought the place and he built a YMCA so he could play pool.

The WTIA had earlier discussed the possibility of raising funds for the construction of a Community House for the use of all of the town's residents. Mr. Bedford's action gave fair promise to provide such a facility for the men and boys of the community, but it seemed to overlook the corresponding needs of the women and girls. The Association was quick to react. The Civic Committee was directed "to meet with Mr. Bedford in the interests of the women and girls of the community to point out to him their needs and to inquire concerning the possibility of extending to them the privileges already promised the men and boys."

The results of this meeting were given in the Association's booklet *High Lights*:

Mr. Bedford was much interested and various conferences followed, the result of which were the beautiful rooms for the use of women and girls which he added to the building (known as Bedford House), and the operation of which he placed in the hands of the Association.

Mr. Bedford, through the YMCA, assumed the expense of operation and maintenance of Bedford House, with the understanding that "the WTIA would contribute annually toward its maintenance such an amount as it conveniently could."

The Bedford House

After some delay due to the inflationary effects of the war, work on the foundations of the building was started on June 12, 1922, with J. B. Lowery, Jr., of New York, as contractor. The building was substantially completed in January 1923 when the WTIA was requested to assist in the selection of furnishings for the Women's Community Rooms in the new facility. The building was formally opened to the public on September 5, 1923, and the Association moved its regular meeting place from the library to Bedford House starting on September 17.

Under the conditions imposed by Mr. Bedford, the WTIA managed Bedford House and paid $1,000 in 1924 and in 1925 towards its upkeep. In 1926, the Bedford Fund endowed "the work of Bedford House and a Public Health Nurse" in a single package amounting to $2,500 annually, with the Association paying the difference between the endowment and the actual cost of operation.

The Association did more than manage the building and use it as a meeting place. For many years it conducted swimming and gym activities for women and girls at the "Y." The WTIA was also greatly pleased to be given its own quarters in the new building. The Club occupied offices there for more than 20 years, running athletic programs for local girls and women.

The YMCA in 1928

A great many artists were connected with projects of the WTIA in one way or another during the 1920s. The list is almost a complete record of the professional artists in the community at that time: Karl Anderson, Percy Anderson, John Taylor Arms, Jules Agramonte, Edmund Ashe, Lowell "Tony" Balcom, Sophie Balcom, Perr Barlow, Caroline Van Hook Bean, Leslie L. Benson, Edward Boyd, Ralph Boyer, Rebecca Boyer, Samuel E. Brown, Jerome Brush, George Clisbee, Homer Conant, Alexander P. Couard, John Steuart Curry, and more. Some of their paintings are shown in these pages.

The Woman's Town Improvement Association was concerned as well with the history and traditions of the community and the honoring of patriotic anniversaries. Thus, in 1921, it sponsored the historical pageant in which artists and other citizens celebrated the Fourth of July. Such entertainments were true community events, a magnet for people from all the strata of Westport. At later Yankee Doodle Fairs, when the age of illustration was still golden, a battery of prominent illustrators would be lined up afternoons and evenings, doing portraits of fellow townspeople for a dollar apiece, the money, of course, going to charity.

The artists who threw themselves into the activities of the WTIA did not bring to these doings the cynicism that might be expected today if a celebrity comparable to John Held were asked to portray the town crier—as he did. The artists were a part of the town. Big events like pageants were important and had to be done expertly; they were carried off with panache in every respect—words and music, direction, costumes, and settings.

Later in the 1920s, the WTIA took on a project more directly involving the artists. The Club mounted annual exhibitions of the artists' work, arranging the displays with their usual attention to detail. The art exhibitions, co-sponsored with the YMCA, took place in the art gallery in Bedford House. Both the art gallery and the women's clubrooms were on the second floor. Primarily a men's preserve, the building had an entrance on Main Street for female use. Relegated though they were to the side entrance, the women showed their mettle in their organization of these art shows. All the local artists exhibited. Their wives helped out. In 1926, several of the artists contributed to another project of the WTIA. They contributed scenes of Westport for postcards that were sold on the premises to raise money for scholarships.

On The Hill
Karl Anderson

Joseph Conrad
Percy Anderson

Medieval
Pageantry
John Taylor Arms

In the Cove
Edmund Ashe

Steel
Alexander P. Couard

THE ANNUAL FAIR RETURNS

After a two-year wartime lapse, the WTIA decided to revive its annual fair. Early in 1919, the Compo Fire Engine Company asked Club members to join with it in a joint fair, with the proceeds to be shared equally by both organizations. A "Fair" was held on the Town Hall grounds on August 27 and 28, 1919, featuring supper, carnival booths, and dancing to an orchestra. Due to poor weather, the proceeds were only $1,481.

MAJOR EVENTS AND THEATRICAL PRODUCTIONS

The following year the membership voted against any further jointly conducted fairs. A "Pageant and Tableau Fair" was held on July 29 and 30, 1920, partly at the Town Hall grounds and partly at "Bayview", the estate of William L. Taylor. In the afternoon, a children's pageant was held, depicting the landing of the Pilgrims in celebration of the tercentenary of the founding of Plymouth. (Many years later, this episode found its way into a 1958 Hollywood movie titled *Rally 'Round the Flag, Boys!* starring Joanne Woodward and Paul Newman, who later became residents of Westport.) In the evening of the fair, a "Phantasy Tableau" written and directed by Mr. Lichtenauer was presented. A full-page ad in the *Westporter-Herald* featured the sale of a "season ticket for $1" that entitled the holder to admission to the afternoon and evening performances, a supper, and a chance at a door prize. Pony rides were also enjoyed by young and old, and the *Westporter-Herald* observed of this feature: "Selectman Wakeman looked like the picture of Mark Twain crossing the Alps on a small jackass."

A most unusual feature of this event was the taking of professional motion pictures of "the fair, the big town and some of its people" on June 29. The film was then shown at the Fine Arts Theater on August l0 and 12. The net profits accruing to the WTIA were $2,133.

In June 1921 a more elaborate theatrical performance was mounted. As reported by the *Westporter-Herald:*

> *Our pageant this year will be shown on a natural stage with a series of beautiful living moving pictures showing the important features of Fairfield County. There will be Indian scenes, dances and battles. The early settlers will appear showing how they worked around here in 1639 when Roger Ludlow and his followers settled Fairfield, Southport and Norwalk. The stirring scenes of 1776–1781 will be reproduced in striking review. There will be a beautiful minuet and a charming wedding party, the whole depicted in 27 tremendous scenes with a large cast at Alden Pond on the estate of Dr. Ruland off Evergreen Avenue."*

Again, full-page ads were placed in the newspaper; and this year a printed program was distributed. Booths were erected at the Town Hall grounds for playing games and for sale of various commodities. In all, the Association netted $1,714 from this event.

RAISING FUNDS AT COMPO BEACH

In May 1922, with the double motive of providing a desirable atmosphere at the beach for the young people while at the same time, raising funds for the Association in lieu of a fair, the WTIA submitted a bid of $1,500 to the selectmen for a franchise to operate the "Nash Pavilion" at Compo Beach. Chairmen were appointed to support the operation for the 14 weeks of the season. Mr. Darrow was hired as manager at $30 per week, and Mrs. Nelson Crawford as his assistant at $25 a week. In addition, a paid cook was engaged. A booth, manned by WTIA members was erected for the sale of "fancy items and food stuffs." As a social supplement to the beach enterprise, a "Garden Fete" was held on September at *Bosco Al Mare*, the Hills Point Estate of Mr. and Mrs. Arnold Schlaet, where an evening of professional dancing and vocal and instrumental music was presented under the management of Miss Helen Smith. The net financial return from both activities was $4,133.

The following year, 1923, an identical pattern was pursued, with the beach pavilion that operated for 14 weeks and with a supplemental *"Festa Della Luna"* held at the Schlaet estate on August 24. In all, the proceeds came to only $1,463, partly because of a season of poor beach weather, and partly because of a dampening in the enthusiasm of the working membership at the pavilion.

The next year on July 17 and 18, 1924, a "Village Mart" was held on Church Lane, where 17 booths were set up to represent old English cottages and shops. A circus was featured, complete with sideshows and vaudeville acts. Souvenir programs *(Ye Village Mart)* were printed and sold for 25 cents a copy. Net returns were $3,330.

On July 31 and August 1, 1925, a "Country Fair and Circus" was held at Dr. Ruland's Pond, featuring "a parade of historical interest" and providing a net return to the Association of $2,100.

EMILY B. FULLER SCHOLARSHIP FUND

On December 17, 1923, Mrs. Robert W. Fuller, a member of two years' standing who had previously been active in school affairs, met a tragic death when her car was struck by a train at a grade crossing north of Wilton Station. Three months later, Mrs. Harris, who later was a president of the Club, led the creation of a fund, designated as the *Emily B. Fuller Scholarship*, to provide each year a $250 grant (later increased to $700) to a "graduate of Staples High School, of either sex, to enable him or her to go on to an institution of higher learning." A capital goal of $5,000 was proposed, to be met by individual subscription and by fund-raising projects. The booklet *High Light* issued in 1932 had this to say:

The committee in charge of raising this money allowed themselves five years in which to complete the fund. Owing to the interest and cooperation of the community, however, this was accomplished in a little over four years. Apart from three large gifts from the WTIA, Mr. E. T. Bedford, and Mr. Algernon T. Burr ($500 each), this money was raised by comparatively small subscriptions from friends of Mrs. Fuller, by those especially interested in such a project, and by entertainments, concerts, etc.

Two unusual projects aided the fund. A booklet entitled *The Town Crier of Westport 1925* was published, containing an illustrated history of Westport, a history of the school system, several poems, drawings and essays of interest contributed by local artists and writers, and some 24 pages of paid advertising. This was sold for 35 cents a copy at the 1925 fair.

Among the projects undertaken to raise money for this fund was the sale of postcards which were printed with copper plates of drawings of Westport scenes, created by Westport artists. One of the artists, the well-known Robert Lambdin, did a drawing for these post cards—a scene of the Westport Country Club (now the Birchwood Country Club). Artist George Wright did a scene of Compo Beach and Oscar Howard, the Fairfield Hunt Club. J. C. Rehber did a Main Street scene looking north from Taylor Place, and Kerr Ely did the YMCA building, then new, flanked with large stately elm trees. There was a sixth scene, the Saugatuck Congregational Church by Henry B. Davis, but the plate for this has not been found. These sketches were reproduced on postcards, copyrighted and sold—first by a drive that realized a goodly sum, and then by distribution through various outlets in town that continued to bring in a little money for the fund each year for several years.

The first scholarship award was made in 1925, and each year thereafter, a special scholarship committee consulted with the principal of Staples High School to decide upon a designee. Two scrolls were made that listed the recipients—one hung in Bedford House and the other in Staples High School. The scholarship committee starts its work in January each year, issuing scholarship forms to the high school. In March, these application forms are returned to the Club. The committee then individually reviews each form and then collectively interviews each qualified candidate. The selected scholarship recipients are invited to attend the June Club luncheon meeting, where they are introduced to the membership. Scholarships are sent directly to the universities or colleges.

Although such a scholarship had been desired for some time, the name of Emily B. Fuller, that tireless and consistent friend of education, crystallized the purpose of accomplishment. The inspiration of her character and the memory of her brilliant and vivid personality moved her best friends to complete a worthy memorial to the name of the woman who was responsible for the forward march of progressive education in Westport.

COMMUNITY GARBAGE COLLECTION SYSTEM EFFORT RENEWED

Despite the WTIA's failure to arouse adequate public support for a community garbage collection system, it decided to try once again in 1922, following a case of typhus which local health authorities traced to improperly handled garbage. Present-day residents of Westport who can rely on a well-regulated commercial operation may not appreciate the problem faced by the average householder of 1920, who had to make his own individual arrangements for this service. In January 1922, the Association entered in a contract with Mr. James, guaranteeing him a salary of $100 per month for the collection and disposal of garbage and ashes at the rate of two barrels per subscriber per week. Costs of operation were divided equally among the town, the residents, and the WTIA. The latter entered in the contract, managed the operation with advice from the town health authorities, and collected the money from the subscribers.

Work was initiated with a roster of 50 families. This rose to a peak of 138 in July under the stimulus of many summer residents, but fell again to 97 during the winter months. At that time, Mr. James encountered great difficulty in effecting collections during periods of heavy snow—a difficulty augmented "by the neglect of people having the proper receptacles." As a result, this project was again abandoned on July 1, 1923, after 18 months of operation. At the next town meeting on August 8, 1923, the Association requested the selectmen to authorize the expenditure of $3,600 to support a public collection system for a period of one year. However, the matter was tabled when President Jennings of the Board of Finance estimated a cost to the town of $35,000 per year.

COMMUNITY ACTIVITIES BEGIN TO DIVERSIFY

In looking back over the period 1919–1925, the number of the Association's activities seems to be myriad indeed. In 1919, the work started in prior years, such as laying sidewalks, landscaping street triangles, and beautifying the railroad stations and cemeteries was continued. In 1920, cash prizes were offered in the schools for the best upper-class essay on the "high cost of living" and for excellence in public speaking. The latter contest was repeated in subsequent years. In January 1921, in a moment of unrestrained enthusiasm, the Association voted to go on record in support of the Volstead Act and the 18th Constitutional Amendment (prohibition legislation). In April, six public lectures were sponsored on the "Machinery of Government." In May, $500 was allotted for playground equipment at the Myrtle Avenue and Bridge Street Schools and in the next year similar action was taken for Greens Farms School and Staples High. In June 1921, the WTIA investigated the possibility of effecting house-to-house mail delivery; but this was declined by the postmaster because the town still lacked a house numbering system.

In June 1922 the Association paid for redecorating the library auditorium. Later in the year, $250 was expended in "planting and beautification" of the Bedford School grounds. School prizes were awarded for the best essay on the subject of Peace. In November, the Art Committee instituted weekly classes in rug making, and by the following year, classes open to the public at a nominal fee were conducted in seat caning, basketry, clay modeling, "nature study for children" at the beach, wood-block printing, wax ornaments, cooking, millinery, painting, sculpturing, and dancing.

In June 1923, $200 was contributed toward the construction of a Clubhouse for the Italian Society of Saugatuck. At about the same time, a pavilion was completed at Burial Hill Park after some delay was encountered due to boys stealing the lumber. That same summer, the WTIA footed the bill to have the library remain open for readers on Sunday afternoons during the summer months.

In January 1924, a Girls' Club was organized and during subsequent months, suppers were served to this club and to the boys' Hi-Y Club. The Connecticut Federation of Women's Clubs was hosted for lunch, and 194 out-of-town guests were served. Prizes were awarded for school essays on music, and an essay entitled "Civic Activities of Federated Clubs" by a member of the WTIA won a $100 prize from the *Pictorial Review* magazine. These proceeds were applied to placing a lighted panel of the Athenian Oath over the mantel in the social room of Bedford House. The Athenian Oath was recited by the citizens of Athens, Greece over 2,000 years ago. It is frequently referenced by civic leaders in modern times as a timeless code of civic responsibility:

> *We will never bring disgrace on this our City by an act of dishonesty or cowardice. We will fight for the ideals and Sacred Things of the City both alone and with many.*
>
> *We will revere and obey the City's laws, and will do our best to incite a like reverence and respect in those above us who are prone to annul them or set them at naught. We will strive increasingly to quicken the public's sense of civic duty.*
>
> *Thus in all these ways, we will transmit this City, not only not less, but greater and more beautiful than it was transmitted to us.*

Courses were given in current events and five lectures by outside specialists supplemented these courses. Metal street signs were substituted for the old wooden ones; and $500 was allotted to the care and spraying of trees, with the town contributing an equal share. Also, in the spring of 1925, $126 was paid to schoolchildren who collected 130,000 tent caterpillar clusters from local trees—a sort of small-fry bounty.

Monday afternoon exhibits of the work of local artists were held in the WTIA building behind the Town Hall, which had been remodeled into a studio for art classes. This building was finally sold to the town in 1923 for $400 to be replaced by an equipment garage.

ESTABLISHING A PUBLIC HEALTH NURSE SERVICE

Since joining the National Organization for Public Health Nursing as an associate member in 1919, the WTIA shared many public health expenses with the town. These included clinics offering free vaccinations, dental clinics, hot lunches for school children, and the purchase of an ambulance for the town. In April 1925, participating with the Bedford grant for a Public Health Nurse, the WTIA hired Miss Fanning for the post and further obligated itself to carry the overhead costs of $225 yearly. The program continued to expand, and by 1939 the Visiting Nurse Committee in its annual report listed: "257 patients treated, 2,227 home visits made, 3,337 children examined at the Well Baby conferences and 97 at the dental clinic, 52 diphtheria immunizations provided, 3,300 quarts of free milk distributed, 15 X-rays taken, and 200 toys distributed to sick and needy children."

The period 1919–1925 closed with 16 standing committees actively engaged within the WTIA. During this period, the presidents were Mrs. Crawford (from 1919–1924), Mrs. Peck (1924–1925), and Mrs. Eager (1925–1926). In 1925, Miss C. E. Thomas, Treasurer of the Association since its founding in 1907 (except for one year), declined re-nomination. In May of 1924, Miss Frances Allen was engaged for secretarial work in place of Miss Lyon, the previous incumbent.

The contemporary reader may find a nostalgic note in the Advisory Board minutes: "The first question, which received a great amount of discussion, was in regard to the non-attendance of the members of the board at meetings."

From WTIA to WWC, 1926–1940

T he years leading up to World War II spawned in turn an era of buoyant prosperity and a period of severe recession and despair. So went the nation, and so, within its own limited sphere, went the Woman's Town Improvement Association. Under the successive presidencies of Mmes. Eager (1925–1926), Harris (1926–1927), and Child (1927–April 1929), a conservative stand-pat policy seems to have prevailed, with a series of fund-raising events to maintain projects started under prior administrations. As stated in the 50th anniversary edition of the *Westporter-Herald,* "These were years of consolidation. Already-founded activities were heightened and brought into sharper focus."

A Shift from Old Town Improvement Projects to New Ones

Some of the older projects were expanded and some were dropped or reduced in impact. Under pressures from an expanding town (population 8,250 in 1940), the Association found itself slowly being squeezed out of the business of "town improvement." Thus, the work of caring for triangles at road intersections was taken over by the town in June of 1926. Street-sign work gradually came to a halt as the town ran out of unnamed streets. Sidewalk-laying also became a town responsibility, as did the maintenance of school libraries in September 1926. The railroad station and cemetery clean-up projects continued on their uneventful way for a while, but even these ultimately became public responsibilities or were relegated to neglect. Apart from the town, many newly organized private agencies entered the civic field in apparent competition with the WTIA.

New Innovative Crusades Mounted

However, with the re-election of Mrs. John Crawford as president (1929–1931), a more aggressive stance was assumed by the Association and several innovative crusades were mounted. One such project that deserved a better fate than it received was sponsored by the "Billboard Committee." First discussion occurred without action at the 1925 annual meeting when it was announced that "The Association goes on record as opposing the placing of billboards and destroying of trees along public highways." Not until 1930 was action taken to implement this declaration by the formation of a joint committee composed of the WTIA, the Chamber of Commerce, the League of Women Voters, the Real Estate Board, the Garden Club, and the DAR to "make Westport one town in Connecticut without a billboard."

Several successes were scored in this enterprise, Mrs. Crawford announced that signs and billboards would not be returned to the newly painted Saugatuck Station, and a sign-less railroad station was maintained through 1933. The town zoning regulations were amended to prohibit billboards except on properties at which the announced activities were actually being conducted, and to require that such signs be at least 15 feet back from the street line. In response to WTIA solicitation, Mr. Merritt of the state legislature wrote to the Association in 1930 "assuring cooperation in *restricting billboards along the proposed (Merritt) highway.*" Prizes were offered to schoolchildren for the best anti-billboard slogans and posters, and stickers were distributed reading, "I favor products not advertised on the landscape." About 120 letters were sent to local property owners, one type for those already possessing billboards and a second type for those with a potential for such advertising but not yet in place.

As a parallel venture in beautification, $100 in prizes were offered to the "gas and wayside stand" which showed the greatest improvement in appearance during the competition period and, in October 1929, the Wayside Stand Committee recommended that prizes be awarded to the Dixie Lunch and to Beers Roadside Market. But despite the Association's yeoman effort in a spirited campaign, the total number of billboards in town was only reduced from 62 to 50 over a period of more than a year until the end of 1930. About that time, the WTIA took under advisement the removal of its own "unsightly" sign in front of Bedford House, but there is no record as to the action taken.

RE-EMPHASIS ON PUBLIC WELFARE

In the health department, the ladies expanded the Well Baby Conference, the first of which had been held some time before, on June 23, 1925. Starting in 1930, these conferences were held on every third Friday of the month. Mothers brought their babies to be weighed and measured, the data being charted by the public health nurse and reviewed by one of the doctors. Pre-natal instruction was given prospective mothers in infant hygiene and in related disciplines. In May 1934, a baby show was held, with 26 babies exhibited, but the record is silent as to whether or not any cried.

In 1932 a Dental Clinic was established in Bedford House. It was initially open one day a week during the summer but by 1955, open two days per week, with Dr.

Bailey of New Haven in charge. During the first year, 178 school children were examined at a nominal fee, the WTIA paying for those unable to do so. Control was vested in a joint committee composed of a town welfare representative, the public health nurse, and a WTIA committee member.

When Westport children needed dental care, school nurses sent a notification to parents. If the family could not afford this care at the time, the children were sent to the Westport Woman's Club

Dental Clinic. In 1952, children such as these made 233 visits. The dental clinic maintained a sporadic existence until 1959 when it was taken over by a group of local dentists.

The WTIA maintained a continuing interest in the ethnic groups of Saugatuck, and in September 1926 it organized a Girls' Club there, largely composed of girls of Italian-born parents. These girls were encouraged to become junior members of the Association upon payment of the 50-cent annual dues.

On May 12, 1932, a three-year lease was signed with the New Haven Railroad to rent for 10 dollars a year a plot of ground near the Saugatuck station at Franklin and Charles streets. It was then cleared, fenced, and furnished with equipment for use as a playground by the boys of Saugatuck. Unfortunately, the project was left unsupervised, and by May 1934, a report was presented to the Association "calling attention to broken apparatus and general untidiness in the Saugatuck Playground." The initial reaction was to discontinue the project, but on second thought it was decided to continue under the supervision of a newly inaugurated committee composed of WTIA members and interested Saugatuck parents. The lease was renewed until May 30, 1936 and with town cooperation, low sections were filled in to enlarge the area available for use as a baseball field.

THE DEPRESSION YEARS

At the end of 1928, the membership had stood at 408. In June 1929, the membership dues were raised from $1 to $5 per year. Unhappily, almost immediately thereafter, came the stock market crash of October 29. Although no immediate effect was had on the membership, shortly thereafter it became apparent that it was a rare woman who could afford $5 yearly, and a mass resignation dropped the Club membership to 55.

President Mrs. Schuyler Carlton (1931–1932), due to poor health, resigned on December 1, 1932 after serving 14 months. Her remaining term was completed by Mrs. Herbert Millard, who refused re-nomination at the next election. It therefore devolved upon the next president, Mrs. Robert T. Baldwin (1933–1936), to take resuscitative action. This she did by reducing the annual dues to a compromise figure of $3 immediately upon her election in September 1933. As a result, many members returned to the fold, and the membership rose again to 350 by the end of 1935.

The Depression years caused a retrenchment in the Association's regular activities but did not dampen its strong determination to help those in need.

In November 1931, a Free Employment Agency was established in Bedford House, "this being a dignified outlet for people in need." The Association also voted in February 1933 to donate 15 percent of all dues (about $175) to a fund for the unemployed.

THE WOMAN'S EXCHANGE AND THE THRIFT SHOP—A PERIPATETIC JOURNEY

The depression years caused a retrenchment in the WTIA's regular activities, but did not dampen its strong determination to help those in need. In January 1931, a temporary thrift shop was conducted in Westport to sell at minimal prices such second-hand articles as might be contributed or consigned. Later, in April 1931, a Woman's Exchange was proposed be established, similar to one conducted seven years earlier in the Bedford House "to help Westport families augment their incomes by selling goods and articles made in the home." Jams, soups, vegetables, and baked goods were sold on consignment, as well as handicrafts, babies' and children's clothes, and home-knit goods. The Exchange, re-christened a "Village Mart", was held on several successive Fridays and Saturdays, beginning on June 27, 1931 on the sidewalk in front of the Central Fire Station. The WTIA financed this effort and collected a 10 percent commission on all sales. But this was largely dissipated in defraying the costs of operation.

THE WOMAN'S EXCHANGE BEGINS ITS SEARCH FOR A HOME

A permanent Woman's Exchange was organized on March, 1932 and opened on February 22, 1933 in rent-free quarters in the Dickson Building at 56 East State Street, where the Elm Tree Shop was. This activity originally was a dependency of the Westport Emergency Unemployment Relief Committee and was organized as a non-profit agency under a committee of nine women, two of whom—Mmes. Baldwin and Wake—were later to serve as presidents of the WTIA. On April 17, only two months after it had been launched, the Exchange lost its free space in the Dickson Building. It moved to "the Pink House," a Westport landmark at the corner of Myrtle Avenue and State Street, adjacent to the Telephone Building, where it continued to enjoy a rent-free status by courtesy of the Southern New England Telephone Company. Here, in addition to selling home products on consignment, a tearoom served lunches for 35 and 50 cents each.

A permanent Thrift Shop was opened on May 10, 1933 at the Westport Unemployment Relief Committee building on State Street at the site of the present post-office, where it shared quarters with the C.W.A. (Federal Relief) Women's Sewing Project, which made garments to be distributed among the needy by the social service worker, the visiting nurse and the Red Cross. At this time, the Thrift Shop devoted all its proceeds to the Westport Unemployment Fund. It was dispossessed of its quarters in September 1935 when construction was started on the new post office. It then followed a nomadic path to 2 West State Street, where it occupied first the ground floor and, later, more spacious quarters on the second floor.

THE WTIA ADOPTS THE WOMAN'S EXCHANGE—A WELCOME SENSE OF SECURITY

Although the Woman's Exchange was a self-contained organization with its own officers, constitution, and bylaws, it very soon requested and received the sponsorship of the WTIA. They formed a permanent Thrift Shop and they established a "Woman's Exchange–Thrift Shop Committee" in January 1934 to help finance the operation and to assist it with volunteer help. The Thrift Shop managed to generate enough income to pay its own rental, the rental of the Exchange, a part of the salary for the manager of the Exchange, and its own rental obligation.

For a while, the Exchange continued its peripatetic course by moving on May 1, 1934, just after its first birthday, to new quarters (rented at $75 per month) in the Sherwood Building at 46 East State Street. The next year to a day, it moved to 8 Taylor Place, where it sponsored a block party with its neighboring enterprises.

The Exchange filed incorporation papers under Connecticut State law on May 3, 1934 with the name "Westport Woman's Exchange, Incorporated." It was re-incorporated about seven years later when it re-filed under the combined name: "Westport Woman's Shop, Incorporated." The Thrift Shop and the Woman's Exchange were reported to have occupied common quarters at some time before 1937, but the Club records do not seem to confirm this.

In February 1942, with characteristic enthusiasm but with a deplorable sense of history, the Exchange announced to the press and celebrated the 10th anniversary of its founding, just *nine* years after the fact.

Food shortages during World War II sharply curtailed the Exchange's operation, but it was the post-war prosperity that finally blunted its mission "to help others to help themselves." Finally, about 1951, it moved to quarters at the corner of West State Street and Riverside Avenue and closed its doors in February 1956.

THE THRIFT SHOP TRIES IT ON THEIR OWN—FOR AWHILE

The Thrift Shop maintained a quasi-independent existence although it was a department of the Woman's Club. The first brochure for the Thrift Shop was published in 1964. However, in February 1970 after mutual agreement, the Thrift Shop separated from the Club. Several Westport Woman's Club volunteers continued to work at the shop and went on to operate as an independent charity. Their landlord, who was able to use his building as a tax write-off and charged the Thrift Shop a modest rent, sold all his buildings on State Street in 1982. The new owner tripled the rent and the Thrift Shop finally closed on June 30, 1982 after 50 years.

THE "BOY PROJECT"—KEEPING JOBLESS YOUNGSTERS BUSY

Another relief project sponsored by the WTIA was the Boy Project" officially the Westport Cooperative Industries, which was established in April 1934 under Mrs. John Crawford as president. It was designed to keep busy the recent high-school graduates who could not find jobs. This was a cooperative factory located on Wilton Road under the supervision of Mr. Coley, the only regularly paid employee, with all the other boys participating as equal partners. Their first quantity order was "500 pallets for the Dolge Company."

THE ANNUAL FAIR GOES "SHOW BIZ"

The time-honored annual fair was continued. On August 19 and 20, 1926, a street fair called "Mother Goose Lane" was held on East Church Street and in Bedford House. Miss Muffet, Mary Contrary, Simple Simon, and all the other Mother Goose characters paraded as a prelude to the fair and then manned the booths. Dancing was featured on the Church Green to a 14-piece orchestra, climaxed with a Charleston dance contest. The net accrual to the treasury was $2,084.

The following year, on July 22 and 23, an "International Circus" was presented instead of a fair. This was a package of the John B. Rogers Producing Company of New York, featuring 200 local citizens in circus costumes and as "wild animals", all comporting on the Myrtle Avenue School grounds. Despite the inclusion of a piquant *Ballet of the Nile,* the affair netted a disappointing $148.50 to the WTIA treasury.

On July 13 and 14, 1928, an attempt was made to return to the former annual fair when "The Old Westport Hotel" (under New Management of the WTIA) was presented in the "Y" auditorium, featuring nine tableaux and netting $2,760 to the WTIA coffers.

On August 1 and 2 of 1929, local talent with a professional nucleus produced Shakespeare's *A Midsummer Night's Dream* on the Schlaet estate at Compo Beach, where 800 spectators viewed three performances. The profit was $1,162.

The following year, on July 24 and 26, 1930, a similar Shakespeare festival featured two performances each of *Midsummer Night's Dream* and *The Merry Wives of Windsor.* Despite a full-page ad in the *Westporter-Herald*, the performances did not draw too great a crowd. The net was only $186.

As a result of the Depression, the WTIA decided to dispense with the fair in 1931 and to hold instead a series of "Diminishing Parties" during the summer months. In spite of their name, these parties were a success to the extent of $1,171 added to the WTIA treasury.

After a hiatus of two years, a supplement to the annual fair was presented in the form of a Fashion Show that was held on April 16, 1934 in Bedford House under the chairmanship of Mrs. Hereward Wake. Ninety models presented the wares of eight Westport shops and two Bridgeport shops, and people attended despite the rain. Later, on July 27–29 of the same year, a Country Fair was held "on the athletic field, between two Westport schools." At this fair, a Chevrolet automobile was raffled off.

On April 8, 1932 a Fashion Show and Art Exhibit was held at Bedford House and elicited a letter from the general secretary of the YMCA deploring the overcrowding and pointing out the hazards which might exist from "a hurried exit." Later that year, on July 25–27, a return was made to the idea of a "package fair" when a Show Boat and Plantation Party was given on a boat anchored "at the old quay opposite the Open Door Inn" (off Taylor Place). Here, the Periwinkle Players presented several *"mellerdrammers"* including "dancing of the Cake Walk." This was presented for a re-run on July 16–18, 1933 under the auspices of the Woman's Exchange–Thrift Shop Committee of the WTIA. One of the performances was somewhat marred by the fact that Mayor and Mrs. LaGuardia of New York City were turned away for lack of seats, after having been especially invited by the Association president.

GAMBLING ALLEGED AT 1937 FAIR—AUDIENCE JEERS POLICE

In 1937, on July 29–31, a "Westport Fair" was held on the grounds of the General Putnam Inn, back of Taylor Place. The WPA Marionette Unit was featured and a Young Women's Beauty and Popularity Contest added zest to the proceedings. A more notorious innovation was the presence of gambling equipment, including two horseracing devices and five jackpot-type machines. State police, responding to complaints from undisclosed sources, braved the jeers of the fashionable Westport charity audience when they arrived to arrest the owner and operator of this equipment. Police said the complaints were based on the charge that small children had patronized the machines. Members of the Women's Town Improvement Association denied the charge. Seven machines, valued at $2,000 were seized by the police, who said they raided the charity fete in response to complaints, the source of which they refused to disclose. Hundreds of prominent Westport residents, many from the exclusive art colony, were on the grounds at the time of the raid.

Subsequent fund-raising activities midway through 1940 included four fashion shows at Bedford House—one given over a period of two days in April 1938 with a net return of $203, two "Fashions by the Clock" shows in March and May of 1939 clearing $529, and a fourth on May 13 and 14, 1940.

The 1938 show set a precedent in that "models making their debuts, average age 5, ran away with the afternoon shows and were missed in the evening performance." A second innovation was the use of several diffident male models. The 1940 Fashion Show also set a precedent, having been broadcast over the local radio station by a paying sponsor—with a net intake of $595.

All in all, the Association maintained a surprisingly stable financial condition despite many vicissitudes. Its annual budget between 1926 and 1940 averaged $4,700 with yearly variations of less than $400 either way.

During this decade and a half, concerts, card parties, and courses in home nursing, drawing, singing, gymnastics, rug-making, dancing, bridge, basketry, swimming, and weaving all contributed to the treasury.

Apart from its basic activities in health and emergency relief, the WTIA found time for other measures. Contributions were made to the Girl Scouts and Boy Scouts (1926) toward the purchase of a curtain for the stage and an electric stove for the lunch room of the Greens Farms School (1917 and 1929), the redecoration of Bedford House using unemployed relief labor (1930), the Norwalk Hospital (1933) and the Greenwich Birth-Control Clinic in Portchester (1935). A spruce tree was planted on Arbor Day in 1934 in front of Bedford Elementary School to be used on Christmas Eve for "children's carol street singing."

In 1926 and 1927, the Association catered the Father and Son "Y" banquet, and the next year meals were served to 150 men and boys attending the "Older Boys Y" convention in March. Starting in November 1931, a chorus of young people gathered one night a week for singing and dancing till 10 PM. In March 1935, badminton tournaments were played, at the conclusion of which "our team had won three out of five matches at Greenwich and are now Metropolitan Champions."

IMPROVING QUALITY OF LIFE IN THE COMMUNITY

The Association went on record in July of 1928 "as favoring the purchase of Taylor's property, by the town of Westport, to be used for Park purposes", but inexplicably, it voted in 1931 to oppose the State Park at Sherwood Island.

In 1938 the WTIA launched "a quiet investigation of housing conditions in Westport as affecting the Negro population." It also investigated "violations of the sanitary ordinances and illegal dumping along the town streets." But little success crowned these latter efforts since "apparently, the distinction between what constitutes a menace to health and what is merely a public nuisance is a delicate one; also there would appear to have been some confusion in the minds of the town fathers as to where the responsibility for dumps and garbage really rests." However, a solution to the garbage problem received a boost from a Yale University health survey of Westport, made at the behest of the WTIA and others, which recommended a full-time town Health Department.

PLAN TO FORM A BEACH COMMISSION UNOPPOSED AT HEARING

In March 1937, the Association pressed for an enabling act to provide a beach commission to regulate Compo Beach. Mrs. Robert T. Baldwin, backed a bill heard by the Cities and Boroughs Committee of the Legislature Wednesday, enabling Westport to appoint a beach commission. Representing 350 members of the newly named Westport Woman's Club, Mrs. Baldwin was introduced at the hearing by Representative Herbert E. Baldwin, who presented the bill.

Mrs. Baldwin made a complete but brief outline of the situations leading up to the request for the enabling act. She stated that the Westport Woman's Club is actively interested in civic problems and as such had received many complaints from Westporters asking them to do something relative to beach conditions. The organization, she stated, has been asked to confer with other Westport civic organizations and town authorities for the past two seasons on ways to improve and protect Westport's beaches. The women's group, she said, had been asked to make a study of possibilities and set-ups that had been provided for Fairfield and Darien. She said that the findings had proven successful and that they indicated a similar system could be handled in Westport for the good of all.

She called attention to the probabilities of the unfortunate expansion of the town and said that the beaches should be handled with this in mind and that the program should be an all-year-round affair. She stressed the point that the great mass of detail resulting from such a program, if it were adopted, should he taken off the shoulders of the selectmen and placed with public-spirited citizens who would have the time to devote to it. In answer to a question from the Chairman, she explained that the funds for operation would have to go through the regular channels of the Board of Finance and town meetings as other items for town expenditure do. This proposal was later approved with minor changes at a subsequent town meeting.

ORGANIZATIONAL AND MEMBERSHIP RULES CHANGE

Perhaps of greatest moment to contemporary readers were the organizational changes made during this period. In September 1927, the Advisory Board was changed to an Executive Board, with power to appoint committee chairmen. Following the resignation of Mrs. Child (1927–1929) in April because of illness in the family, Sara B. Crawford, as First Vice-President, once again took over the helm until 1931. Under her energetic leadership, many changes in the membership rules were adopted. In November 1929, the constitution was revised to provide free life membership to any member of ten years' standing who attained the age of 80 years. In 1928, Mrs. John Baker was voted an Associate membership "until such time that she feels she can take an active part", and in the following year, a second Associate Member was added to the roster although no formal change appears to have been made in the bylaws or the constitution to regularize such action. Similarly, eight "midget" members were listed on the roster for 1930.

By way of digression, it might here be mentioned that Mrs. Crawford, after her retirement from the Association presidency, went on to serve six two-year terms (1925–1938) as Westport's representative in the General Assembly of the State Legislature, and subsequently (1939–1941) as Connecticut's first woman Secretary of State.

A SPECIAL ROLE FOR "YOUNG MARRIEDS"—THE JUNIOR WOMAN'S CLUB

A Business Girls' Club was organized in 1928 from among 25 young working members of the WTIA. This group possibly became the nucleus of the Junior Woman's Club (JWC), which became a department of the WTIA in 1937 and was composed largely of young marrieds between 18 and 30 years of age. This group should not be confused with the Junior membership of an earlier period who paid reduced dues and had no voting privileges. The JWC ran the children's activities at the fairs, held a dance for the benefit of the Dental Clinic (1937), dressed dolls and repaired toys for needy towns-children (1946), and staffed the mobile chest X-ray unit of the State Tuberculosis (TB) Commission (1947). The group participated in the TB seals campaigns, held white elephant sales, food sales, card parties and dances, the proceeds of which provided clothing for needy local and overseas children through the "Children's Friendly Service." The Junior Club also serviced the scholarship fund, the Norwalk Hospital and the "Y" girls. For many years the Juniors conducted the sale of Easter seals in town and also sponsored locally the *New York Herald's* "Friendly Town Project", whereby underprivileged city children were brought to Westport homes for a week's vacation. The Junior membership reached 155 in 1948.

Is a Woman Over 35 Still a Junior?

Club says no. So 62 members quit to form own organization. The Junior Woman's Club sowed the seeds of its own ultimate disjunction. This came about partly by virtue of the fact that many of the members refused to attain "retirement age" and partly because the group began to operate as a "couples' club" with disparate aims from the parent organization. The Juniors resolved the age problem by the simple expediency of raising the age limit for members to 35, then to 40, and finally—in quiet desperation—the age limit was removed entirely in February 1952. The *raison d'être* of the JWC group initially grew out of the fact that most of the younger women, because of babies and jobs, could not attend the afternoon meetings scheduled by the senior membership. Slowly, however, the JWC grew in self-sufficiency, electing its own officers, setting up its own bylaws, and maintaining its own treasury. When the parent group belatedly woke up to the fact that there were virtually two clubs under its roof, it was too late for effective action.

But such action was attempted nonetheless. A first palliative was tried in July 1956 when the Club president announced: "To serve the needs of women from both Clubs who cannot meet during the day, a new group called the P.M. Club will be formed to provide a vehicle for community-minded individuals who cannot meet during the daytime." To permit husbands to attend with their wives, membership in the Club was waived as a prior condition of attendance. The new organization was not accepted by the Juniors as a substitute for their own club.

Finally, on July 24, 1956, the seniors pulled the reins too hard, too fast, and they snapped. The triggering action was a resolution by the Executive Committee that the membership of the "Junior Department" be limited to age 35, that its body of officers be reduced to a chairman and vice-chairman, and that its treasury be absorbed into that of the parent organization. On September 12, 1956, after several futile attempts at reconciliation by both Seniors and Juniors, 62 Juniors resigned en masse, reducing the membership of the Club from 556 to 494 in one fell swoop. The Juniors thereupon set up an independent organization, named The Westport Junior Woman's League, which affiliated itself with the YMCA Woman's Division, and met at Bedford House for some years.

Rumblings within the WTIA, indicative of a maladjustment with the times, were first heard in 1931 at the September meeting of the Executive Board, when it was moved "that the Woman's Town Improvement Association be and hereby is dissolved. Be it also moved that this meeting appoint a committee to organize a Public Health Nursing Association to which shall be transferred the funds of the WTIA remaining after all obligations shall have been met." Concurrently, it was proposed that all activities other than those pertaining to public health be given up, including the maintenance of Bedford House, which had lately greatly increased in cost.

A luncheon was held on September 16, 1931, with one delegate from each civic organization in town "to get the consensus…as to whether or not the WTIA should be dissolved, as other organizations have taken over a large part of their work." The *Westporter-Herald* of September 29 unfurled the headline: "WTIA May Change Name to Westport Woman's Club." However, no further definitive action was taken at this time.

Under Mrs. Baldwin (1933–1936), the regular business meetings were changed to the first Monday of each month (with a lecture on the third Monday). In February 1934, the constitution was revised to provide for biennial elections in lieu of annual elections. The annual meeting was changed from September to June, with the report year from April 1 to March 31. Consequently Mrs. Baldwin's first term was for only nine months. She was re-elected for a succeeding term of two years but resigned for reasons of health, and Mrs. Meyers filled out the remaining six months of her term. Mrs. Buell, who succeeded to the presidency in June 1936, also resigned because of illness in January 1937, and Mrs. Hereward Wake, first vice-president, assumed the duties of president until June 1938.

A four-page printed monthly newsletter was authorized in August 1934, replacing the postcards used until then to announce the monthly meetings. This was named the *WTIA News Letter*, and Mrs. Allan Dodd was its first editor. Later, after February 1928, the name was changed to the *Westport Woman's Club Newsletter* and it is now *The Bulletin*. Somewhat earlier—February 1928—membership cards were first issued. These were marked "non transferable."

The WTIA Becomes the Westport Woman's Club

It was during the administration of Mrs. Wake that the name of the WTIA was finally changed to the Westport Woman's Club, after much debate as to whether "Woman's" or "Women's" was appropriate. This change became effective on February 1, 1938. But the new constitution and bylaws were not formally adopted until the following month. Business meetings continued to be held on the first Monday of each month, but the annual meeting was changed from June to May. There were four classes of membership: Regular ($3 per year), Athletic ($2 per year additional), Life ($25 lump sum or $10 for each of three successive years), and

Junior—up to 25 years of age—($1 dues plus $3 for athletic privileges).

The Westport Woman's Club was organized along departmental lines: Athletic and Recreational, Civics and Legislation, Fine Arts (including committees on drama, art, literature, and music), Garden, Junior Woman's Club, Public Health, Social, and Woman's Exchange–Thrift Shop. In addition to these departments, there were committees on Bedford House, Membership, Press, Program, and Scholarship. Frequent changes and additions were made in this list each succeeding year.

Finally, on December 1, 1939 (with legal filing on December 4), the Westport Woman's Club was incorporated under Connecticut State Law as a non-profit organization "to provide residents of the town of Westport, County of Fairfield and State of Connecticut, and adjoining towns, with educational, medical, dental and other charitable facilities that may directly or indirectly promote health, standards of living or well-being of the people and their communities." The principal address of the corporation was listed as "No. 3 North Main Street" (the YMCA).

COMMUNITY FORUM STARTED—NOTED, PROMINENT SPEAKERS

In 1935, a community forum was sponsored by the Club with such speakers as Roger Baldwin (civil rights activist and founder of the American Civil Liberties Union), Norman Thomas (social reformer and frequent candidate for political office), and Clarence Darrow (defense counsel in many dramatic trials including the famous Scopes Trial, in which he defended John T. Scopes against prosecutor William Jennings Bryan). The subjects of these lectures were the controversial ones of that period. At each monthly meeting of the Club, there was always a speaker of prominence lecturing on timely subjects.

The War Years and After, 1941–1950

O n September 1, 1939, the Germans invaded Poland, thereby precipitating World War II. Although the United States abstained for two years, it ultimately was drawn into the conflict by the Japanese attack on Pearl Harbor on December 7, 1941.

The Woman's Club was not lax in the war effort. The Club formed a Home Defense Committee on June 11, 1941, devoting a full measure of energy to defense projects from 1940 onwards. Funds were appropriated to adopt both a British war orphan and a needy American child. A mammoth "Revue" took place, featuring Westporters of stage and concert hall. Even a "ski patrol" was organized.

Then, there was "Bundles for America," a group with headquarters in the State Drive-in Cleaners store that collected and repaired clothing for servicemen and needy families. Over 3,800 pieces were distributed. And it continued after the war, when the project became the Club's Clothing Relief Committee.

The war put a severe crimp in other endeavors. A daytime playschool formed in 1941 to entertain some 25 youngsters while their mothers took jobs in defense plants. The playschool was dropped the following year because of transportation difficulties.

The effect of the war on the town of Westport and its Woman's Club was not immediate. For a time, the usual bridges, dances, luncheons, and benefits continued apace. However, the war brought on a reassessment of priorities by the Club. One of the first issues to be considered was whether to continue the spring fashion shows and summer fairs. This question was finally decided in the affirmative because, in the words of Fashion Show Chairman Mrs. Baldwin, "you can stop manufacture of civilian luxuries in wartime, but you can't stop babies from needing milk."

And under her strong influence, starting with "The Fashion Market—1940" given in the "Y" auditorium in May 1941, the fashion shows became elaborate affairs with printed programs and paid commercial advertising. This particular event featured 80 models and 21 door prizes. Booth space was rented to 15 exhibitors and a raised runway was built to promenade the models. Proceeds were $595.

The next fashion show, the seventh, came ten months later and unfurled before 400 spectators "fashion trends towards South American colors...and flowing peasant lines." The amount realized was $1,169. The "8th Annual Fashion Mart", presented in March 1942, highlighted "women in uniform" but netted only $475 to the Club treasury.

FASHION SHOWS SUSPENDED 1943–1946

Because of war-generated difficulties, the fashion shows were suspended for the next three years. And at this point, the arithmetic of counting successive shows becomes somewhat fuzzy. Thus, while the "8th Annual Fashion Show" was in 1942, the "9th Annual Fashion Mart" was in May of 1947. And the "10th Annual Fashion Show" was held in March 1950.

The 9th show in 1947 was by far the most successful of all, bringing the Club a net profit of $2,394. Perhaps a particular boost was given to this affair by the *Westporter-Herald*, which issued a special eight-page fashion supplement on May 8th, just before the show. It may be that the Club's own news release: "Husbands May Find the Exhibit of Corsets on Living Models an Attraction" was responsible for drawing the 1,400 spectators, each of whom paid $2 for an afternoon luncheon view or $1.50 for an evening pastry-and-coffee peek.

The *Town Crier* newspaper laid the grounds for the ultimate abandonment of the large fashion shows in the "Y" with an editorial on May 23, 1947 which pointed out the fire hazard inherent in an overcrowded auditorium with potential for a "Coconut Grove disaster" in Westport. Although the "10th Annual Fashion Show" was held in the "Y" after this editorial, subsequent shows were limited events held in the Clubhouse on Imperial Avenue, with a much smaller return.

THE BIRTH OF A WESTPORT INSTITUTION—THE YANKEE DOODLE FAIR

As in years before, the backbone event that provided most of the wherewithal to support the Club's activities was the annual fair. The first such fair, held after a two-year lapse, was a "Country Fair" scheduled for August 15–17, 1940, at the Thayer estate on Boston Post Road West and Sylvan Road. This property was of special historical interest, having been owned at one time by the great-grandfather of P. T. Barnum. As a further drawing card for prospective patrons, it was announced that "you may bowl on the green where Washington and Lafayette once drank from the old well, while waiting to have their horses shod at the old smithy."

Suzanne Conn, a board member, suggested that the motif of the fair be patriotic and that it be sponsored by "Yankee Doodle." From this suggestion came the Yankee Doodle Fair of 1940, the progenitor of a long and fecund line.

Admission to the 1940 fair was free, and a small brochure issued at the time listed thirty booths including some very familiar standbys: Bingo, Fish Pond, Attic Booth, and Hoop-la.

The grand prize was a Chevrolet automobile, and a contest was held to select the "most popular matron, man, and debutante in Westport"—a contest that the *Town Crier* later deplored as "a gyp game won by the person commanding the biggest bankroll." (But then, the *Town Crier* loved to needle the establishment.) This fair netted $4,962.

In August 1941, the fair was repeated at the Thayer place, this time with a western motif featuring a barbecued steer. A series of pithy cartoon announcements, "Yankee Doodle Says" was published in the newspapers, creating a publicity breakthrough for the fair. This event realized $6,477.

For the next five years, a Yankee Doodle Fair was held annually on Jesup Green "back of the Westport Town Hall where the old General Putnam Inn was." In 1942, the first children's fair—"A Fair Within a Fair"—was innovated. Also, arrangements were made to have a plane drop leaflets on the local beaches advertising the fair. Some of these leaflets bore numbers that entitled the holder to $5 in War Savings Stamps.

In 1943, and for some years thereafter, the *Farmers Almanac* was consulted before setting the fair dates. So successful was this method that not a drop of rain marred the proceedings for years—until the precedent-shattering fair of 1950, when a downpour on the first day suspended operations for four hours, and a transformer failure on the second night caused a further loss of time. A vacant store next to the Fine Arts Theatre was made available to the Club in 1943 for use as a fair office and storage depot. That same year, tickets were issued to servicemen allowing them $1 each in free food and games. Wartime conditions were further in evidence by the presence of a WAC (Women's Army Corps) recruiting booth, by the requirement that "red rationing coupons" be surrendered for a chicken dinner, and by the grand prize, a $500 war bond.

The August 1944 fair was—if the reader will pardon the expression—serendipitous. A "Fanny Farm" had been designated as a rest area on the Green. The *Town Crier* seized this idea to editorialize on the need for such facilities elsewhere. As a result, benches were placed on the library green to afford passengers using the bus stops at Main and State streets similar benefits.

The 1945 fair was uneventful, but the 1946 frolic produced some innovation. A nightclub atmosphere was fostered by engaging two specialty dancers for the 6:30 supper show. A "G.I. Pin-Up Baby Contest" was inaugurated; and the proceeds from one hour of the fair on its second day ($1,500) were donated to a fund for the care of several firemen who were victims of a recent truck explosion in town. It was estimated that 20,000 persons attended this fair.

Because of an increase in the size and cost of the fair, the next several events were held on the grounds of Bedford Junior High School. Here, from 1947 through 1950, the fairs had as their respective motifs a "Big Top Circus", a "Salute to Westport Artists", "The Forty-niners", and "Westport–1900."

The growth of the fair as a Westport institution led to its incorporation as a non-profit organization under Connecticut state law. Articles of association were filed with the secretary of state on February 28, 1947, under the name "The Yankee Doodle Fair, Incorporated." At the same time a four-page set of bylaws was prepared.

Although the fair was a uniformly successful operation, its course had not been entirely smooth. In 1946, a patron brought suit jointly against the Woman's Club and the town (finally settled by surety) because of injuries sustained at Jesup Green from stumbling "over a depression in the ground." A more endemic problem was lack of workers. Although the Club membership had topped 750 including the JWC by May 1948, only about 50 dedicated club-women bore the brunt of the fair work and through their leadership, hard work, and high morale, gave this Westport tradition both form and substance. As many as 650 people were involved in mounting the larger fairs, and as a result, many non-members were invited to participate as a means of community involvement. On August 14, 1948, the *Town Crier* took note of this state of affairs and editorialized that "it is surprising to an outsider how many of the members of the Woman's Club were not connected in any manner with the fair and how many men and women who have no connection with the Club worked themselves practically into the hospital to put the carnival across."

GAMES OF CHANCE CONVERTED TO GAMES OF SKILL

Other troubles were less serious in retrospect. A law of long standing on the state statute books proscribed gambling; but by common consent the authorities had become quite myopic in respect to charitable endeavors. In accordance with this unwritten understanding, the Games Chairman of the 1942 fair had rented some devices commonly called "one-armed bandits." Almost immediately some never-revealed ill-wisher lodged a telephone complaint with the State Police that they couldn't very well ignore. So, willy-nilly, they descended on the offending gaming booth and carted off the poor male operator to the local lockup. The Games Chairman became paralyzed with consternation, and only the glib tongue of the offender and the sympathetic response of the local police saved him from a booking.

This same problem reared its head some nine years later when Fairfield County District Attorney Lorin W. Willis of Bridgeport took it upon himself (with some needling from the clergy) to announce on June 30, 1949 that henceforth he would enforce rigorously the state ban on "wheels of chance which gave money, merchandise or liquor as prizes." Thus Fairfield County suffered a charitable blackout due to the indefatigable dedication of one man, while elsewhere throughout the state, carnivals for charity were rife. Mrs. Bradley, the Fair Chairman, refused to be nonplussed. "We have already put $7,000 in the fair," she stated, "and are depending on our friends and neighbors to support us as enthusiastically as they have in the past." So the fair went ahead, and in the two weeks remaining before opening date, the games of chance were all converted to games of skill. At the final reckoning it was found that the amount realized was slightly more than $16,000. This was $2,000 less than the year before, possibly because of Mr. Willis' ruling. Such is the perversity of legislators that a bill, introduced in the 1950 session of the Legislature by Assemblyman Serena of Westport to legalize certain types of games at charity-sponsored carnivals, failed to pass.

Another incident of the July 1946 fair was recounted by the *Norwalk Hour:* "Yankee Doodle is credited with riding to town on a pony, but it was the pony that reversed the tables yesterday by going to town at the Yankee Doodle Fair."

The pony at the Children's Carnival became frightened at the popping of a balloon in front of his nose and bolted. When Mrs. J. D. Lodge, former ballerina, attempted to stop the runaway, she was thrown beneath the wheels of the cart, which passed over her chest. The pony was finally corralled after snarling early evening traffic in the center of crowded Westport. Fortunately Mrs. Lodge was not badly hurt, and like the trooper she was, continued to handle the pony rides after a day of rest.

Not a little of the success of the fairs in the late 1940s was due to the pert and piquant columns created by Mrs. Bradley just before each fair. Starting in 1947 and for four years thereafter, she wrote two weekly columns that appeared in the *Town Crier* and the *Westporter-Herald*. In a regular weekly column that she later wrote for the *Westport Town Crier*, she frequently devoted space to Club activities.

The State Federation of Women's Clubs made awards for the high quality of the Club's publicity for the years ending 1945, 1947, 1948, and 1949. The third award conferred on the Club the right to permanent retention of the trophy cup. In September 1948, the Club's press book of that year topped all others by winning both the State and the General Federation of Women's Clubs awards, thus achieving "best in the nation."

CLUB EXPENSES DOUBLE AFTER THE WAR

The Club expenditures during the 1949s showed the effects of wartime activity and inflation. The pre-war budget for the year 1940–1941 was slightly over $11,000. The following year it jumped to $15,700. Thereafter, it rose steadily to a peak of $38,900 in 1948–1949, dropping to $31,400 the next year. The receipts from the Yankee Doodle Fair followed a parallel course: $4,961 in 1940, followed by $6,476 the next year. Similarly, the fair income peaked in 1948 at $18,000, dropping to just over $16,000 in 1949 (thanks to Mr. Tillis' war on games of chance).

The principal Club outlay was for salaries, and the defect between the income from the fairs and fashion shows on the one hand and the total expenditures on the other hand, was supplied by receipts from the Bedford Fund, Club dues, visiting nurses' fees, and Drama Department ticket sales, in descending order of magnitude. A stable fund-raising activity during the whole of the 1940s was the *TB (Tuberculosis) Seal Campaign* conducted each year in Westport by the Woman's Club. Eighty-five percent of the gross sales of these seals reverted to the public health activities of the Club.

In the early 1940s, the Woman's Club responded promptly once the call had been issued for home services in support of the war effort. On June 11, 1941, the Club formed a Home Defense Committee, which immediately set up a broad spectrum of activity within the scope of its available resources: a civilian motor corps, nutrition and "canteen" courses to insure balanced diets despite war shortages, a telephone squad of women to handle emergency calls, and a bicycle squadron of boys and girls for emergency messenger service. Some of these programs strained a bit: a women's marksmanship course under police tutelage, a women's ski corps, and incredible enough, a women's cavalry. Of more immediate pertinence, was an aluminum scrap collection conducted in July 1942 with the help of local Girl Scouts and Boy Scouts, who garnered nearly a ton of this critical metal, giving the town the highest per capita collection rate of all in Fairfield County. In October 1942 the Club was awarded a "bronze certificate" by the governor and the Connecticut Defense Council in recognition of the fact that more than 10 percent of the Club members had passed the first-aid examination and were accredited "first-aiders."

In May 1942, the Club sponsored a two-year old British child—and then an American child—by contributing an amount sufficient to provide each with room and board. About the same time, fuel economy became an issue, and as a result, Bedford House was closed on Mondays.

The working mothers employed at defense plants also received support when the Club conducted at Bedford Junior High School a series of 6-week Play School sessions for girls 6 to 14 years of age. About 50 girls were registered the first year; but, by 1943, the project was abandoned because of transportation difficulties. However, correlative athletic activities were continued in junior life-saving courses, a co-ed sports club for teenagers, and basketball and bowling tournaments for intermediates.

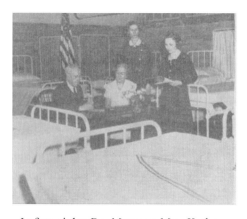

Left to right: *Dr. Munson; Mrs. Kathryn McCormick, public school nurse; Mrs. Hazel Rosenau and Mrs. John Guidera, visiting nurses of the Westport Woman's Club, who supervised the operation of the hospital.*

In the early 1940s, the Medical Corps, headed by Dr. William R. Munson, local health officer under the Westport Civilian Defense Council, established a 16-bed hospital in the basement of the Bedford Elementary School. The hospital included an operating table and other essential medical supplies for use in an emergency or disaster and could be expanded to include 40 beds. The hospital was created as a preparatory war measure and was supervised by the Westport Woman's Club.

A SPECIAL WAR SERVICES COMMITTEE FORMED—"BUNDLES" FOR AMERICAN SERVICEMEN AND THEIR FAMILIES

In May 1942 the Club's Home Defense Committee was disbanded because the Red Cross, the Civil Defense Council and a host of other organizations had pre-empted the field. In its stead a *Special War Services Committee* was appointed in November 1942, whose principal effort was focused on the "Bundles for America" program. This was a national organization that was an outgrowth of the earlier "Bundles for

Britain." This program was dedicated "to winning the war by strengthening and vitalizing the home front...offering aid to servicemen and their families as well as to discharged veterans."

At the outset of its existence, the Special War Services Committee opened a Westport branch of the Bundles for America on East State Street, next to the First National Store. Its first project, completed in less than a month, was to make 95 layettes for Service wives and to assemble 1,000 Christmas stockings for the "forgotten men of the Navy"—the gunners of the merchant fleet. This program operated largely in response to requests by the Army and Navy for specific items on a pre-set schedule. Twelve dozen pairs of special mittens were made for men on the mine-sweepers; and a Clothing Bank was established to provide warm clothing for Army storage in the event of a national disaster. To facilitate the collection and storage of clothing, a branch office of Bundles for America was opened at the Saugatuck Elementary School in February 1943. As reported by Mrs. Bradley in 1944, "In Westport and vicinity over 400 women have been giving their time to this project turning out 1,000 knitted garments for the Army, Navy, and Merchant Marine, 1,050 layettes, more than 3,800 pieces of reconstructed clothing, and more than 200 miscellaneous articles."

In February 1945 the Westport office of Bundles for America was moved to Bedford House, where it headed up branch offices in Saugatuck and Weston as well as home operations in Westport, Darien, and Norwalk. Toward the end of the war, emphasis was shifted to aiding discharged veterans. Finally, in September 1945, after V-J Day, the Bundles program closed its doors.

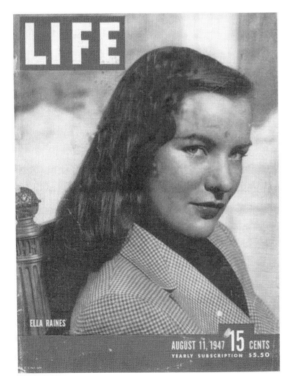

LIFE MAGAZINE CELEBRATES "A RARE WOMAN'S CLUB" ON ITS 40TH ANNIVERSARY— UNPRECEDENTED RECOGNITION FROM THE NATIONAL PRESS

Apparently the Club, on its own merits, was considered very newsworthy by the press, as over 7,000 column-inches of space were devoted to Club activities in the local and national press during both 1947 and 1948. *Life* magazine featured the Westport Woman's Club in its August 11, 1947 issue with the following characterization of its members: "The Ladies of Westport, Connecticut Like Sidewalks and Street Signs Better than

Teas." In a three-page article including photographs of the Club's officers, the Yankee Doodle Fair, and club members' children playing on a sidewalk that had resulted from the WWC campaign, *Life* summarized the Club's many contributions to the community and featured the fair's role in financing these programs. Apparently impressed with the Club's uniqueness among women's clubs in general, *Life* characterized it as "A Rare Woman's Club."

After being featured in this issue of *Life* magazine, many direct appeals for help were received from all over Europe. These were investigated and accommodated in turn.

SIX OF EXECUTIVE COMMITTEE MEET TO DISCUSS THE CLUB BUDGET AT HOME OF PRESIDENT INA BRADLEY (SEATED ON TABLE)

A RARE WOMAN'S CLUB
The ladies of Westport, Conn. like sidewalks and street signs better than teas

A Rare Woman's Club
The ladies of Westport, Conn. like sidewalks and street signs better than teas

Westport, Conn., a town of 8,258 on Long Island Sound 45 miles from Manhattan, pleasantly combines the charm of New England and the up-to-date bustle of a commuting population. Like most U.S. towns, Westport has a woman's club. But unlike many woman's clubs, Westport's has little time for lectures, cards and teas, the traditional woman's club activities which have provided Cartoonist Helen Hokinson with a lucrative lifework. Its membership has worked to make Westport a better town rather than toying with culture by entertaining visiting literati and appointing committees to study delphinium-raising. Over the years the club has provided once somnolent Westport with its first street signs, public drinking fountains, garbage collections and rubbish cans, playgrounds, concrete sidewalks and all-night street illumination. It introduced hot lunches to the Westport schools and brought about the development of Compo Beach, where it provided life-saving equipment and helped buy a bathhouse pavilion. It has accomplished these things mainly through annual fund-raising fair for which many of its members work hard, sometimes in costumes. Profits from this year's fair, staged successfully last month, will finance the even more ambitious program on which the Club is now embarked.

Fair Buys Schooling, Milk and Clinics for Westport

In this, its 40th year, the Westport Woman's Club is, among other things, providing its town with free visiting-nurse service, free milk for underprivileged children, a children's free dental clinic. Its members, always active in community government, are currently serving on the town Traffic Committee, the Board of Education, the town Planning Commission and hold the offices of town Clerk and State Legislator. The scholarships the Club annually offers amount to $1,100 yearly. With a membership of only 693 and annual dues of $3, the Club must employ various methods to finance its philanthropies. One is publication of *The Connecticut Cook Book,* a compilation of recipes used in Connecticut kitchens. But the chief method is the Yankee Doodle Fair, which annually offers such rich raffle prizes as automobiles, washing machines, luggage, watches and cases of Scotch. The approximately $18,000 raised at this year's fair, plus the members' enormous energy and cooperation they cajole from other organizations, will keep the Club program rolling another year without difficulty. Cooperation was not always so easy. When the Club sought to install concrete sidewalks in Westport 40 years ago, the town fathers protested stoutly. People would slip and fall, they, argued, on such smooth walks.

"PARCEL PACKING MAMAS"—PREDECESSOR TO THE CLOTHING RELIEF COMMITTEE

For many years, one day each week a group of "Parcel Packing Mamas" met at the Woman's Club to make up packages of clothing for shipment throughout the world. They gathered donated clothing from as far away as Ohio, mended it, cleaned it, and packed it for shipment. Since it started as part of British War Relief before America's entry into World War II, the group expanded its activities to include outfitting returning servicemen who had outgrown their civilian clothes, and continued to send packages overseas.

Some of the women involved in this program decided that the need for this service was far from over. Out of this nucleus the *Clothing Relief Committee* of the Westport Woman's Club evolved. After being featured in the August 11, 1947 issue of *Life* magazine, many direct appeals for help were received from all over Europe. These were investigated and accommodated in turn. Clothing was also sent to the Sioux and Navaho Indians in South Dakota; and the people of Holland sent tulip bulbs in appreciation for clothing received.

As the need for clothing decreased, the committee, under the dedicated chairmanship of Lillian Lambdin, devoted itself to making new clothes for Connecticut Children's Aid, and later toys were repaired and sent to children in Norwalk Hospital. In 1949 the committee moved to the Clubhouse on Imperial Avenue where it continued in operation until 1961.

WESTPORT LOAN CLOSET STARTED

In October 1943, a *Westport Loan Closet* was started by the Public Health Committee of the Woman's Club. Later it was placed under the *Community Services Committee* where it continues to reside. This unit was to maintain a stock of seldom used items such as wheelchairs, crutches, commodes, and, at times, an inhalator, a walker, leg braces, and bathinettes, for loan to residents of the town and its environs without charge. The supply is replenished from time to time by purchases and donations.

THE NEW CONNECTICUT COOK BOOK

Another wartime effort of the Woman's Club was the publication of *The New Connecticut Cook Book*, initially proposed as early as 1927. This 261-page paperback, spiral-bound book, contained 600 recipes garnered from 200 Connecticut cooks, local housewives, and famous personalities, including Lawrence Tibbett's Chicken Casserole, Lily Pons' Crêpes de Boeuf, and Edna Ferber's Crème Brûlée.

Original Cookbook

Second printing Cookbook

About 90 percent of the recipes were designed "to promote the preparation of good food under trying wartime conditions." The book was compiled under the chairmanship of Mrs. Dorr, edited by Mrs. Fry and illustrated by 26 local artists. A first printing of 5,000 copies was ordered at a cost of $3,000, with the book to retail at $2.50 a copy. After some delay, which unfortunately virtually ruined the Christmas sale of the book, the printer made an initial delivery of 500 copies on December 13, 1943. Copyright was approved on January 20, 1944.

Reviews of the book were broadcast over two national radio hook-ups and published in several national women's magazines. Newspapers in Bridgeport, New Haven, Hartford, New York, Philadelphia, and Cleveland gave it notice. The proceeds from the sale of the first printing were allocated to the War Service Committee, and about $1,000 was turned over to the Bundles for America project. Late in 1944, the Club designated Harper & Brothers, publishers, as sole agent for a reprint edition with the Club to receive a royalty of 25 cents a copy or 10 percent of the retail price. A second printing with corrections was run in 1945.

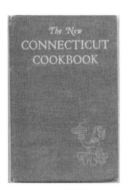

Second edition cookbook

A second edition, revised to reflect the post-war food market, was compiled by Margot Stewart and published by Harper & Brothers in April 1947. This was touted as "a volume whose 734 taste thrills are spiced with literary gems and fine art work." Among these gems is "Do you weep when you cut onions? Try holding an ordinary kitchen match between your teeth while you are handling them." Copies sold at $3.00 each, with a 25 cent royalty to the Club. In all, the cookbook grossed nearly $10,000.

Major organizations in town wasted no time in getting back to normal. The postwar period was "a well-ordered one" for the Westport Woman's Club, for example. Mrs. Helen Warnock, whose presidency (1944–1946) spanned the transition period from war to peace, also served in the General Assembly of the state legislature for two terms (1945–1949). At this time a new club slogan emerged: "We, the women of this organization, dedicate ourselves to truth, service, and cooperation. We will enter no activity that cannot fulfill this pledge." The Club's colors were established as blue and white, and the lilac became the Club flower.

In 1945, V-E Day in May was followed by V-J Day in September, and transport of soldiers back home was soon underway. The post-war period of the 1940s was a well-ordered one for the Westport Woman's Club. Its leadership for the most part was in exceptionally able hands. Mrs. Bradley, who succeeded Mrs. Warnock, was similarly oriented. Her first term was from 1946 to 1948 and her second term from 1950 to 1952. Organizational changes were few in this decade. The 1940 bylaws introduced a new class of "special" membership. This class paid dues of $15, was non-active and non-voting, and by virtue of its higher dues was relieved "from the call of the Hospitality Committee for donations." At about the same time, the Executive Board created a set of Standing Rules. One Standing Rule provided that any "qualified" member may bring a guest to any regular meeting of the Club on payment of 50 cents for each guest. In 1943 all past presidents of the Club were voted to be "Honorary Members."

In the early 1940s the Club also appears to have receded from its long-standing proscription against male members when certain men (not all husbands) associated with the Drama Group, the Civics Committee, and some Yankee Doodle Fair Committees were designated as "Associate Members." However, these names do not appear in either the yearbook or the Club membership roster. Later, men associated with the Drama Department were required to pay the Drama Department dues of $2, but were otherwise not designated as Club members. Years later, from 1957 through 1959, a tiny breach was made temporarily in the fortress walls when about 12 men were officially listed as "Associate Members" by virtue of joining the P.M. Bridge group and on payment of $5 annual dues.

THE NEW CLUBHOUSE ON IMPERIAL AVENUE

Probably the most important single postwar project of the Woman's Club, in terms of impact on the organization, was its new clubhouse. Membership mushroomed after World War II and a larger meeting hall was needed. This doubtlessly received its triggering impulse from YMCA planning for a greatly expanded program to accommodate returning servicemen. But it also culminated a long-standing groundswell of dissatisfaction on the part of both the Woman's Club and the YMCA staff over their competitive use of the "Y" facilities.

In any event, in September 1944, through Mr. Frederick T. Bedford, the Bedford Fund offered to finance the purchase of the Watts House at 87 Imperial Avenue for use by the Woman's Club in lieu of the Bedford House. In a letter dated September 13, 1944, the Bedford Fund offered this property with "additional monies available for some necessary repairs and alterations." Mr. Bedford subsequently clarified this phrase to limit its application to "alterations to the house for a larger meeting room." On September 18, 1944 the Club membership voted to accept this offer.

The house in question was a three-story frame structure with eleven rooms, an attic and a basement. It had a wide porch on three sides—removed during rehabilitation—and occupied a one and three-quarter plot of upland on the west side of Imperial Avenue extending to the Saugatuck River. Since the property was at that time leased to a third party who ran it as a boarding house, occupancy by the Woman's Club was scheduled for May 1, 1945, the terminal date of the lease.

The building's origin is somewhat cloudy. The town records list it merely as "very old." It is known that the property originally was farmland owned by Henry R. Treadwell, and that he sold two-and-a-half acres to Sidney Watts in 1881. The house was in existence in 1883 when Imperial Avenue was extended to Saugatuck, so it must have been constructed either in 1881 or 1882. The house remained in the Watts family until June 13, 1940 when it was sold to Morris Marks for $14,500. As shown on a survey map on file in Town Hall (Map #1471 dated 1940) the plot then consisted of 2.58 acres of upland. This was subdivided by Marks by a line parallel to and one foot north of the small utility building between the main residence and the old carriage house. The northerly portion, comprising about three-fourths of an acre, was sold on January to the Banfe's, who converted the carriage house into a residence. The southerly portion (about one and three-fourths acres) with a frontage of about 340 feet on Imperial Avenue was sold to the Westport Woman's Club on December 30, 1944 for a price of $16,450, as indicated by the tax stamps on the deed. However, the actual cost to the Woman's Club was somewhat less, as the real estate brokers, Baldwin and Vermilya, remitted their commission in favor of the Club.

Although the house was available for Club use in 1945, actual occupancy was delayed for several years by post-war shortages of material and labor. In the interim, the place was rented to Howard Cool.

By early 1948, Mr. Bedford, in discussions with Mrs. Bradley, evidenced some misgivings over the wisdom of the purchase, citing "the location, parking and lack of auditorium" as defects which might warrant selling the property and canvassing for a new facility. However, in spite of these compunctions, he paid $2,500 to replace the furnace that had failed beyond repair. Subsequently, a Woman's Club committee was appointed to look into other sites but terminated its mission by recommending that the Imperial Avenue property be retained. Club occupancy finally took place on April 22, 1949 when the building was formally dedicated during a spring downpour.

THE DISASSOCIATION FROM THE BEDFORD HOUSE

On May 31, 1949, the Woman's Club terminated its "Teenage and Woman's Program" at Bedford House, and at the same time the "Y" staff inaugurated its own program in this area on receipt of a $300 donation from the Club.

The disassociation of the Woman's Club from Bedford House raised some questions: Who was to inherit the $2,500 annual contribution made by the Bedford Fund since 1926 in support of Bedford House and the Visiting Nurse Service? What rent-free rights for large gatherings did the Woman's Club retain in the "Y" building pending the addition of an auditorium to the new clubhouse?

Both of these questions were answered largely through the efforts of Mrs. Bradley. The first was resolved by arranging in 1951 for the conversion of the Bedford annuity into a trust fund whose income would be payable to the Woman's Club "so long as the Club continues its existence and continues to carry on public health and welfare activities." The second question was answered less directly.

THE NEED FOR A MEETING ROOM AND OTHER FACILITIES

The school building being prepared for the move

Since the new clubhouse lacked a meeting room and other facilities, a temporary arrangement was made with the "Y" to permit Club use of the auditorium for general meetings and other rooms on request. However, overcrowded conditions at the "Y" soon made a shambles of this arrangement; general meetings of the Club soon had to be held in the crowded space of the Clubhouse.

In 1950, auspiciously for the Woman's Club, the Saugatuck Congregational Church on East

State Street decided to move its original building (constructed in 1832) to a new site on the other side of the street. But its Sunday School Meeting House, a later addition of Civil War vintage, was offered to the Club at a knock-down price of $2,000 because the church felt—in the words of Mrs. George R. Trafton, Auditorium Committee Chairman—"that our use of it in the service of the community is most closely allied to the original purpose of the building."

SAUGATUCK CONGREGATIONAL CHURCH MEETING HOUSE BOUGHT AND MOVED

A plan was conceived by the Club to move this structure to the new clubhouse where it could serve as an auditorium—at a total estimated cost of $20,000. Again, through Mrs. Bradley's efforts, the Bedford Fund was persuaded to donate $10,000 toward the project. The purchase took place in September 1950, and on September 21, the building was moved in two sections from the old location on East State Street to Imperial Avenue where it was reassembled as an auditorium. *Life* magazine came to Westport

One-half of the building starting on the way from the old location on East State Street.

to cover this event. It seemed the whole citizenry turned out to watch the day-long transporting procedure, rolling across the Post Road down to Imperial Avenue and attaching it to the back of the Clubhouse.

With this large-scale addition, all kinds of events could take place. The Club now was able to rent spacious rooms for wedding receptions, dances, lectures, concerts and many other affairs.

By an odd coincidence, when the work was finished, it was found that the exterior clapboards of the original building and the new addition matched exactly. The auditorium was dedicated on March 5, 1951 "to the service of the Westport Woman's Club as a place of meeting, where members may plan their labors on behalf of a better Westport," and to the generosity of the Bedford family who made it possible.

The final cost of the work was $20,600 exclusive of landscaping, which was done by the Garden Department under the direction of Mrs. Eloise Ray, a local landscape architect. Several builders estimated "that the new wing could not be duplicated for $40,000 to $50,000—especially in these times." Gibson Daniels, pastor of the Saugatuck Congregational Church, expressed pleasure at the use to which the church building had been put, noting that it had certain historical value as it had been constructed during the Civil War.

The Clubhouse has always been available either free of charge or at a nominal rental to philanthropic and educational organizations. And it has been used in the past for church services and as a Sunday school by the Unitarian Church of Fairfield County, by the Society of Friends, and by Trinity Church after its fire in 1950. The Clubhouse was also rented for a fee for private and public functions to assist financially in its upkeep. However, the annual maintenance cost of this facility added about $4,000 to the Club budget, and it was nearly twenty years before outside rentals were sufficient to carry this burden without a deficit.

Major Clubhouse Improvements

Many major improvements were made in the building apart from painting and the provision of furnishings. In 1952 the ceiling in the auditorium showed signs of distress and had to be reinforced. A new stage was built by the Westport Players in 1954. Four years later, under the stress of several successful dances, the auditorium floor had to be reinforced. In September 1963, the Clubhouse was connected to the new sewerage system on Imperial Avenue at town expense (as a by-product of town filling operations west of the Clubhouse). In 1967, a loudspeaker was installed; and two years later, the "rotary" entrance driveway was rearranged as a safety measure on the advice of the town police. In August 1968, work was started on a new all-electric kitchen that was constructed adjacent to the auditorium. This added 675 square feet to the area of the first floor that subsequently was converted to a secretary's office. This total operation cost about $27,500, with the kitchen being formally opened on March 3, 1969. In the summer of 1970, the Clubhouse roof was re-shingled and new gutters were installed. At the same time, a new acoustical ceiling and new lighting fixtures were hung in the auditorium, adding considerably to the attractiveness and utility of this facility.

In 1971, the trust committee of the Grace Salmon estate voted a donation of $1,000 to the Woman's Club; and part of this was used to rehabilitate the cloakroom off the entrance hall of the Clubhouse.

One of the perennial headaches of the House Chairman was housekeeping. For a time, hourly labor was used cleaning and dusting. In June 1952 John Sherry was given quarters on the second floor rent-free in exchange for performing light housekeeping duties. He left in May 1953, followed in turn by William Jones who resigned in September 1954, and by the latter's wife, who left in May 1956. Thurman McClinton was the live-in houseman for the next years, and when he left, professional hourly cleaning service was again retained for a while. In February 1963 the second floor apartment and third floor studio was leased to Miss Anne Ogden, an artist. In 1966 she agreed to perform light housekeeping on remission of her rent, and this arrangement continued in effect until the summer of 1967 when she moved to New York City. In September 1967 an agreement was signed with Stuart Bigley on the same terms as his predecessor.

The Clubhouse now contained on the first floor an entrance foyer, with adjacent coatroom and lavatories, the secretary's office, a large lounge or living room, a small lounge or dining room, the auditorium and the new kitchen. On the second floor is a bride's room used also for board meetings, three rooms and a lavatory leased to Junior Years, a young ladies' group, aged 14 to 16. A third room was rented to the Junior Woman's League (vide supra) and the remaining two rooms and bath, with third floor studio, were occupied by Stuart Bigley. The basement area housed the Connecticut Braille Association, the Loan Closet and some storage space.

Adequate parking was now available for about 35 cars at the front and side entrances to the Clubhouse, and additional space for about 100 cars on a lower level south of the Clubhouse on land owned by the town and provided rent-free to the Club.

The large grandfather clock in the hall was purchased by the Club in 1950 in memory of past president Sara B. Crawford. A second clock in the large lounge was presented by the Junior Woman's Club as a tribute to Sarah Payne Butcher, one of its most active members. A third clock in the auditorium was presented in 1971 as a gift from the 16 living past presidents of the Club.

CIVIC ACTIVITIES RESUME IN ABUNDANCE

The civic activities of the Club during the 1940s were almost too numerous to mention. The Garden Department was particularly active, campaigning energetically against ragweed in the summer of 1942, and against poison ivy in 1948 and 1949. The Club, the Westport Garden Club, and the town shared the cost of spraying roadsides, the Boston Post Road and wherever there was poison ivy on town property. One notable activity that might be called the *Veterans' Housing Caper* involved an $80,000 temporary housing project for 21 veterans' families that was being erected by the Westport Housing Authority on North Compo Road. In the fall of 1946, red tape threatened to delay completion of the housing by Christmas as promised.

The citizens of Westport became irate over the situation and banded together from all walks of life to finish the project after receiving an approving nod from the labor unions. The Club helped at this "community barn raising" by serving hot coffee and sandwiches at the work site. Despite the contributed labor, however, the Housing Authority ran out of funds before landscaping could be accomplished. The sight of a small child floundering in a sea of mud in the spring aroused the Club to action. With the cooperation of a local nurseryman and a contractor, the Garden Department graded and seeded the area and planted 150 rose bushes and dogwood trees. For this effort, the Club was awarded a "Certificate for Special Achievement" by the National Council of State Garden Clubs in the summer of 1949.

The first groundswell of a Connecticut "All-purpose Highway" burst upon the surprised citizenry of Westport when State Highway Commissioner Cox announced at a Chamber of Commerce meeting on September 15, 1943 that he had received legislative authority to acquire property for a new limited-access road, initially to be four lanes wide, but later to be expanded to ten lanes. It developed that the enabling legislation had been a "sleeper" rushed through the last days of the legislative session under a mountain of routine measures. The Woman's Club took strong exception to the "limited access" feature of the improvement and to its proposed routing through Westport. Through the Club's efforts, spearheaded by Club President Helen Warnock—then also an Assemblyman in the State Legislature—an amendment was passed limiting the authority of the Highway Commissioner to study purposes only.

EXTENDING PUBLIC HEALTH ACTIVITIES

In the area of public health, the Club was no less active. By the end of the decade, under the supervision of Hazel Rosenau, RN, the staff of the Visiting Nurse Service had expanded to three full-time nurses who made 3,879 visits to the sick during the Club year 1949–1950 vs. 3,312 the previous year. In March 1949, the visiting nurses were moved to a large, attractively decorated, well-equipped office, a modern workroom, and a waiting room. Using funds from Tuberculosis Seals Campaign sales, the Club enrolled the nurses for further training in public health work at the University of Bridgeport.

Nurse Hazel Rosenau comforting a young patient

In April 1949, the Club awarded a $300 Nurses' Scholarship at the Norwalk Hospital School of Nursing. At the request of the director of nurses at the hospital, two student nurses visited the nurse service at the Woman's Club in order to observe the visiting nurse in her daily routine. This was seen as an opportunity to sensitize the student to community needs. By that time, the fee had climbed to $2.00 for a house call. The Metropolitan Life Insurance Company and the John Hancock Mutual Life Insurance Company used the Club's nurses for their policyholders.

The Dental Clinic for school children was also continued, as was the annual Tuberculosis Seals Campaign. During the school year 1948–1949, free dental service was offered to all children who needed it.

As a result of funds derived from the sale of these seals, the Club was able to bring to Westport in the fall of 1948 a mobile X-ray unit of the state Tuberculosis Commission to provide free X-ray examinations for more than 2,000 persons. Subsequently, the state reported that the incidence of tuberculosis in Westport was among the lowest in the state.

A smallpox scare occurred in April 1947, when several cases of the disease broke out in New York City, and it was feared that commuters might act as carriers in bringing the infection to Westport. The State Health Department lacked adequate serum, so the Health Committee of the Club arranged through the General Federation of Women' Clubs to fly 1,060 units here from Wisconsin for local use, as a result of which 838 persons were vaccinated either free or at nominal cost.

THAYER ART SCHOLARSHIP ESTABLISHED

After the death of Mrs. John Adams Thayer in 1943, a fund was established in her memory for awarding Art Scholarships annually. Originally, a $50 scholarship was awarded annually to Westport or Weston sophomore and junior high school boys or girls. In 1946–1947 a $250 Art Scholarship award was added for award to a senior at Staples High School who wins the annual competition arranged under Club direction. This award was presented on graduation night. The $50 Thayer Art Award continued to be offered annually to Westport school sophomores and juniors. This award included studying with a Westport artist of the winner's choice. And over the years of its existence, special awards in the form of art books or materials were added.

The competition took place in May just before graduation. An exhibition at the Club House showing the work done during the year by the art award winners of the previous year was added so that Club members may see how the young artists they sponsored are progressing.

STIMULATING FURTHER INTEREST IN LOCAL ART ACTIVITY

In December 1949, a special exhibition of the work of Westport photographers was held in the art gallery of the YMCA for two weeks with the public invited to see it. A final exhibition of the paintings by Westport women artists was shown in the new Club House, a feature of the formal opening to the public in April.

Art classes for club members run by well known professional artists were held during the year: landscape painting outdoors, weather permitting; during inclement weather, still life painting indoors; a sculpture class with models; and a class in practical ceramics (i.e., making of dishes, vases, etc.). To help stimulate interest in public school art, the Club held annual public exhibitions of the artwork of our public schools.

MONTMARTRE IN WESTPORT—A SALUTE TO WESTPORT ARTISTS

To further stimulate civic interest in art, the Club decided to honor the artists in a unique way. They made the theme of their Yankee Doodle Fair "A Salute to Westport Artists." An entrance gate modeled after the *Arc de Triomphe* in Paris set the keynote of the fair. A replica of the Eiffel Tower dominated the center of the green, with colorful flags, pennants, and lights radiated to all the booths that were decorated to resemble artists' studios and French sidewalk cafes. The artists themselves were the chief attraction as they took turns sketching portraits that were then sold.

The Art Department also helped establish a new art gallery on Main Street. Special lighting and background effects were arranged by the owner of a new hardware store to set up special lighting in two long mezzanine galleries. Subsequent art displays attracted throngs of people and many artists reported success in selling their paintings there.

The public library then began to hold monthly exhibitions of the works of these artists. Local restaurants soon followed suit and a new form of appreciating the works of Westport artists was born.

THE RISE AND FALL OF THE WESTPORT PLAYERS

One of the most active and durable cultural programs of the Club was conducted by its Drama Department. Drama has always had a deeply rooted tradition in Westport, and the Woman's Club's Drama Department provided a workshop for anyone in the community interested in dramatic production. In 1938 the Club picked up the torch from an earlier organization known as the "Westport Players", which was started in 1927 by some local artists and writers and which presented a number of original plays in Nash's Barn on King's Highway until 1935 when, for some reason, it disbanded. Three years later its embers were rekindled and subsidized by the Club, who managed it as the "Westport Woman's Club Players", initially composed only of women who limited their productions to one-act plays.

Westport Players on steps of Nash's Barn

The Players' first venture was a one-act mystery play titled *White Iris,* which was presented competitively in the spring of 1939 at the Hotel Taft in New Haven, where it won the State Federation championship hands-down. Later that year, the Players presented their first three-act play *Night Fall*. This time there were men in the cast. The next year, the group's presentation of *Ladies, I Address You Privately* earned second place at the State Federation contest. Thenceforth, the Players produced an average of four plays each season, with men playing key roles in acting, building scenery, and directing, along with the ladies. Male members were required to pay dues only to the Westport Woman's Club Players.

Early in 1941, Velma Knox (then Drama Department Chairman) received from England the manuscript of *Me Pink 'at,* a review in which she had appeared in London. This was presented before the State Federation in May, with the players repeating their initial triumph by again taking first place in the state competition. The following year saw the highly successful *Victory Review of '42* featuring the "Westportettes" in a precision ballet at the Bedford Junior High. The proceeds from this affair—more than $1,800—were all applied to the support of the Club's war services.

The Westport Players symbol used for many years

During the remainder of the war the drama group lapsed; but it was revived again in November 1945 as "Westport Theatre Guild" under the leadership of Ruth Dolge and Bryan Randolf. The Guild's initial presentation was a one-act play, *Oh, Brother,* written by two members of the Woman's Club and presented in March 1946.

So successful was the group that early in 1947, the Westport Country Playhouse—which held a local option on Theatre Guild plays—suggested that the Club group change its name to avoid possible misunderstanding by the public. Out of this name change came the new "Westport Players."

The Players seem to have had their greatest successes with vehicles portraying villains. Perhaps the most noteworthy of these was *Dirty Work at the Crossroads,* presented originally in 1947 and repeated twice the next year. Advance publicity for the show was largely effected through widespread display of handbills for which special drawings were made by local artists. The play itself was lively and well paced with a wicked villain, a sweet young thing, and a hero tied to a railway track. The entr'actes were can-can dancers, singers, and comedians, who kept things moving during scene changes. The first-night audience caught the spirit of the show from its advance publicity, and many appeared dressed in costumes of the 1890s. On the last night of its performance, an over-enthusiastic stagehand gave the audience an extra show when he pulled the curtain too far back, revealing Munroe Murgetroyd (erstwhile David Poor) in the somewhat altogether during a costume change.

THE

WESTPORT PLAYERS

OF THE WESTPORT WOMAN'S CLUB

PRESENT

A DOUBLE BILL
OF
THE MEDIEVAL FARCE IN TWO ACTS
"THE MAN WHO MARRIED
A DUMB WIFE"
By ANATOLE FRANCE

AND

THE CURTAIN RAISER
"WHY I AM A BACHELOR"
A Comedy in One Act
By CONRAD SEILER

February 10th and 11th, 1950
BEDFORD ELEMENTARY SCHOOL — WESTPORT

Waxing in its symbiosis with the Woman's Club, the Players produced their first musical in 1951—the 1944 Broadway smash hit *Sing Out Sweet Land.* In 1952, for the third time, they won the State Federation's drama contest with their production of *The Witch,* thereby earning permanent retention of the trophy cup. In 1951 and 1952, several plays were produced as theatre-in-the-round, and in the following year, *Born Yesterday* was innovated in cabaret style, with the audience sitting around the tables with refreshments but without conversation. The best of Broadway were brought to Westport with *Mr. Roberts, Pursuit of Happiness, January Thaw, Voice of the Turtle,* and *East Lynne*—all resounding successes.

Not a little of the Players' fame came from the publication of a weekly column on their activities prepared by members of this talented group and published in the *Town Crier* and the *Westporter-Herald* starting in 1949.

In 1956, as a result of a disagreement with the Executive Board over the handling of funds coupled with the non-payment of Club dues by this impecunious group, the Players separated from the Woman's Club by mutual consent, continued a short independent existence as the Westport Community Theatre, and then quietly expired. On May 24, 1956, William Harrar, their envoi to the Club, wrote a most exquisite reflection on this relationship:

> *Open Letter to The Westport Woman's Club*
> *May 24, 1956*
> *Imperial Avenue*
> *Westport, Conn.*
>
> *Mesdames:*
>
> *This is an elegy on The Westport Players, the child whom you Spawned and weaned, but who, in the moment of death and dissolution, is not ungrateful.*
>
> *We started life quietly and circumspectly and once in a while made you a little money, never enough, but some. (Our female members never could quite get around to paying you your $10 membership fee. This was not ingratitude, but was based, partly on tradition, partly on economics. Almost no little theatre group in Fairfield County has charged its members more than $2. And our females were not all wedded to account executives. There were the spouses of machinists, mates, postmen, electrician's apprentices, and small grocers, and there were schoolteachers. They could act, or paint, or choreograph, or design, and we had to have them.) We always did our stint for the Yankee Doodle Fair, and in the days of the Beer Booth the pleasure was more than mutual.*
>
> *But the little theatre bug, a filterable virus, began to grow. We came, in time, to abuse you. There was the day an officer of one of your good-paying tenants told us he would kick the set down if we "didn't get it off the stage—right now." We broke the leg off the piano, which weighs megatons, particularly after a three-act play. We kept the Clubhouse in a constant din. Never will we forget the night a studious member of the Zoning and Planning Association wandered into a*

rehearsal of an especially strident play, muttering to himself of variances and gravel-pits, stared vacantly and fled, a shaken man caught in a hell not of his own making. The lights burned late, the oil-burner worked overtime and the beer cans clanked grittily on the auditorium floor.

Nevertheless, we who have died are grateful to you, for you gave us the means to practice a humble art form. Although some of our productions set the theatre back a hundred years, in others we felt the authentic thrills, such as good lighting working on cue, the successful milking of an obscure line for an unexpected laugh and the sight of real tears in the front row. When one has the time, little theatre is worth it, and if we took from you more than we gave, we surely owe you thanks for making it possible.

All of the foregoing leads me to the promulgation of a law, which I shall call Harrar's Law: "Ham will out, or, if you prefer, Smithfield Rides Again." As the peace and quiet settle over the Clubhouse at last, keep your eyes on The Westport Community Theatre, Inc.

Gratefully and sincerely yours,
William H. Harrar,
Ex-Director of Workshop for
The Westport Players

SCHOLARSHIP PROGRAM EXPANDED

During the 1940s, the Club's scholarship program was expanded. The Emily B. Fuller annual award to help a Staples High graduate attend college was increased to $500. A $250 Thayer art scholarship was first awarded in 1947 to a Staples graduate. A $50 "junior" Thayer art scholarship was available to a Westport or Weston boy or girl of sophomore grade for study under a local artist. In 1947 the sum of $300 was voted for a music scholarship to be awarded "on the basis of talent, worthiness and need." This scholarship did not find a qualified recipient every year.

To stimulate the supply of nurses during the war, two nursing scholarships of $250 each were made available in 1943 for study at Norwalk Hospital. These were repeated in 1946, and again in 1950.

In closing the narrative of the 1940s, mention might be made of the Club's memorial to its founding president, Mrs. William Staples. When such a memorial was first proposed in 1937, it was voted to plant a row of dogwood trees in her memory. However, no suitable site having been found, the plan was abandoned in favor of a "double silver service of 12 pieces" for coffee and tea for use at Club meetings. This was purchased on March 27, 1941 from the International Silver Company who provided a suitably engraved inscription thereon.

T he 1950s were burgeoning years for the town of Westport. Some 9,300 new people moved to town, bringing the 1960 population to 21,000—an increase of 80 percent over the decade. Henceforth, growth was to slow down as land use approached the point of saturation, and the first signs of big city problems began to rear their heads. The success with which the town met these problems under Selectman Baldwin became evident when Westport was designated as "All-American City", one of eleven in the nation selected by the National Municipal League and its co-sponsor, *Look* magazine, for "progress achieved through intelligent citizen action" during 1958. This was the first time that a Connecticut city had been so honored.

This decade was in many respects a banner period for the Westport Woman's Club as well. Under the competent leadership of Mrs. Bradley (whose second term covered 1950–1952), the Club attained a peak in its activity. It plateaued—with some ups and downs—but still maintained its paramount position under her successors, Mrs. Schuck (1952–1956) and Mrs. Lue (1956–1960).

In 1957 the Club celebrated its golden anniversary and the *Westport Town Crier & Herald* issued a special 16-page supplement on March 7, titled "Westport's Helping Hands." This extolled at length the Club's history and its good deeds. The year 1955 also brought many accolades to an already extended list by making the Club recipient of five State Federation awards. At the 58th Annual Convention in Hartford, all prior Federation records were broken when the Club captured first place with its press book, first and second places with its submission of light verse, first place for playwriting, and an honorable mention for serious poetry. About the same time *McCall's* magazine gave the Club national recognition through its award for "general excellent service to the community." President Schuck accepted this honor on behalf of the Club on the Maggie McNellis television program.

New Competition and a Serious Erosion in Membership

The nineteen-fifties were not, however, free from vicissitude for the Club. Under post-war inflationary pressures, the annual Club expenditures rose from about $27,000 to $37,000 over the decade. Unhappily, during this same period there was a serious erosion of dues-paying members—from 726 in 1951 to 328 in 1959. Only a small part of this decrease was due to the schism with the Junior Woman's Club and the Westport Players in 1956. Mostly, it was due to competition from other organizations. Thus, by 1959 there were no fewer than 54 non-profit organizations in Westport, all offering some form of community service and most seeking support from the townspeople.

To offset the loss of membership income, the annual dues were raised three times: from $3 to $5 in 1952, to $10 in 1954, and to $15 in 1958. However, a financial deficit still remained, and various plans were devised both to economize and to raise funds.

TIME-OUT FOR THE YANKEE DOODLE FAIR

As in prior years, the largest source of income to the Club was the Yankee Doodle Fair. During the 1950s, a fair was held each year through 1958. For a period of five years thereafter, an annual Yankee Doodle Charity Ball was held instead.

The 1950 fair, featuring Westport at the turn of the twentieth century, was held at Bedford Junior High School from July 27 to 29. This was to have been a mammoth event, with over 250 local business and 50 out-of-town concerns lending their support with donations and prizes. Unhappily, for the first time in years, fair-time was marred by rain, with the result that the proceeds totaled only $11,400. The next year a "Country Carnival" held at Jesup Green was again marred by rain—this time, a four-hour downpour that served to discredit for the second year in a row the Farmers' Almanac prediction for fair and sunny skies. Despite the handicap of weather, some 20,000 persons were estimated to have attended this fair, bringing the proceeds to $14,000, the best return since 1949. In 1952 the fair was again held at Jesup Green, but the return was only an unexplained $12,000.

During the 1952 fair, an incident occurred that is still recalled with indignation by some "old timers." On July 17 the town prosecutor, Attorney Virginia P. Boyd (until that time a Club member in good standing), filed charges of fraud against the Woman's Club as a result of a dispute over a prize won at the fair. "The alleged offense," said Miss Boyd, "occurred at the 'Fish Pond' where tickets with numbers printed on them were fished out of a bowl by patrons. There was a prize, also numbered and displayed, to correspond with each ticket drawn." What actually took place was never fully revealed. It seems, however, that on the second day of the fair, a fourteen-year old boy drew the winning number for an on-display $175 tape recorder that he carted home. It then developed that the number in question "was being saved for Saturday" and had not yet been placed in the bowl. It appeared, therefore, that the boy had won the prize through a ruse. And indeed, when the tape recorder was retrieved by the police, the boy was quoted as saying, "I'm sorry—it was just a prank." Nonetheless, his parents proceeded to file charges against the Club "for obtaining money under false pretenses" and for "conducting a lottery." Not a judge in Westport would hear the case, so it was tried before a New Canaan jurist instead. He dismissed the first charge as unproven but found the Club guilty of the second. Facing a prospect that all of the Club members might have to go to jail, the judge tempered justice with mercy, and merely fined the Club $100—with $90 remitted. The case made the New York City newspapers, and a Chicago firm, anxious to bask in reflected publicity, presented the boy with a $235 tape recorder. At the conclusion of the trial, the boy is alleged to have said, "Well, crime *does* pay after all."

The 1953 fair at Bedford Junior High realized $12,000 but was otherwise uneventful. President Schuck had previously enunciated her policy concerning the fair: "The members of the Woman's Club who are responsible for the fair each year have watched it 'just grow' like Topsy. Most of us feel now that it would be wise to curtail it." In support of this position, it might be noted that an estimated 650 persons worked at the 1951 fair—most of them non-members. In accord with the new policy, the 1954, 1955, and 1956 fairs were "smaller and more intimate" events held on the Clubhouse grounds. The amounts realized were $9,000, $7,700, and $11,800 respectively.

The 1955 event was sparked with a Bingo game run by Doug Edwards, TV news commentator, and Art Hannes, announcer on Ed Sullivan's *Toast of the Town* program. The 1956 fair was handicapped for lack of a Ferris wheel and a merry-go-round—these items having burned the week before in the owner's barn. Despite this apparently fatal drawback, the 1956 return was larger than the others as a consequence of a new state law that authorized certain lotteries and games of chance conducted by charitable organizations. Another input in support of the 1956 fair was a weekly column in the local press titled "Yankee Doodles", written by Roz Hannes, Publicity Chairman for the fair, and the first publicity of this kind to appear since Ina Bradley's column in 1953.

The next two years saw the fair back at the Bedford Junior High School grounds. The 1957 event, most naturally, featured a "gold" theme, and brought in $10,500. *Yankee Doodle Goes to Paris,* the following year, produced about $9,200 despite some rain.

LUCY RICARDO—CHAIRWOMAN OF THE YANKEE DOODLE FAIR?

In the final season of the popular television show *I Love Lucy*, the Ricardos (and, of course, the Mertzes) move from New York City to Westport—just as comedy series writer Bob Weiskopf had done after his son was born. An article in the *Connecticut Post* on October 22, 2001 covered Bob Weiskopf's hilarious misrepresentations:

The final "I Love Lucy" show, broadcast May 6, 1957, featured many references—some accurate, some not—to Lucy and Ricky Ricardo's new country hometown of Westport. The plot had Lucy volunteering as Chairwoman of the Westport Historical Society's "Yankee Doodle Day Celebration." The show's producers were unaware that in real life,

81

Westport's annual Yankee Doodle Fair is run by the Westport Woman's Club, not the Historical Society.

In the episode, part of the celebration involves dedicating a Revolutionary War statue depicting a Minuteman soldier to be unveiled on "Jesup" Green. Westport's Jesup Green is downtown, near the library and Main Street, but the town's landmark Minuteman statue is located miles away on Compo Road South. While making the dedication speech, Ricky commemorates the Battle of Compo in 1777 (when local Minutemen militia battled British redcoats) and notes that many ancestors of those who fought in the battle still live in the community. "The references to the battle and its descendants are accurate," said Alice Shelton, education director of the Westport Historical Society. "But the actual statue was dedicated in 1910." Also in the last episode, Fred Mertz dresses up as a town crier. "A nice touch, since Westport's newspaper at the time was called *The Town Crier*."

YANKEE DOODLE BALL REPLACES 1959 YANKEE DOODLE FAIR

On January 31, 1959, a *Yankee Doodle Charity Ball* was held at Longshore Country Club, with Emil Coleman's orchestra as entertainment. Participants paid $15 per couple. In the words of President Lue, "the high costs of operation, the long months of labor, the time and energy involved—to say nothing of the hazard of bad weather—are too great for the small income derived from the Yankee Doodle Fair." The ball netted $8,100. The next ball was held in December 1959 because the Longshore Country Club was to be closed for the first three months of 1960. This was even less remunerative than the previous year—only $7,000 being realized. Nonetheless, the practice of holding a ball in lieu of the fair continued for some years to come.

EXPANDING EDUCATION FOR DEVELOPMENTALLY CHALLENGED CHILDREN

One of the most important projects of the Westport Woman's Club in 1954 and 1955 was the establishment and continuance of the special education class located at Hurlbutt School in Weston.

The Westport Woman's Club had long realized the need of an educational program *outside* of institutions for mentally challenged children, where they could be trained with special help to get along independently. Also needed was a program for the semi-dependent group who previously had been excluded from public school entirely.

After months of work by the committee and the school superintendents of the towns of Weston, Wilton, and Westport, a class was started in Westport. The Woman's Club paid the $5,000 salary of the instructor of the special education class. The agreement was that these towns would take over the salary of a teacher in September 1955.

Mr. George Brabner, Jr. was the first teacher of this class. There were two children from Wilton, four from Weston, and five from Westport. They ate lunch with the other children, went to the auditorium programs, and took part in some of the school programs and events. The program, intended to encourage other children and teachers to accept these children and allow participation in and out of school, was highly successful. The class was well regarded and drew many visitors who wanted to gain experience and guidance from it.

When the "Committee for the Mentally Retarded" found that the class was well established and progressing, it decided to form another class for younger children. These younger children could not be placed in the existing class, as the ages ranged from 9 to 14, and the state law stated that it could not exceed a range of five years in age. The Committee had heard of ten children who would be eligible for this new younger class. The three school superintendents agreed that if these children could have training at an earlier age, they would progress much further. Many problems that could arise would be eliminated.

The best classroom solution was to find a place that was already established as a nursery school. In that way, the issues of equipment, teachers, and resources would be, in the most part, solved. After several weeks of searching, the Reverend Frederic Lorentzen offered the Club the facilities of the Christ and Holy Trinity Church. A large room downstairs was near both the lavatories and the kitchen. It was excellent for these purposes and the Club was very grateful to the Church for solving the location question.

The Westport Woman's Club selected and agreed to pay the salary of the teacher of this new group. Members of the Junior Woman's Club worked as aides and handled the transportation. The three town school systems helped with supervision and supplied the equipment. In a short time, the towns were to take over this class so that every child from Westport, Wilton, and Weston who needed help would have an opportunity to enroll in a special education class.

NEW FUND-RAISING PROJECTS NARROW THE FINANCIAL GAP

To relieve its financially straitened condition, the various departments of the Club undertook a multitude of fund-raising projects: white elephant sales, bridge parties, teas, and selling soap, stationery, books, personalized paper, and some residuals of the Club cookbook. Fashion shows were held in the Clubhouse. Antique shows were staged and art goods were sold, including a posthumous exhibition and sale of the works of George Wright, which netted $1,100. None of these closed the financial gap.

In 1952 the Club suggested to local merchants that they conduct a "give while you buy" sale. Greenberg's, a local retail store, agreed to sponsor this effort whereby five percent of all sales over $1 in amount, during the month of February, would accrue to any one of four organizations designated by the purchaser.

This drive produced over $1,100, shared by the Club, the Boy Scouts, the Girl Scouts, and the YMCA. The following year, this was repeated with the Westport

Hardware store as sponsor. A similar *Good Neighbor Week* in April 1954, involving 40 participating stores, netted $385 to the Club.

In April 1957 the Club initiated a new form of fund solicitation. Tear sheets and envelopes were distributed to schoolchildren in the fifth to the ninth grades, after Board of Education approval had been obtained "on a one-time basis." This *Helping Hands Fund* drive netted about $3,800 in 1957 and $2,000 in 1958.

BUSY 1950S WITH MANY ACHIEVEMENTS AND NEW ACTIVITIES

The year 1953, under President Gladys Schuck's aegis, saw the Club brimming with new activities: the railroad station parking lot was enlarged, six trophies were awarded to the Little League baseball teams, and ten memberships were purchased in the Metropolitan Opera Guild, permitting 40 Westport youngsters to attend operatic performances at half price. A course of instruction was initiated to teach patients at the West Haven Hospital how to make Christmas cards. Through the efforts of the Public Health Committee under Mrs. Joyner, a town-wide X-ray survey was conducted in the spring of 1953 in cooperation with the State Tuberculosis Commission, and over 2700 persons were examined, with all costs borne by the Club. Examinations were concentrated on school students over 15 years of age and on food handlers. As a result of this effort, 13 cases of tuberculosis were discovered, and 63 other abnormalities were revealed. This was the first such survey since 1948, and in terms of its findings, was 50 percent more effective.

ART HISTORY IS MADE

Art history was made in November 1952 by the sponsorship of a retrospective fifty years of painting by Karl Anderson, Westport's dean of artists—an artist whose portraits are represented in all the important art museums of the country. Many out-of-state visitors were among the large attendance at the Sunday afternoon reception. A souvenir program that pictured a number of Mr. Anderson's paintings was given to the guests.

A SENIOR ARTS CLUB IS STARTED—A NEW LIFE FOR SENIOR SHUT-INS

In the early 1950s, President Schuck felt there was a role for the Westport Woman's Club in helping to improve the lot of the town's seniors 60 years of age and older who were living alone or in serious need for interests and companionship. She appointed member Sophie Bascho as chairman of what was called The Gerontology Project. Before starting, they visited organizations they could find in Connecticut and New York that performed such services in order to decide what services they might consider. So many of these groups looked so desolate—seniors meeting in basements, just sitting around and playing cards, or just sitting.

The Gerontology Project decided to form a group that would be an active one, with results to show for it. Their first step was to set out to get a volunteer group of teachers in crafts and arts on a trial basis. They started with the teachers in art, ceramics, rug hooking, textile design, leatherwork, and block printing. They called this project the "Senior Arts and Crafts Club." There would be no charge.

They aggressively recruited teachers and prospects for enrollment and initiated the program on November 7, 1952 with a party attended by about 50 prospects. Exhibits of paintings, drawings, block printing, and leather craft, hook rug making, textile printing and ceramics procedures were demonstrated by the respective instructors. Over 20 seniors enrolled in the program and got to know one another during a social hour that followed. The program was off to a fast start.

The Club paid for all materials and refreshments. Mrs. Schuck observed that "the Club put $500 in the budget for the first year but it never cost over $200 a year. It is amazing how much one can do with so little." The seniors met at 1:30 every Friday and worked at their chosen craft until 3:30 when they were served tea, coffee, and cake. They usually left at 4:30. When participants first arrived, they were introduced to everyone and encouraged to do whatever they wished. Sometimes new seniors were shy and felt they would not do the work well enough and were afraid to try—so they watched. But before long, they joined in the work. They went on to develop many talents and made beautiful things they never dreamed they were capable of creating.

New participants were solicited through churches, doctors, and everyone else Shuck and Bascho could think of. Sometimes it was difficult to get older persons to come but once they did, they enjoyed it so much that they became regulars. One of the new members told Mrs. Schuck that she had lived in town over ten years and this was the first time she had made a friend. Many times lonely people under 60 requested to come—people who needed companionship badly. So they were invited to come to be hosts, and in helping others, they helped themselves.

As the program developed, the output of these seniors received awards at exhibits and were offered for sale at the Yankee Doodle Fairs. More than 50 persons had registered with this department by the end of 1953. And that year, the State Federation awarded a "certificate of achievement" to the Club for the best gerontology program in the state. Then later that same year, at the General Federation meeting in Washington, it won "best in the nation."

Mrs. Bascho totally dedicated herself to this program every week for seven successful years with steady growth in membership and enthusiasm. Three years thereafter, the group ceased to exist. In her final report, as she retired from the project she created, she described what she considered "the major event of all its existence—a New England Patchwork Quilt, charming and original in design." Each square was sewn by a different senior woman and carried her signature in testimony to her presence and achievements.

The railroad parking project was a brainchild of the Club's Civics Committee. This Committee was first established during 1937–1938. It lapsed in the early 1940s, and was revived in 1953 under the chairmanship of Mrs. Wintraub. One of its first acts was to persuade the New Haven Railroad to spend $20,000 in leveling, draining, paving and marking the area between the tracks and Ferry Lane, to enlarge the commuters' parking capacity from 120 to 327 cars. Then, by diligent maneuvering under the zoning laws, the Committee forestalled the possible installation of parking meters and the levy of a daily charge for parking.

In 1954 under Mrs. Speaks, the Civics Committee instituted a series of forums designed to bring to public notice a variety of pressing problems facing both local and national governments. The first such forum on November 10 was titled "River Fill-in", a euphemism for garbage and sewage disposal. The next forum, a rowdy affair in January 1955, concerned the pros and cons of a Nike missile site for the defense of Bridgeport that was proposed for construction on the May property adjacent to a recently acquired school site. CBS television news-film crews came to Westport to film this forum for later presentation on the Eric Sevareid Sunday afternoon program "American Week."

A number of other forums were held in co-sponsorship with local organizations, such as the League of Women Voters and others, to provide a broader base for discussion. The Civics Committee lapsed again early in 1957 without rhyme or reason for its demise.

SOLVING THE GARBAGE DISPOSAL PROBLEM

One of the tritest of clichés, and perhaps the truest, is that history repeats itself. And this time the theme was garbage, a perennial town headache. In 1955 the town dump off Taylor Place was "filled to capacity," and a new location was being sought. For the third time in its history, the Club came to the aid of beleaguered Westport with an assist toward a solution of the garbage disposal problem.

In September 1955 the Club, at Gladys Schuck's suggestion, agreed to cede its riparian rights to the town for construction of dikes and a sanitary garbage fill, in return for making available to the Club a new parking area on the newly filled site. Immediately, an avalanche of objections spewed forth from the other selectmen and from adjacent property owners who, unhappily, had not been informed of the plan. Of this babel the *Westport Town Crier & Herald* wrote: "We wonder whether the Woman's Club shouldn't be running the dumping, and perhaps leave the Yankee Doodle Fair to the town fathers." Be that as it may, nearly six months elapsed before local injunctions could be lifted, money appropriated ($33,260) for dike construction and a permit secured from the Army Engineers.

Finally, on February 4, 1956, a formal agreement was signed between Club President Marjorie Lue and Selectmen Crossman and Selectman Parker. Under the terms of this agreement, the Club quit-claimed its riparian rights over about two acres of "land under water" south and west of the Clubhouse in return for use "in perpetuity" of a new 100-car parking lot to be built by the town on the new fill. The agreement further provided that no garbage trucks would use Imperial Avenue as access to the fill area, that no dumping would be permitted during the summer, and that the sanitary fill operations would at all times be under the control of the town Health Department. This fill, when completed, was to comprise a portion of a new park between Imperial Avenue and the river.

However, delays continued to plague the project and defer its initiation. To mollify public opinion, Irwin Elliot, radio sportscaster, decided to use the "soft sell" on behalf of the project by issuing a public invitation to attend a gala reception and tea (the latter dubbed "Tiffin for Sniffin'") atop the dump on October 6, 1957. Amy Vanderbilt presided as hostess, backed up by a grand piano, some contributed furniture and a sterling silver tea set. Declared Elliot: "At a well-run dump you can hold a tea or a formal ball—there is absolutely no smell." And none there was.

By July 1958 the dump had been filled to the height specified in the agreement, and the town moved its disposal operations to a new four-acre tract "on the former Thompson property off Saugatuck Avenue." For a short time at least, there was peace and quiet on Imperial Avenue.

EXPANDING LEADERSHIP IN PUBLIC HEALTH SERVICES

In 1956 the town health director requested visiting nurse assistance in following up convalescent cases of polio, tuberculosis, and other maladies. Nurses' visits were now totaling nearly 6,000 a year, and the Club conducted and financed a TB X-ray survey of 2,704 local residents. As a result of this experience, the town authorized $4,200 "for a full-time public health nurse" and car on the staff of the town health director beginning July 1, 1958. To implement this authorization and to prevent conflict, the Club thereupon turned over its own nurses to the operational control of the health director, even though it continued to bear most of the cost. Following a study in January 1960, which recommended that a nursing bureau be added to the town health department, the 1960–1961 budget provided for eight nurses to perform school duties in the mornings and home-visiting duties in the afternoons. At this juncture (July 1960), after 35 years of continuous community service, the Westport Woman's Club Visiting Nurse Service ceased to exist.

Also under the auspices of the WWC Public Health Committee were the *Well Child* conferences, revived in 1951 after several years of lapse. These provided free monthly examinations of babies and pre-school children at the Clubhouse under several local pediatricians who volunteered their services on a three-month basis, to conduct physical check-ups and to administer vaccinations and polio shots.

Even in Westport, availability of fresh milk could become a problem for many children. When the visiting nurses in their rounds found a child whose parents were unable to supply adequate milk, the Club took over, furnishing free milk as required—some 2,000 quarts annually.

As in prior years, the Club operated a dental clinic for children in cooperation with the school dental hygienist. Treatment was provided, at Club expense when necessary, by local dentists for about 100 children annually. The Club expense for this service ending in 1959 averaged $1,500 per year.

The Public Health Committee also continued to supervise the award of the annual nursing scholarships and instituted the Loan Closet. The latter, a stock-room of hospital and surgical equipment, available for loan without cost to visiting nurse patients, afforded hospital beds—the most popular item—wheelchairs, crutches, and even bed pans.

A little heralded but much needed service for the sick and aged of Westport was provided by the Visiting Homemaker Service. This project, an offshoot of a national movement, was instituted in Westport in 1956 by the National Council of Jewish Women in co-sponsorship with the Woman's Club. After three years of joint operation, the Club became sole sponsor during the period October 1960 to January 1965. The group was incorporated under Connecticut state law in December 1956, and began operation in January to "provide experienced homemakers to work in the homes of neighbors and keep the household running on an even keel when a parent is sick, disabled, or hospitalized by a personal emergency." The project was supported in part by special fund drives, by the United Fund, and by fees paid by subscribers on an hourly rate, depending upon their ability to pay. The Visiting Homemaker Service worked in close cooperation with many agencies, including the town health department, the Red Cross, the Norwalk Hospital, the American Cancer Society, Alcoholics Anonymous, and Hall-Brooke Sanitarium. Without this service, many patients would have had to give up their homes, and in some instances husbands and wives would have had to separate. On January 1, 1965, the Visiting Homemaker Service began an independent existence.

HAS WESTPORT OUTGROWN THE WOMAN'S CLUB?

The 1950s saw a spate of publicity for the Club, much of it generated by the Yankee Doodle Fair. Perhaps the greatest single stir in the press of the fifties came from an "old-time member" who sought a forum in the *Town Crier* of November 21, 1957, with an anonymous letter asking "Has Westport Outgrown the Woman's Club?" The "old-timer" contended in somewhat chauvinist terms that the Club's budget was too large to be sustained by the annual Yankee Doodle Fair, that its Visiting Nurse Service should revert to the town, that a number of Club officers were from communities other than Westport, and that the Club was becoming more social than civic. But tacitly, beneath it all was the plaint that the Club was losing its small-town flavor, and possibly its democratic process. An avalanche of rejoinders quickly smothered the "old-timer" and the Club went on its way much as before.

One of the quietest adjuncts of the Club was its Garden Department. In cooperation with three other local garden clubs, the Garden Department planted 691 trees in the Westport area over the period 1951–1959 in a roadside planting program. Property owners paid for half the cost, with the town and the Garden Clubs carrying the remainder.

All told, this decade was a generally successful period for the Club. Many worthwhile projects were initiated, and its financial burdens were either relieved or headed toward an ultimate solution. The membership not only served the community through Club projects, but during this period scarcely a town committee failed to list a Woman's Club member on its roster: the School Study Council; Board of Education; Zoning Commission; Zoning Board of Appeals; the town Clerk's Office; the Library Trustees; the Beach Commission; the Traffic Control and Regulation Committee; and a committee to investigate the need for a new town hall. In such able hands, we can safely drop the curtain on the 1950s.

The Westport Woman's Club's history is rife with its achievements in the development of public health services in Westport and Weston. And unlike most other activities, they are timeless. Beginning with a drive to sanitize conditions at Compo Beach's bathhouses in 1908, creating the first school lunch program in 1918, sponsoring smallpox vaccinations during the 1922 epidemic, helping to start a school dental clinic, and establishing a public health nurse service in 1925, WWC went on to create public health initiatives that led to the highly regarded Westport Weston Health District we now have. Its members have participated and taken initiatives in health issues, opportunities, and crises virtually every year of the Club's existence, and it continues to do so today.

A HISTORY WORTH TELLING

Visiting nurses preparing kits for their daily rounds

In April 1925, participating with the Bedford grant for a public health nurse, the WTIA hired Miss Fanning for the post and further obligated itself to carry the overhead costs of $225 yearly. A car was purchased for the nurse's use and brochures were mailed advising the public of the availability of this service at a charge of 75 cents per visit. This rate was increased to $1 in 1929. The idea was well received, and by 1930, a second nurse was hired on a part-time basis to relieve Miss Fanning of emergency schoolwork. The program continued to expand, and by 1939 the Visiting Nurse Committee in its annual report listed 257 patients treated, 2,227 home visits made, 3,337 children examined at the Well Baby conferences and 97 at the dental clinic, 52 diphtheria immunizations provided, 3,300 quarts of free milk distributed, 15 X-rays taken, and 200 toys distributed to sick and needy children.

By 1958, the service had expanded to four nurses, all provided with cars, teaching health hygiene and pre-natal care to expectant mothers as additional duties. In 1946, a psychiatric consultant was employed on a part-time basis, available to any of the townspeople by referral of the visiting nurse and the town welfare director. The nurses helped with polio shots in 1954 and with Asian flu shots in 1957, when school children and employees of the town were all immunized.

Between 1926 and 1953, the John Hancock Insurance Company, later followed by the Metropolitan Life Insurance Company, used the Visiting Nurse Service to perform routine physical examinations of their policyholders in consideration of a small fee paid to the WTIA. In 1928, $107 was paid by the John Hancock Company for this service.

With the passage of time, the town became more and more conscious of the public obligation involved in public nursing care, so by 1958 it had assumed about a quarter of the cost of salaries and other expenses, and by 1960 it took over full financial responsibility.

From the start of this service, the nurse operated out of Bedford House as a rent-free tenant of the YMCA, but in 1949, the nurse's office was moved to a room on the second floor of the Westport Woman's Club building on Imperial Avenue. Here it remained until 1965, when it was transferred to the quarters of the Aspetuck Valley Health District Office on Bayberry Lane.

HOW THE WESTPORT WOMAN'S CLUB EVOLVED AS A COMMUNITY HEALTH SERVICE

First came the Well Baby Conference. In 1925, the WTIA began to co-sponsor a monthly Well Baby Conference with the state health department and the assistance of the Bureau of Child Hygiene. These services were free and directed toward the residents of Westport but Weston residents were included for a small fee. The Well Baby Conferences were expanded to twice a month ten years later, as residents in the Saugatuck area evidenced a great enough need for a conference of their own. One full-time and one part-time nurse were involved as well as a state dental hygienist who was brought in three times a year. The Well Baby Conferences were discontinued in 1948 as the number and use of private physicians increased.

Then came a dental clinic. The Dental Clinic was jointly established by the WTIA and the American Red Cross in 1937 as part of the public health program. Its services included extractions and fillings, at 25 cents per visit. An office was equipped at the Bedford House and a local dentist was employed part time. By the end of the 1930s, the Club was contributing approximately $3,600 per year for public health services. During the war years, the emphasis was on quality care for servicemen's wives and babies, with service available to any resident of Westport or Weston at a small charge.

Finally, there was bedside care of chronic patients. In 1945 Red Cross aides, trained at Norwalk Hospital, began assisting the visiting nurses in bedside care of chronic patients. The visiting nurses at this time were Mrs. H. Rosenau and Mrs. R. Pritchard.

THE WESTPORT WOMAN'S CLUB PRAISED FOR PRE-EMPTING SMALLPOX OUTBREAK

Due to an outbreak of smallpox in New York City, Westport launched an all-out protective campaign against smallpox with a vaccination clinic on a Saturday in April 1947 at the headquarters of the health department on Wilton Road. With local doctors cooperating with the Public Health Committee of the Westport Woman's

Club, the clinic was open from 10:00 AM to noon and from 4:00 to 6:00 PM. Dr. C. W. Gillette, health officer, urged that everyone who had not been vaccinated and all commuters to attend the clinic. Everyone else who had not been vaccinated within the past ten years was also urged to attend.

With the outbreak of smallpox in New York, it had been pointed out that the disease is airborne, that contact with a smallpox victim is not necessary in order to get it, that there is no treatment for it, and that there is no such thing as a light case. Westport had 540 commuters who traveled to New York, center of the present outbreak, every day.

On their way by plane to Westport from Wisconsin were 1,060 units of smallpox vaccine for use in the clinic. They were obtained through the Westport Woman's Club, whose Mrs. Mary Baldwin wired the Wisconsin Federation of Women's Clubs on a Monday asking for help in obtaining 2,500 units. Word that the 1,060 units would be on their way was received from the state chairman of public health for the Wisconsin Federation, who added, "Wire me if you need more. This amount is all I could get quickly."

There was no charge for vaccination at the clinics, but many of those who attended made a contribution. Children were accompanied by their parents or guardians. Other clinics for junior high school and high school children were set up the following week.

Plans for the clinic were made at a special meeting called by Mrs. John B. Warnock, Public Health chairman, on a Wednesday night. Detained in Hartford, Mrs. Warnock was not able to attend, and Mrs. G. C. Mullen, former public health chairman, presided. Attending were Mrs. J. Kenneth Bradley, WWC president; Dr. Gillette, superintendent of schools; G. E. Rast, welfare director; Howell F. Fuller; Dr. C. William Janson; Kathryn McCormick, school nurse; and visiting nurses Hazel P. Rosenau and Esther Veronica Rempl. The following is a letter from Mrs. Warnock to the *Westport Herald* dated April 24, 1947:

> *Dear Sir:*
>
> *Thanks to the splendid news story you gave the smallpox vaccine clinic recently held by the Woman's Club, we think it was a great success. In addition to the help 838 people received who came to be vaccinated, we feel that the clinic, together with the prominence you gave it, no doubt impressed many others with the importance of going to their doctors for vaccinations.*
>
> *You, yourself, deserve much of the credit because it was your idea that the Woman's Club try through its outside connections to obtain some vaccine which has been so scarce in Connecticut. As you know, this is exactly what we did, and as a result received 1,060 units from Wisconsin. We are most grateful for all your help and cooperation.*
>
> *I would also like this opportunity of thanking publicly the doctors, nurses and others whose names appear elsewhere who volunteered their*

*time and services to this project. The town should in-deed be most
grateful to them all.*

> *Sincerely,*
> *Helen H. Warnock*
> *Chairman, Public Health Committee*
> *Westport Woman's Club*

SCREENING FOR TUBERCULOSIS

In 1948, the Woman's Club brought a mobile unit to Westport and 2,047 residents
were x-rayed for tuberculosis—approximately 20 percent of Westport's population.
In 1955, the discovery of five cases of tuberculosis in a single Westport school
resulted in the visiting nurses doing patch tests on the entire student body as well as
on teachers and all others known to have been in contact with the children.

THE PRESSURE TO EXPAND INTO FULL-TIME HEALTH SERVICES BEGINS

A by-product of the Westport Woman's Club's success with its Public Health
programs was growing pressure by the state health department and others to build on
the Westport Woman's Club nursing program and to create a Health District in
combination with neighboring communities.

WESTPORT WOMAN'S CLUB CREDITED WITH CHILDREN'S SAFETY IN DIPHTHERIA EPIDEMIC THREAT

In May 1947, after the Connecticut Department of Public Health had issued a
statement warning of an increase in diphtheria in the state, Dr. C. W. Gillette, health
officer, said that, with over 95 percent of the children in Westport immunized
against diphtheria, he believed that an epidemic of that disease was unlikely here.
The *Town Crier* in May 8, 1947 cited Dr. Gillette's endorsement of the state
department's urging that all children be immunized, but pointed out that most
Westport parents had already had their children inoculated against diphtheria and
whooping cough.

He attributed the high percentage of immunization in Westport to the work of
the visiting nurses, sponsored by the Westport Woman's Club, and the school nurse,
and also pointed out that the town had taken official action to assist in prevention of
the disease by including in the health department's budget an appropriation for
immunization.

In 1949, an estimated 98 percent of Westport's children were vaccinated against
diphtheria due to the joint efforts of the visiting and school nurses. The Woman's
Club set up monthly meetings and bi-weekly meetings with the school nurses to
review cases and to avoid duplication.

SALK POLIO VACCINE TESTS INTRODUCED

Early in 1953 eleven cases of polio occurred in town; perhaps it was this fact that prompted Columbia University to request the Club to cooperate in a study to determine certain inheritance factors in polio susceptibility. In December, daily saliva samples were taken for a period of five days from members of 175 families having two or more children. These samples were collected by the Red Cross and the Visiting Nurse Service, refrigerated at the Clubhouse, and delivered to Columbia University by the Club. In January 1954, the Club was awarded a "certificate of appreciation" by the Sister Kenny Foundation for its participation in these experiments.

In 1954 when nationwide plans were formulated for Salk polio vaccine tests, 84 percent of eligible children took advantage of this precautionary measure through the efforts of the visiting nurses headed by supervisor Mrs. Louis Rosenau. She set up all the procedures, worked out all the schedules of doctors, nurses, and other personnel, and obtained the necessary syringes. She also took the blood samples, along with Norwalk's, to New Haven.

PRESSURE TO CREATE A FULL-TIME HEALTH DEPARTMENT

Arguments for the town's hiring a full-time, well-paid health official were put forth in December 1944 at Bedford House by Professor Philip E. Nelbach of Yale University. He was invited by a group of citizens who had formed what they called the "better health committee."

The speaker said that the health problem in the town was not, at the time, a serious one but he did feel that there should be a closer coordination among the three groups now serving as public health agencies. These were the health officer and his staff, the public school employees, and the visiting nurses who were paid in part by the Woman's Club. He did not advocate bringing them all into a single department but did wish they might work closer together under a full-time health officer. He said, "Public health is a dynamic science and art. In the last two or three decades particularly, many new administrative practices have been developed. Are we in Westport taking full advantage of this new knowledge? Our purpose is to do a thorough research job to answer that question before coming to any definite conclusion."

HEALTH COMMITTEE CONCLUDES THAT A PUBLIC HEALTH DISTRICT WOULD OFFER NO MORE IN SERVICE. SAYS TOWN SERVICES NOW EXCEED TOTAL AVAILABLE IN STATE'S PROPOSED SET-UP

"Westport would probably have fewer public health services under a health district, as proposed by the state department of health, than it has now…" according to the conclusion of a group of citizens asked by First Selectman Emerson F. Parker to look into the matter. Mrs. J. Kenneth Bradley, president of the WWC, spokesman for the group, announced this conclusion in March 1948 in a statement that suggested securing a combination school doctor and public health officer.

Included in the committee named by the selectmen were Mrs. Hazel Rosenau, Dr. N. F. Lebhar, Dr. C. W. Gillette, Mrs. Gerald C. Mullen, Dr. H. A. DiBlanda, C. William Janson, First Selectman Emerson F Parker (who set up the committee), Clarke W. Crossman, Hereward Wake, G. B. Rast and Mrs. Bradley. Mrs. Bradley's statement read:

> *The meeting was held to determine what greater advantages a district would provide than those which the community now enjoys. At our request, Dr. James A. Dolce of the State Department of Health met with us to explain the health district bill, as passed by the legislature, and to describe the benefits of it.*

> *On the basis of the information which Dr. Dolce gave us, it appears that we would probably have, in the last analysis, less public health service than we now have. He stated that under the district plan a minimum of one public health nurse per 5,000 population is required, not including bedside care. In Westport we have better than one nurse per 5,000—and we include bedside care. We have a school nurse; the district plan unit does not include one. We have a children's dental clinic and also a school dental hygienist; these are not included in the district plan. We now have a part time health officer; under the district plan, we would still have only a part time health officer since we would have to share him with other communities.*

> *Through the Woman's Club, we also have a family counseling service, with a trained psychiatric consultant in charge. (Dr. Dolce declared that this was "an ideal of the future" which few communities could enjoy.) The Woman's Club is also set up to organize and operate emergency clinics, such as the vaccination clinic during the smallpox scare some months ago. Well-child conferences have also been run by the Club and although these have lately been discontinued because mothers now feel that they can afford to take their children to private doctors, they will be resumed whenever the need arises.*

> *It is important to note one outstanding fact with which a number of people do not seem to be familiar with in connection with the public health bill. It is stipulated by the State Department of Health that a minimum aggregate population of 30,000 is necessary before a health unit can be formed. Obviously, Westport would have to join with Norwalk or with Fairfield in order to form such a unit. It could not take in the towns to the northward, such as Easton, Wilton and Weston, because the aggregate population would not meet the required 30,000. It is our understanding that neither Fairfield nor Norwalk would join with Westport in a unit since they have their own public health plans.*

> *Attention is also called to the fact that there is apparently a*

misunderstanding in some quarters in regard to the financial set-up of such a district. It has been said that the state would finance a health unit up to 50 percent of the cost, with the towns sharing the remainder. The fact is that the state would pay $4,000 per town. A suggested budget submitted to us by Dr. Dolce shows that the total cost per year of a unit composed of Westport and Norwalk would be $57,620, of which amount the state would pay $8,000. This is hardly a "fifty-fifty" basis.

The committee which was asked to consider this matter concluded that a public health district as proposed and regulated by the State Department of Health would offer no more in scope and kind of service than that which the Community now has through the school system, the town and the Woman's Club. The department itself has set up limitations that would make it impossible to form a unit even if one were necessary.

A development which has come out of the conference is the suggestion that an effort be made to secure a combination school doctor and public health officer, a man qualified to fill each position equally well and to divide his time between the two. It was brought out at the first meeting, and a later one, that there is a need for the part-time services of a school doctor and that probably the most effective and practical solution would be to employ someone who could do that job and the work of a public health officer for the town. It is important to note that there is no provision for school nurses or doctors in the proposed health district and suggested budget.

THE 1950s AND A RENEWED CONCERN IN PUBLIC HEALTH SERVICES

The first part of the 1950s saw a renewed concern in public health services, which led to a complete reorganization of the nursing services. An outbreak of measles and chicken pox in 1951 was one factor that led the *Westport-Herald* to call for a "streamlining" of Westport's health services. The part-time health officer in Westport was in his eighties and refused to step down. The Woman's Club absorbed the responsibilities of the insurance nurse and by 1953 was spending $14,000 annually on their public health programs. Their staff was expanded to two nurses and they continued to sponsor medical and dental clinics, a free milk fund, consulting services, as well as the home nursing.

At the same time the school nursing program had reached $13,500 per year, with two full-time nurses and a dental hygienist. The school program continued vision screening, chest X-rays, home visits to absent students, and prophylactic dental care. In addition, the school nurses were involved in hearing tests, cumulative record keeping, checking for contagious diseases, and referrals of indigent medical cases to the Woman's Club. Yet, 1953 also brought the threat of a statewide polio epidemic and once again a selectmen's committee was called to review public health programs and policies. The 1953 selectman's study committee again had no members that were named to previous groups. However, the Woman's Club was represented as well as the League of Women Voters. The report, urging the appointments of a new qualified health officer, an adequate staff and a health council, outlines many of the "angles" that the committee had to take into consideration.

The committee reached two general conclusions: 1) public health is no longer "a routine, part-time corrective type of work—carried out by a partially-retired physician with no specific training in public health work," and 2) experience has shown "the great desirability for the preventive and educational aspects of the work."

The report went on to enumerate Westport's present public health services offered by the Woman's Club volunteer service, the school health services, and the health department. Services provided by the Woman's Club included home nursing, free milk fund, dental clinic, well child conferences, X-rays, clinical supplies, doctors, and special aid.

The five-month study resulted in recommendations that led to the replacement of Westport's part-time health officer. Dr. R. MacCalmont assumed the dual role of health officer and school physician in 1955. Dr. MacCalmont was finally able to bring the school and visiting nurses under the Health Department in 1960. It was not until 1965 when the department of health in Westport acquired the present Westport Weston Health District offices at Bayberry Lane that the nurses moved physically under the health department's roof.

The Golden Anniversary—1957—A Celebrated Milestone

T he 1950s were not only a decade of extraordinary achievement for the Westport Woman's Club, but a period of transition from a focus on the town's physical improvement and preservation to providing and improving much-needed community services. And the entire town rose to the occasion in 1957 on this golden anniversary to reflect on and celebrate what these women had achieved in the first fifty years.

The town's newspaper, the *Westport Town Crier & Herald*, published a supplement on February 28, 1957. It celebrated this constructive history and publicized the Westport Women's Club, challenging re-dedication to continue to provide critical services that would prove to be as profound as those of its past. The following are excerpts from this publication:

A Proclamation—Official Community Recognition

> On the Golden Anniversary of this Woman's organization dedicated to community service, the Westport Woman's Club is recognized in the town of Westport as an organization working for civic betterment.
>
> In their numerous programs for the welfare of the community— Visiting Nurses, Mentally Retarded Class, Free Milk Fund, Well Child Conference, Dental Clinic, Six Annual Scholarships, Loan Closet, Senior Arts and Crafts, Clothing Relief and Woman's Exchange-Thrift Shop, this organization is to be commended for 50 years of voluntary service.
>
> The Westport Woman's Club has set aside the Month of March 1957 to observe the founding of this organization as the Woman's Town Improvement Association in 1907 and to commemorate such founding by re-dedicating ourselves to community service through their list of Helping Hands.
>
> As First Selectman of the town of Westport, I am designating the Month of March 1957 as Westport Woman's Club Month and urge all citizens of our community to give full consideration to the past and future services of the Westport Woman's Club, which has done so much for the town of Westport during the past half-century.
>
> Clarke Crossman
> First Selectman

*Nineteen hundred and fifty-seven marks the 50th Anniversary of the
Westport Woman's Club. If this had been an ordinary woman's
organization, a routine editorial would have sufficed—commending the
group largely for its persistence. One might have cast a nostalgic
backward glance at a succession of pink teas and gay parties, and an
amused one at dull meetings concerned with less than world-shattering
affairs.*

*But as a number of national publications have also discovered, The
Westport Woman's Club is no usual ladies group, concerned mostly with
ways to combat boredom, and promote pleasant social intercourse, and
populated by Helen Hokinson clubwomen. It has, on the contrary, been
an exceedingly potent force in the history of Westport, and has
contributed so much to our town that even the present members have
forgotten nine-tenths of their own story.*

*The record of the Woman's Club can perhaps be better understood
by recalling its original name—the Woman's Town Improvement
Association. It took the name seriously—and the jobs that went with it.
In reading the history of our town during the last fifty years, one cannot
avoid coming away with the impression that most of the truly
progressive things that happened stemmed directly or indirectly from the
ladies of the WTIA, and later, the Woman's Club. On the one hand, they
fought to keep Westport's charm—and, on the other, to convince the
town fathers to meet the new needs of a growing community.*

*In more recent years, as other groups formed to take on the job of
improving and preserving Westport, the Club shifted its emphasis from
improvement* to *service. It became the focal point of Westport
community services functioning very much like a home-based community
chest. It still supplies more than half of all the town's health services—
and supports a list of activities that would put many a town's whole
efforts in this direction to shame.*

*Now, in its Golden Anniversary Year, the Woman's Club is
launching its first major fund drive. It can no longer depend entirely
upon a Yankee Doodle Fair to extract, relatively painlessly, the
necessary dollars for all of its activities in a growing community.*

The Town Crier & Herald *is publishing this supplement for two
reasons: First, we want to salute this truly remarkable organization on
its Golden Anniversary, and to tell Westport's many newcomers of its
constructive history. And second, we are offering this edition as our way
of getting the first Westport "Helping Hands" drive off to a good start.*

This edition has been made possible by the advertising of many

Westport merchants, contractors, and professional men—and a good many from neighboring Norwalk. The Town Crier & Herald *is donating 25 percent of the gross proceeds to the "Helping Hands" drive; the remainder defrays the cost of the supplement that you are about to read, And as you read of the Woman's Club's history, departments, and services, we suspect that you will agree that this Golden Anniversary is really a Golden Wedding celebrating a remarkable union between Westport and its Woman's Club.*

It is our profound hope that the happy marriage will continue for another fifty years of good and constructive works. You can contribute to this future by the simple device of—helping the "Helping Hands."

The Years of Consolidation, 1960–1972

For the Westport Woman's Club, the 1960s were years of consolidation, of self-appraisal, and of re-orientation. In keeping with Club policy, many projects of earlier years had been developed to a point where they either became self-sustaining or were integrated into the town government. So, with the changing times, new goals had to be developed and new activities ordered.

In September 1960, three months after turning over the Visiting Nurse Service to the town, the Woman's Club took over full sponsorship of the Visiting Homemaker Service from the Westport Section of the National Council of Jewish Women. In 1961, five new homemakers were added to the staff totaling 17 and placing a homemaker with 119 different families. No family was denied services due to inability to pay a fee. The prevalent need for this service was due to old age. But other hardships were well represented: Respiratory difficulties, bone and joint infections, mental and nervous disorders, post-operative disabilities, cancer victims, pregnancy complications, and family emergencies. This was a most fulfilling effort to the members in general and the participants in particular. Simply knowing we were able to allow an aging person to remain in his or her home; help a father feel his children were sufficiently cared for while he was at work and his wife bedridden; lessen the anxiety of small children who were suddenly deprived of their mother's care due to her hospitalization or enforced absence—made this program a source of great satisfaction and pride to all members.

Seeking other community projects, we learned the Connecticut Braille Association was looking for a single location in which to consolidate the various phases of its program. The membership voted to assume the cost of housing this outstanding organization. After completing alterations in the basement of the Clubhouse, the Connecticut Braille Association moved into its new quarters in September 1963 and has remained there rent-free—except for the cost of utilities—consolidated and better able to serve the entire state of Connecticut.

During this period, the Club membership was fairly stable, averaging 275 members. However, 1963 bottomed-out with an all-time low of only 230 members, which represented an astonishing loss of more than 550 since the peak year of 1948. This ran sharply counter to the town's general population increase from about 10,000 to 23,000 during the same period. In retrospect, it would appear that the causes of this attrition lay in the increase in dues over the period 1952–1958, in the competition from other organizations in town and from the gradual urbanization of the population which tended to eschew private enterprise as a vehicle for community betterment.

Mrs. Jo Destino, Club president from 1959 to 1960, recognized that the most effective resuscitative measure would be an increase in membership, so in September 1960 she effected reconciliation with the Young Woman's League—at that time 120 strong. Under the terms of their agreement, the League was to pay to the Club $10 annual dues for each of its members. And in return, it was to have the free use of the Clubhouse.

The League retained its own officers, assigning a liaison representative (Mrs. McGilvray) to work with the Club. This arrangement ran into difficulties after its first year of operation, primarily because the Young Woman's League began to schedule evening social activities far in excess of its prior use, with the result that revenue from clubhouse rentals to outsiders was seriously curtailed and the Club budget adversely affected. So once again, the League separated from the Woman's Club (in 1963) and was made a rent-paying tenant, with space on the second floor of the Clubhouse, which it continues to occupy at the present time.

President Helen Patch (1962–1964) tried a new approach to stimulating public interest in the Club. In March 1962, a professional public relations officer was hired at $20 per month to assist in obtaining better press for the Club. But this venture seems to have failed as the service was terminated in 1963.

Mrs. Patch took a further step in December 1963 by the appointment of an Evaluation Committee to investigate "the Woman's Club role in Westport and ways in which it might update and increase its civic and social activities." The idea was well received, and the committee's recommendations were adopted (with considerable brouhaha) by the general membership early in 1964. Unhappily, the committee's proposals may never be known to posterity, as someone forgot to place them in the file. Nonetheless, some positive effect became apparent in succeeding years, as the Club membership climbed steadily to a peak of over 350 by the Club in 1966–1967. This state of affairs earned for the Club two State Federation awards for increase in membership—one for the current year, and one for the preceding year.

A CRISIS IN LEADERSHIP: REVAMPING THE ORGANIZATION

A further product of the Club's self-reappraisal effort was a complete revision of the old constitution and bylaws by a Rules Committee under the chairmanship of Ruth Paine. A new consolidated document produced by this committee was approved by the general membership at the February 1965 annual meeting. This was followed by a new set of Standing Rules in May of the same year, House Rules and definitions of duties and responsibilities of Committees and Departments.

The changes effected by the new bylaws were considerable, based upon information obtained from a number of women's clubs, considerable library research, and the advice of three attorneys.

The Club year was changed from a calendar to a fiscal year basis. Officers, until then elected biennially, would now be elected annually, and no individual was to hold the same office for more than two years consecutively. Officers were to be nominated in May, voted upon in June, and installed at the annual meeting in September after a two-month summer recess. The former redundant Executive Committee and Executive Board were now combined into a single Board of Directors consisting of the six elected officers and five members-at-large, each of whom was to serve as chairman of a Standing Committee. Vice-presidents were also vested with committee chairmanships to relieve the president of her current overload. A junior membership was established with an age bracket of 16 to 21, and life membership dues were raised from $100 to $200.

President Iris Nolan, whose administration (January 1964 through September 1965) straddled the introduction of the new bylaws, came into office on one wing. Her debut was announced by a headline in the *Westport Town Crier:* "Woman's Club Without President." And, in point of fact, for the first time in its 56-year history, the Westport Woman's Club was indeed without a president. At the November 4, 1963 general membership meeting, the nominating committee presented a slate topped by three vice presidents but no president. It developed that the presidential nominee, Mrs. Philip Michel, decided at the last moment not to accept the office for personal reasons. Rather than hustle in a Johnny-Come-Lately, the nominating committee decided to ride it out with what was left of their slate. So at the first Executive Committee meeting in December 1963, Mrs. Nolan was unanimously designated acting president, and in March of 1964 she was declared president. Because of the new bylaws, her term was only 20 months. In September 1965 she was succeeded by Mrs. Carol Schnack (1965–1967). Mrs. Betty Chase was the next president (September 1967) but resigned on August 1 of the following year, one month before the expiration of her term, because her husband was transferred out of town. At the next annual meeting in September 1968, Mrs. Rita Keneally was installed and served two successive terms. She was succeeded by Mrs. Myrtle Cuneo in 1970.

The resignation of Mrs. Chase during the summer recess in 1968 had left the Club without a president for the second time in its history. Then followed a further re-examination of the bylaws by a committee appointed by Mrs. Cuneo and chaired by Mrs. Ina Bradley. The proposed revisions were approved by the general membership in March 1971. The principal changes involved the addition of three members-at-large (now totaling eight) on the board of directors, the deletion of the junior membership classification, and a provision that officers elected at the May general meeting would assume the duties of office immediately upon election. Somewhat before this, the annual dues were increased to $20, effective September 1970.

TAX-EXEMPT STATUS CHALLENGED

During the 1950s, the Club's annual operating budget stabilized at about $30,000, of which between one-quarter and one-third was dispensed for charitable purposes. The salary of the executive secretary (Miss Allen) and the operation of the Clubhouse constituted the largest part of the fixed expense, but the pattern of expenditure remained within the range considered appropriate by the federal Internal Revenue Service for a charitable organization. This benevolent status was not, however, free from challenge. In April 1966 a computer in the Hartford IRS office rejected the Club's 1964 revenue report. After every record in the Clubhouse had been thoroughly thumbed through, President Schnack was finally able to announce that "the Club has been declared a non-profit charitable tax-exempt organization—a status enjoyed since January 27, 1945." In addition to filing annually a federal income tax exemption Form 990A, the Club was now required to file every four years with the town assessor a state Form M-22 claiming exemption from property taxes.

THE YANKEE DOODLE FAIR RETURNS

The Yankee Doodle Fair was given up in 1959 in favor of a Yankee Doodle Ball, held annually at the Longshore Country Club. This policy remained in force for four years, the fourth Ball being held in April 1962, with a net return of $5,800. President Patch, however, wasn't happy. "At this time," she announced, "we realized that there were just too many charity balls in Westport (there were four in a 4-week period) and we voted to return the Yankee Doodle Fair in 1963." The fair was held at the Clubhouse each June thereafter.

Unhappily, the first revival in 1963 got off to a bad start. Fair equipment that had lain in storage for the past four years had literally disintegrated from disuse, and new equipment had to be procured. Due to a reorganization of the local newspaper, the publicity had not been as effective as had been planned. To add to the problems, the truck carrying the carousel jack-knifed on its way from Massachusetts, wrecking beyond repair the children's favorite ride. On top of this, two days of torrid heat and humidity and a third day of rain scarcely induced people to want to "come to the fair." Perhaps it was the feature attraction—First Selectman Herbert Baldwin as lead singer in a barbershop quartet—that helped overcome these deficiencies, or the fact that the Club bought its own electric equipment, thereby reducing the rental drain-off. In any event, despite the gloomy expectations, the fair netted a handsome $6,200 that year.

In 1964 Selectman Baldwin was recalled for an encore by popular demand, and a new twist was added to the fair by the presence of a psychologist "to read doodles." As on previous occasions, the Young Woman's League manfully braved the dust and the heat of the lower parking area to run the "Young Yankee Doodles" children's fair at the fair. The 1966 event was run for one day only, and despite four combo bands and a "pistol booth" where more than a dozen belles held lighted candles in their mouths to be fired at by sharpshooters with water pistols, the proceeds were only $3,800. In 1967, the Zoning Board of Appeals instituted a policy of requiring a permit for the temporary location of carnival rides on Imperial Avenue as a non-conforming use. But the $75 fee was later remitted. The first day of the 1968 fair was "in the Irish idiom—a 'fine soft day', but the hard working committee would have been happier with a little less rain and a few days of sun."

In 1969, *The Town Crier* devoted much of its June 28 issue displaying the fair's events and promoting attendance. It made special reference to a final appearance of a picture annually submitted in the 1930s for competition in the "unusual hobby" category by local artist John Grahn, an avid stamp collector. It was created from his stamp collection showing various American birds and won so consistently that he was finally asked by the Club not to enter it again to give someone else a chance to win. Recalling that his late father considered this gesture as his highest compliment, Grahn's son, William, resubmitted it in 1969 in his honor.

The Town Crier paid a special tribute to the Westport Woman's Club by displaying a drawing executed by Famous School Founder Albert Dorne, symbolizing the Club's role in the community and editorializing:

His *[Dorne's]* concept could not have been more accurate. We've come to know and respect them for their imagination, energy and long record of good works. Many of the good things our community enjoys got their start with the busy gals of the Woman's Club or its predecessor organization, the Woman's Town Improvement Association.

As the town has grown, some of its services have had to be taken over by government—but it still has plenty left to do and to finance.

The traditional Yankee Doodle Fair has long been one of the highlights of Westport's summer. Its proceeds keep flowing. We urge you to be on hand anon the 27th and 28th, to help the 'Helping Hand'.

The 1970 fair was spiced with a live interview program "over Westport's Educational Station WSRB 640 on your dial" plus a net income of nearly $5,000. The 1971 fair, with a European vacation as first prize, produced $4,800.

ADDING NEW SOURCES OF INCOME

To supplement the fair, a variety of income-producing activities was generated by the membership. Starting anew a practice of prior years, a *Preview of Easter* fashion show and champagne luncheon were held at the Clubhouse in March 1961. In 1963, five luncheon-fashion shows were held at the Westport New England Motor Hotel, each sponsored by a different local dress shop. A second series of four "beauty-fashion luncheons" was held the following year. Similar shows were continued during the years 1966 through 1970, some at the Club and some at the Longshore Country Club. Of the latter, the most successful was a *Fashionata* held in February 1968 at $6.50 a seat, producing $878 for the Club.

Antiques Flea Markets were introduced in September of 1969 and held annually through 1976 at the lower-level parking lot, where rentals to dealers from neighboring states provided additional revenue each year. Club members provided a

hospitable ambience with a booth selling homemade baked goods, an Attic Treasures booth, a refreshments stand, and club members' children wholesomely promoting the event in flea market finery. Bridge tournaments, consignment and rummage sales, cake sales, and luncheons all helped to reduce the budgetary gap. Dances on New Year's Eve, starting in 1962, as well as on other occasions, managed to combine conviviality with money-raising.

During the early 1960s, about eight art exhibits were held in the auditorium each year, and some of these netted a 20 percent commission to the Club from sales. Unhappily, a discouraging note was sounded in the fall of 1963 when a painting valued at $300 was stolen. While insurance coverage was adequate for this contingency, the incident pointed up the need for greater security and control at the Clubhouse.

THE BEDFORD FUND GROWS—AURORA FRASER AND JULIA FARNUM QUINN SCHOLARSHIP FUNDS CREATED

Bequests and gifts were another source of income to the Club. Mention has already been made of the large gifts donated by Mr. Frederick T. Bedford, president of the Bedford Fund. An additional $10,000 was donated by the Mary A. Bedford estate in 1954. This was designated by the Club as a special "Community Services Fund." On January 22, 1968, Mrs. Aurora Frazer of Rye, New York, a former Club member, died and left $10,000 in cash and other effects, which realized $6,200 additional on being sold. This bequest was dedicated to a scholarship fund, the first of which was awarded in 1968. A plaque in Miss Allen's office lists the recipients to date.

In December 1967 a donation was made to the Club in memory of Julia Farnum Quinn. This also was voted to be used for a scholarship to further the education of a Westport boy or girl, and it was first awarded in 1968.

The scholarship program of the Westport Woman's Club began with the Emily B. Fuller award in the late 1920s. By the late 1960s, scholarships had become a major item of charitable endeavor by the Club. The amount and number of awards varied from year to year, but the list for 1969 is typical: Emily B. Fuller award, $750; Mrs. John Adams Thayer Art award, $300; music award, $300; a special one-time grant to a Vietnam veteran, $300; four Thrift Shop vocational awards, $500 each; two practical nursing awards, $100 each; and two special tuition grants of $500 each from the Aurora Frazer Fund.

COMMUNITY SERVICES RE-EMPHASIZED

Many contributions were made by the Club in 1969 to youth-oriented agencies such as Silvermine College, Norwalk Community College, Mid-Fairfield County Youth Museum, Shakespeare Students Program, and Renaissance. In other years, contributions were made to the Save the Children Federation, YMCA, the Mansfield State Training School, the Mid-Fairfield Child Guidance Center, the Student Aid Fund, and the Westport Youth Ecology Workshop—to mention just a few.

On March 9, 1967, the Board of Directors approved the "adoption" of two Indian children at a cost of $300 yearly. This was part of the "Save the Children Federation" program that selected a boy and a girl, one in New Mexico and one in Arizona. Apart from direct sponsorship, several gifts were also sent both to these children and to their parents.

A major beneficiary of the Club donations was the United Fund of Westport, but in keeping with the Club's orientation toward public health assistance, the Norwalk Hospital was an even larger recipient. On the Hospital's 75th anniversary "diamond jubilee" in 1958, the Woman's Club pledged $7,500, payable over a three-year period, to underwrite the cost of a patient's room in the Bedford Pavilion. In addition, a Thrift Shop pledge of $14,700 in 1967, and a down payment of $3,000 toward the cost of a unit in the hospital's intensive care pavilion, brought the Club's total contributions to the Norwalk Hospital "in recent years" to $27,700. Donations are now being made to the hospital annually.

In 1961 the Club still maintained several continuing projects that were managed by its own personnel: the Visiting Homemaker Service, Loan Closet, Clothing Relief, Free Milk, Thrift Shop, and Senior Arts and Crafts. But by 1971 all of these had been discontinued except the Loan Closet, and the Club's charitable endeavors became largely directed to supporting the work of others rather than work of its own.

However, several sporadic operational projects occurred which will bear mention: A town immunization program for administering polio and other oral vaccines, inaugurated in 1963, was based at the Clubhouse and at several schools. Nearly 8,000 Westporters took Sabine oral polio vaccine at this time.

In April 1962 the town revived the Well Child clinic that had lapsed in 1960, and the Woman's Club was requested to accommodate this facility along with the Visiting Nurse Service that still maintained—at that time—its base of operations at the Clubhouse.

In 1967 and again in 1971, the Club co-sponsored the Westport Red Cross blood bank, which met its quota of 225 pints.

In its quiet way, the Garden Department also nurtured several gainful projects. In the fall of 1961, the Canal Street municipal sewage pumping plant was provided with a screen of planting—and a plaque was affixed to the fence announcing the

Club as donor. In April 1963 the Garden group effected a "spring rejuvenation" of the same project. And in 1970, continuing its co-sponsorship of the "Roadside Conservation Association Program", the Garden Department planted its 2,000th tree in Westport.

A NEW ROLE IN SAFEGUARDING THE ENVIRONMENT—CONSERVATION COMMITTEE APPOINTED

Conservation was becoming of public concern at this time, so early in 1963 the Club appointed a Conservation Committee. A delegation from this group sought to induce First Selectman Baldwin to appoint a town Conservation Commission as authorized by recent state legislation. Shortly thereafter, a sub-committee of the Planning and Zoning Board was requested to make an investigation and prepare a report on action needed. The report of this "Committee on Open Space, Conservation and Beautification" was completed in November of 1963 and resulted in the appointment of a permanent town Conservation Commission. Lack of funds precluded the undertaking of any major work; but in 1967 the Commission did organize a joint community clean-up project of the Saugatuck River area, for which the Garden Department operated a fleet of station wagons serving iced coffee and tea to 500 volunteer workers on the east bank of the river over a 10-mile reach.

Ecology also came in for its share of attention. In 1970 the Club was asked to serve on the Ecology Workshop, a work-study program of the Westport Recreation Commission.

At about the same time, the Garden Department promoted and sold to the membership low-phosphate, non-polluting household cleaners. And early in 1971, before the town started its own recycling program, the Garden group came again to the fore, instructing members in the proper procedures for saving glass, cans, and newspapers. Members brought their glass to the Club garage and when a town depot was finally established, ten station-wagon loads of glass were taken there. In November 1971 a *Clean-Up Westport* project was initiated, and Mrs. Jacky Booth was cited by the Club as Westport's "Woman of the Year" for her work in this and related projects.

In 1972 the Garden Department again demonstrated its deep involvement with conservation and environmental protection by distributing to each appropriate instructor in the town's public and private school systems a copy of a teachers' guide known as PATE (People And Their Environment). These books were edited for use at eight different grade levels, from first grade through high school, having been field tested by more than 2,000 teachers and approved by the education departments of all fifty states. In all, 154 guides were distributed by the Club "the purpose of which is to make environmental awareness and appreciation a part of the daily lives of all our children."

A Helping Hand to the Connecticut Braille Association

Assistance by the Club was also accorded to the Connecticut Braille Association in 1966. At that time, the Association operated partly in the basement of the Adams Academy and partly in the home of one of its staff. This group is a service organization, staffed by volunteers, who compile, print and distribute textbooks for blind and near-blind students, and also supply leisure-reading books in the same category to the local public libraries. About 200 students were serviced in the state. All attended regular classes with sighted children and who therefore required the same textbooks. Texts were produced either in Braille for the sightless students, or in enlarged photocopy for the near-blind. The Association was invited to occupy rent-free quarters in the Clubhouse basement where the old ceramic studio used to be. To obtain funds for remodeling, the Club held a "Fashion Show Brunch and Bridge" on March 31, 1966 at the Longshore Country Club at $5 a plate. Concurrently, the Thrift Shop donated funds for remodeling additional basement space for the Loan Closet. The combined work was accomplished at a cost of about $3,700 and the Connecticut Braille Association moved into its new quarters on September 9, 1966, where it has remained since.

A World Class Kitchen Added to the Clubhouse

For some time, it was apparent that the old kitchen was inadequate to serve the Club membership and inhibited others who were attracted by the location but would not contract to use the facilities due to lack of space or unsatisfactory equipment.

In 1968, during the presidency of Betty Chase, the board appointed a building committee to resolve the problem. The committee met with several builders and architects and chose to work with architectural firm of Edward O'Dwyer, who developed drawings and specifications for an attractive kitchen addition to the Clubhouse that the committee enthusiastically approved. They and Mr. O'Dwyer submitted these plans to the Club membership on May 1968, and the plan was approve unanimously. The architect then proceeded with the more detailed working drawings and specifications that were offered for bids to a number of contractors.

Construction began on August 1968 and after several delays, the addition was completed in February for a total of $19,349 for the construction and $6,560 for utilities, equipment, appliances, and the architect's fee.

The Woman's Club new kitchen quickly attracted many new activities and users—by members and other organizations seeking attractive facilities for their varied purposes.

THE SANITARY FILL SITE GETS BIGGER—BUT SO DOES THE CLUB'S PARKING SPACE

The "good old days" were revived again in 1958 when the town—up to its nose in garbage and unable to find a disposal area—appealed to the Woman's Club to permit the addition of another 10 feet of sanitary fill on top of the 10 to 12 feet of fill previously placed under the agreement made with the Club in 1956 on lands then under water along the Saugatuck River. A new agreement was therefore signed on October 15, 1968 by President Rita Keneally and selectmen Kemish and Veazie, permitting the town to make the additional fill—with a target completion date of June 1, 1969—in return for the town's repairing and marking the 100-car parking area on the lower level to which the Club had previously been given "in perpetuity."

As a by-product of this agreement, the executive board authorized a boundary survey of the Club property. A final survey dated October 8, 1970 (map #6883, filed June 30, 1971) was prepared by Mr. Lyman. This showed that the Club property consisted of about 1.65 acres with a 337-foot front on Imperial Avenue. Additionally, a new appraisal of Club property was prepared in November 1969, and insurance coverage was adjusted based upon the new appraisal. To complete the record, a certificate of title for the Club property was completed on April 22, 1970.

The title certificate and boundary survey both brought out that the west boundary of the Club property was an ill-defined line that could not be staked out on the ground with any degree of accuracy. This boundary, originally the shoreline of Dead Man's Brook, had been obscured by the town's filling operations and diversion of the brook from its original location. To rectify this anomalous condition, President Myrtle Cuneo offered in March 1972 to trade to the town a small triangular area west of the Clubhouse (0.33 acre) for that portion of the lower level parking lot (0.48 acre) that was still in town ownership. The town Zoning and Planning Commission rejected the offer in April 1972 for undisclosed reasons.

CONTINUED PARTICIPATION AT THE STATE FEDERATION OF WOMAN'S CLUBS

During the 1960s, the Woman's Club maintained an active participation in the affairs of the State Federation of Women's Clubs, and kept up a "Federation Committee" to further this relationship. Over the years, the Club had been the frequent recipient of many Federation awards, and the 1960s were no exception in this regard. Witness the impressive list for 1960: 1st and 2nd place for hand-made articles, 1st place for woodworking, 2nd place for painting, for copper work and for toleware, 3rd place for silver work, and an honorable mention for the general category of metal crafts. At the State Federation Convention in May 1960, Mrs. Ina Bradley was elected first vice-president. At the same time—and quite unrelated to her election—she captured first place in the poetry competition, with Mrs. Stephen Kiss taking second place for essay writing.

At the State Federation Convention in May 1962, Ina Bradley was elected Federation president, and in her remarks to the Woman's Club in February 1964, she told of the work of the Federation and urged the Club to "take a more active interest in statewide projects."

On the lighter side, art and ceramics courses were provided by the Club in the early 1960s. A Music Department was established in 1960 and a Gourmet Department in 1964. For a time, a Drama and Literature group was activated. Bowling was begun in 1964, a Craft Workshop in 1968, and yoga classes in 1971. Bridge was a perennial activity, both in tournament and social play. In 1966 a Heritage group met to study the history of Westport. By 1971 there were eleven Standing Committees, seven Sub-Committees, five Special Committees, and five Departments, all more or less active.

Woman's Exchange and Thrift Shop Cut the Knot with WWC

Although the Woman's Club organized and sponsored the Woman's Exchange and Thrift shop as a department of the Club in the 1940s, they had been operating independently for some time. The Club was again revising its bylaws and President Myrtle W. Cuneo met with them to discuss their obligations under these revisions. The Woman's Exchange and Thrift Shop chose to separate from the Woman's Club. Because their bylaws established them as a Westport Women's Club department, their severance required a vote of the WWC membership. At the February 1970 meeting, it was unanimously approved. The separation was amicable as the Club took satisfaction in having served as the "torch that lighted the way." The Thrift Shop had done a fine job for the community and everyone wished them a very successful future.

After 65 Years, a Pledge to "Transmit This Town Greater and More Beautiful"

In the fall of 1972 the Westport Woman's Club attained the grand young age of 65. Behind it lay a proud history of intensive and unselfish service to its community and to its fellow men. In forging ahead into the future, it continued to make its mark in the betterment of Westport. As was pledged long ago for another city in the Athenian Oath, which once was ensconced over the mantle in the social room of Bedford House: "I will strive increasingly to quicken the public sense of civic duty, thus transmit this town greater, better and more beautiful than it was transmitted to us."

The Greening of the Post Road Begins, 1972–1982

Late in April 1973, a tree was planted to mark the realization of the Westport Beautification Committee's long-standing dream that project members called the "Greening of the Post Road." Phase One of the project called for the planting of 70 trees this year, with the future greening spanning from the Norwalk town line to the Southport town line.

Mrs. Eloise Ray, landscape architect and long-time crusader, was on hand to watch the first tree planted Wednesday afternoon. "My hope," Mrs. Ray said, "is that in a very few years as we drive down the Post Road, we will see a long vista framed with tall trees, bringing greenery and beauty to the community. We are responsible for the stretch of the Post Road of our town where commercialism has been allowed to take over, and the original charm and history of this old road has been swallowed up. This area could be the birthplace of the restoration of the Old Post Road."

On hand for the beginning of the tree-planting program were Frank Geiger of Parsell's Garden Mart, who was in charge of the planting, Mrs. Nicholas Cardell, committee member, holding five-month-old Catherine; George Newman, assistant town engineer; Mrs. Eloise Ray, landscape architect; and Mrs. Milton Rusk, President of the Garden Department of the Westport Woman's Club.

As early as 1703, colonists had become concerned about the destruction of trees along the road followed by post riders between New York and Boston. When plans were made for the highway from the City of New York to the "Colony of Connecticut," provisions were made for the issuing of fines to anyone (other than a tree warden) who cut down trees. "Connecticut" had a similar provision. The

112

historic road traversing Westport from Southport to Norwalk once was lined with old and beautiful trees. Protected or not, the trees disappeared. The path that had been followed by Indians, frontier backpackers, post skiers and stagecoaches became Route 1 for cars and trucks. Repeated widenings, installation of utility lines, and parking lots took a heavy toll on the graceful trees that had lined it.

This greening of the Post Road project was the beginning of the realization of some dreams many townspeople had for a long time to return its once former beauty. It came about through the Garden Department as a result of the imagination of its chairman, Elaine Rusk. The Post Road project was born in 1970. Mrs. Rusk met with Eloise Ray, a landscape architect, at a luncheon meeting at Chubby Lane's restaurant and the plan for the Greening of the Post Road began to take form. Mrs. Rusk, chairman of the Westport Beautification Committee and a member of the Roadside Conservation Association, said, "We strike a nostalgic note when we remember what this old road was in the past, when it was a major artery between New York and Boston, lined with stately trees and greenery. Even as short a time ago as the 1930s, old maps showed almost solid rows of fine oaks, maples and elms on both sides of the road."

The original objective was to plant trees on the commercial stretch of the Post Road in Westport in order to replace the visual monotony of the highway. The Club's National Bicentennial Celebration was already being discussed, and it was decided to plant two hundred trees (one for each year of our country) on town, state, and private sites as planned by Eloise Ray.

Many of the trees would have to be planted on state property. An application was filed through the town of Westport with the state of Connecticut for permission to plant on the state road, but there were no state funds to obtain. Any tree planted on state property would have to be financed by funds from other donors. The Beautification Committee of the town of Westport was authorized to use funds only for town and private properties. The Roadside Conservation Committee could be involved only with private properties on town roads.

Nursery men who were consulted were pessimistic: the cost of planting and maintaining 200 trees would be prohibitive. The estimated cost of "The Greening" came to a staggering $30,000.

When the two organizations presented the plan to the Garden Department of the Westport Woman's Club, the ladies responded with a vote to sponsor it. The first encouragement came when the Beautification Committee allotted $3,000 "seed money" for trees to be planted on private property.

This became a Community project and eventually was paid for by the Club's Ways and Means, The Garden Department, The Beautification Committee of Westport, The Westport Garden Club, The Young Woman's League as well as donations from individuals and businesses facing the Post Road.

''The Greening of the Post Road" had been a major ongoing project of the Garden Department of the Westport Woman's Club since the fall of 1972. As a result of the program, approximately 1,000 trees were planted on the four-mile stretch of Route 1 between the Fairfield and Norwalk town lines. The tree-planting program dramatically influenced the improvement of the quality of commercial plantings along the Post Road.

Eloise Ray selected the varieties of trees and drew up the plans for the landscaping. Members of the Garden Department made all the arrangements to execute her designs and to see that each tree was properly planted. (The Beautification Committee continues to devote more than 50 percent of its budget annually to maintain these trees.) The program had the approval of the state and town officials and received the backing and support of the town beautification committee. Property owners, local and regional garden clubs, civic organizations, and many individuals contributed to the Greening.

Ginkgos, Honey Locusts, Hopa Crabapples, London Planes, Norway and Red Maples, Red Oaks, and Washington Hawthorns were planted by Russell Greaves. All trees chosen for the Greening of the Post Road would withstand highway fumes, dust, glare, and salt. They were "clean" trees—without obnoxious fruit and relatively resistant to pests and disease. Smaller trees were planted under utility wires. After the final phase of planting was completed, members of the Garden Department continued to serve as "tree watchers" to be sure that trees would remain in healthy condition and receive prompt attention if damaged.

A parade of young trees soon lined State Street, where just a few years earlier there were monotonous, tree-less stretches along this heavily traveled four miles. The greening of Post Road was becoming a reality.

In 1974, a Book of Evidence on the Greening of the Post Road was entered in the Environmental Improvement Contest, co-sponsored by the National Council of Garden Clubs, Inc., and Sears Roebuck and Company on May 11, 1975. Elaine Rusk went out to Salt Lake City to accept the award of $2,500 and a large engraved silver tray. On June 29, 1974, *The New York Times* praised the Westport Woman's Club on this achievement in a major article that covered the entire history of the "Greening." On October 25, 1975 in Hartford, the Garden Department also received the State Environmental Improvement Award of $300 and a plaque for First Place. Elaine Rusk was awarded the Club's "Woman of the Year" plaque in appreciation for her imagination and efforts with this project. Nearly $2,000 in prize money was earmarked for civic

Elaine Rusk (center) *receiving a silver tray and $2,500 check at National Council of State Garden Clubs convention*

114

improvement, and the Garden Department channeled the sum into the Post Road project, the Westport Garden Club's Grace Salmon Park on Imperial Avenue, and for planting trees on Avery Place. The trees were now well established. Today, Westport's Beautification Committee Members are appointed by the first selectman and serve two-year terms. The committee oversees care of some 300 "Greening of the Post Road" trees, originally planted by the Garden Department of the Westport Woman's Club.

Despite town regulations, many of these trees have been cut down by business and property owners while others are still carefully maintained.

THEY CALLED HER "MISS ALLEN" FOR FIFTY YEARS

In 1974, after serving fifty years as executive secretary, Frances Allen decided to retire. The April 12th luncheon was designated as "Frances Allen Day." The program consisted of several amusing skits portraying past events of the Westport Woman's Club, such as "The Tea Party on the town Dump" and "The Destruction of the Private Beach Houses" at Compo Beach. Frances was presented with a trip for two to the British Isles, given with deep affection from her many friends. The gift represented contributions from members, the Young Woman's League, the Connecticut Braille Association, the Roadside Conservation Committee, and the Thrift Shop. Frances had served us well for half a century.

"Ask Miss Allen" was a phrase frequently heard among members of the Westport Woman's Club for those fifty years. "Miss Allen", who served as part-time secretary to the group beginning in 1924, always seemed to have the answers. When her duties became more numerous, she was made the Club's first executive secretary during Mrs. John B. Warnock's presidency in 1945. Even her best friends addressed her as Miss Allen, and she, in turn, used their formal names.

Strangely enough, Miss Allen did not become a member of the Club until she retired. Then she was made an honorary lifetime member. Subsequently known as "Frances", she took an active part in club endeavors and served as the elected secretary of the Garden Department.

THE FOOD CLOSET—HOW IT STARTED

In 1975, a food closet was created at the Clubhouse to be used for distribution of food supplies to local needy families upon request from authorized sources. The Westport Woman's Club was authorized in writing by the town to receive and handle all monies collected from individuals or groups who cared to contribute to the Westport Thanksgiving and Christmas baskets.

The next year, through the inspired leadership of Kay Rooney, the project became a significant addition to our community services. Thirty Thanksgiving baskets were delivered and 166 people were given a happier Christmas through distribution of food baskets, plants to the elderly in nursing homes, catered dinners,

money, and gift certificates. With the help of donations from members, St. Luke's Church, and the townspeople, many emergency food deliveries were also made. This resulted in the Community Services going back to the original purpose of the Club of helping citizens of the community during emergencies of the times. For several years the main help had been in the form of financial donations. The Community Services Committee added a Volunteer Services sub-committee and it has become one of the Club's most satisfying activities in providing a logistical supplement to the many programs the Woman's Club sponsors or supports.

CELEBRATING THE AMERICAN REVOLUTION BICENTENNIAL

Westport was selected as a bicentennial town in January 1975. The steering committee consisted of individuals from various town organizations. Myrtle Cuneo represented the Westport Woman's Club. The general committee set up a series of art shows called *Prism '76* at the Westport Public Library in February 1975 and furnished refreshments and flower arrangements made by the Garden Department.

After a gala opening, each exhibit continued for three weeks. Calendars showing local scenes were printed and sold. Members of the Club staffed the exhibition for its duration. Hard copies of our new history were presented to the public library and to the Westport Historical Society. Sunday guided historical tours of the town were given, using one of the town's mini-buses. The Performers of Southern Connecticut put on two concerts of American music at Levitt Pavilion in July 1975. The Westport Historical Society completed a commemorative quilt. On Patriot's Day, April 18, there was a re-enactment of the arrival of the news of the beginning of the revolution. There was a *Great American Issues* lecture series. At a memorable Ball held at the home of Ernest Eckstein on Cross Highway on July 3, 1976, everyone wore eighteenth century costumes, After dinner, which was served around the pool, dancing took place in the large entrance hall, and the evening was climaxed with hundreds of sparklers on the front lawn. Westport was bubbling with patriotism.

Our Club was not content without doing something special for this important event. Myrtle Cuneo presented to the board the idea of making a diorama of the Battle of Compo Hill. This project was met with enthusiasm by both the board and the membership. Using the Club kitchen as a workshop, a committee consisting of Rita Keneally, (chairman), Nan Headley, Harriet Bryniczka, Marne Mayne, and Bea Kelly worked evenings under the technical and historical guidance of Myrtle's husband, John R. Cuneo, and made a very realistic diorama. It was unveiled at the

November 1975 meeting, and was exhibited at the Prism Art Show and later at the Nature Center. In March it was given to the Westport Historical Society and later transferred to the Adams Academy to be viewed by children and adults for years to follow.

To conclude the bicentennial year, the Westport Historical Society buried a time capsule to be opened in 2076. The Club history and the 1976 membership book were included among the items in the capsule.

THE CLUB—70 YEARS OLD

In 1977, the Westport Historical Society claimed the Club House qualified for a historical plaque. The plaque was placed on the front of the Club House. It reads: "Sidney Watts—1881".

At the March 1977 meeting, Ruth Harley of the Garden Department presented a plan to landscape the hillside between the Clubhouse and the lower parking lot as an anniversary gift to the Club. Members' donations, added to the Garden Department funds, made it possible to plant 40 exbury azaleas, as well as wiltoni junipers, upright yews, and myrtle. Eloise Ray was director of planning and Russell Greaves advisor of the planting. The Garden Department maintains the area during the summer and it is now well established.

The highlight of the year centered on the Celebration of the Club's 70th Birthday. The occasion was officially celebrated at the April 1977 Club Day meeting and the Club was honored by the presence of several former presidents: Jacqueline Heneage (first selectman of Westport and a member of the Club), Ursula Kolb (president of the Connecticut State Federation of Women's Clubs—CSFWC), Ann Bradley (first vice president of CSFWC), and Rita Leyden (president of the Westport Young Woman's League). At this meeting, Eloise Ray, professional landscape architect and consultant for the Westport Woman's Club for the past 25 years, was made an honorary life member.

THE JESUP GREEN/LOWER PARKING LOT ISSUE RE-EMERGES

Because of a proposed plan to develop the Jesup Green area, the perennial problem of the Club's rights to the lower parking lot was raised again. John Cuneo, the Club's attorney, researched and wrote a legal opinion confirming the Woman's Club's exclusive rights and hoping that the Jesup Green Planning Committee would settle the matter permanently. But three new plans were discussed at a Jesup Green Planning Committee public information meeting on January 4 1978. They were unacceptable to the Woman's Club board in their current form for the following reasons. Two plans called for the location of a new fire department headquarters building and a new access road from across Dead Man's Brook to Imperial Avenue next to or on the Club's lower parking lot. The third plan called for a new access road through the center of the Club's lower parking lot. These plans would infringe on the Club's current use of this parking lot and violate agreements signed by the Westport Woman's Club and the town of Westport in 1956 and 1968.

At this meeting, Club President Dorothea Citti noted these objections and referred to the agreement signed in 1956 that stated that a parking area would be prepared "to be available at all times in perpetuity for utilization by the Woman's Club and which area shall contain room for not less than one hundred (100) cars." The agreement in 1968 again affirmed the Club's right to the parking lot and further stated that the area between the parking lot and the proposed new road to the dump site could be used "for all lawful purposes," thus enabling the Club to use this area for such functions as the Flea Market and Yankee Doodle Fair, in addition to parking purposes.

What was the background of these agreements? Before 1956, the area consisting of the lower parking lot, the service road, and the landfill behind the parking lot was owned by the Westport Woman's Club. The town of Westport needed a place for sanitary landfill and asked the Club for permission to use the area described above for dumping. The 1956 agreement was the result. The Club gave the town title to the property (except for about one-third of the lower parking lot area) and received use of the parking lot in exchange.

Also noted at the January 4 meeting was the ratification of the 1956 agreement by the RTM, and approval of the 1968 agreement by the Planning and Zoning Commission. Kathy Roach, Rentals chairman, explained they could not rent the Club without adequate parking, and that the lot is essential to fund raising and regular club activities, or, in other words, to its existence. Jackie Heneage, Westport's first selectman, felt the Club made its point very clearly and urged we wait until one final plan is developed before taking any further action. The Jesup Green Planning Committee began working on this final plan for presentation at a future meeting open to the public.

The proposed plan was never carried out.

THE CANAL STREET PROJECT STARTED

The big new civic improvement project in 1981 was the Canal Street project chaired by The Garden Department's chairman Lois Lenfest. Lois and her committee worked with the town Committee, the Planning & Zoning department, RTM, town Beautification Committee and Eloise Ray Landscape Architect. After most of the work had been completed, the plan had to await the re-routing of the street in front of the project directly across from the elderly housing complex. Canal Green was completed and dedicated on June 24, 1985. It provides a pleasant park for the residents to spend leisure time. A statue created by Eloise Ray's son was placed near the sewer pumping station until it was stolen. Fortunately, the original molds were located and a new statue was made and replaced the original.

Jacky Booth chaired a committee consisting of past presidents Ina Bradley, Jo Destino, Rita Keneally, Myrtle Cuneo, Joan Croarkin, Dot Citti, Adele Collins, and Mona McKiernan, to make plans for a 75th Anniversary Celebration in 1982. The official celebration was held at the April 5 Club Day Luncheon and had a record attendance. First Selectman William Seiden was a guest. He gave a short talk and proclaimed the month of April 1982 as "Woman's Club Month."

Proclamation [1982]

On the Diamond Anniversary of this Woman's organization dedicated to community service, the Westport Woman's Club is recognized in the town of Westport as an organization working for civic betterment.

The Westport Woman's Club has set aside the month of April 1982 to observe the founding of this organization as the Woman's Town Improvement Association in 1907 and to commemorate such founding by rededicating itself to community service.

The Westport Woman's Club's numerous programs include the Food Closet, the Loan Closet and Scholarships for graduating seniors of Staples High School, as well as support of the United Fund, Norwalk Hospital, American Field Services, Staples WWPT, the Nature Center, Home Delivered Meals, the Lion's Club, Rescue 8, the Wheeler House Fund, Levitt Pavilion, the YMCA, STAR, and the Elder House.

As First Selectman of the town of Westport, I hereby designate the month of April 1982 as Westport Woman's Club Month and urge all citizens of our community to give full consideration to the past and future services of the Westport Woman's Club, which has done so much for the town of Westport during the past three quarters of a century.

Dated at Westport, Connecticut this 1st day of April, 1982.

William Seiden
First Selectman

Ruth Dolge was introduced as the Club member of longest standing. The Clubhouse looked very festive for the occasion, with flower arrangements made by the Garden Department, artist easels displaying the news books of past years and balloons. The highlight was a cake replica of the Clubhouse, which was exhibited on the stage and later served as dessert.

Many members marched in the Memorial Day Parade as a climax to the Westport Woman's Club 75th Anniversary Celebration. The *Westport News* dedicated a special section of its April 2, 1982 edition to this anniversary and expressed appreciation of the Woman's Club community service over the years:

Merci Beaucoup! Muchas Graçias! Thanks a Million! How DO We Say Thank You for 75 Years of Dedication?

By Addie Wagner

To outsiders, the name "Westport Woman's Club" might bring to mind one of Franklin Folger's cartoons of "The Girls"—affluent dowagers congregating in a birds-of-a-feather flock to discuss only the airiest of lightweight subjects, whiling away idle hours until their similarly-caricatured executive husbands come home from the office.

Westport residents know how false that scenario is! As far back as 1907, the ad hoc committee members had a very important and altruistic goal for their new group: to improve the quality of life for all Westport residents. That's why they chose the name "The Women's Town Improvement Association" 75 years ago. Improve the community they did, despite stubborn resistance from town officials and the public who looked upon the women's "dangerous" ideas with a conglomerate jaundiced eye.

Undeterred, the women took up the banner of "in union there is strength", rolled up their lady-like sleeves, and in relatively short period of time, began to surprise the Westport townsmen with their improvements which started from the ground up with sidewalks and reached to the skies with beautiful trees. The Association, later to be known as the Westport Woman's Club, meant business in 1907!

Today, the mustard seed of faith planted by those women has flourished into a tree laden with the fruits of civic, cultural and charitable contributions that have improved and enriched the community of Westport. We would certainly be remiss if we let this important occasion go by without an anniversary bouquet of appreciation and thanks to the 400 Westport Woman's Club members who continue, as their sisters have for the past 75 years, in the zealous pursuit of community service to Westport. Here, in the pages which follow, is a series of vignettes on their history of accomplishments and service, charitable works, personality and character, industry and ingenuity, and patriotism and pride in their community.

The year 1982–1983 was a most successful year for the Club. Membership grew to 401 members and the Club House and grounds were improved. Philanthropic donations within the community continued to rise.

The major improvement to the house and grounds was the installation of a flagstone patio in the side yard. The Garden Department did some planting of shrubs in the area that added the finishing touch. Within the Clubhouse, a new floor covering was installed in the kitchen, as well as having the cabinets and woodwork painted. The worn carpet on the stage and stairs to the stage was replaced.

Community Services Department met their usual commitments but also gave an additional $2,000 to the Emergency Medical Services. WWC had given them money for equipment the previous year in celebration of the 75th Anniversary. The largest single donation was for scholarships for Staples High School seniors. In addition to their usual activities, they helped with the distribution of Federal Surplus Food to the needy under the supervision of the town of Westport.

The first fund raising event of the year was a Silent Auction with items donated by members. Wine and finger foods were served during the viewing and bidding. The evening was a fun way of raising $2,300. In April a special Book Sale was conducted at the Club. The 2,500 new books were donated by a subsidiary of W. R. Grace. This successful fund-raiser has evolved successfully in other forms.

A "Soup Kitchen in Affluent Westport"—In Search of a Home

In January 1982, two young men brought to the attention of the citizens of Westport that there were homeless people in town and suggested a "soup kitchen." When no action was taken, the two men began a hunger strike, which quickly caught the attention of the national media. Ted Hoskins, pastor of the Saugatuck Congregational Church and David Kennedy, chairman of the Human Resources Services, were invited to appear on the Phil Donahue Show. After much controversy as to whether "affluent" Westport truly needed a soup kitchen, a cold meal project was begun at the new Post Road Fire Station. A group of enthusiastic high school students appeared for lunch. The two hunger strikers continued their fast until Save the Children building was offered as a home for the kitchen.

The Community Kitchen served soup, bread, beverage and fruit between 5 and 7 PM, Monday through Friday at Save the Children on Wilton Road. This was a volunteer project under the sponsorship of the Critical Human Needs Coalition. From 9 to 25 people—with an average of about 12—appeared each day for a meal.

Though the Westport Woman's Club was approached as the home for the kitchen, it was felt that our Food Closet and Holiday Project and other efforts were alternative programs performing similar services but with greater outreach. In 1982 the Club helped one hundred families with food baskets, food certificates, gifts and catered dinners during the holidays, and all year we gave food to needy people on an emergency basis from our Food Closet.

During the summer, nineteen Club members helped the town's Human Resources Services distribute almost six tons of food to some 199 families. They then helped set up Governor O'Neil's "Operation Feed a Friend" program, took applications, processed paperwork, manned the distribution site and home-delivered to the handicapped on an ongoing monthly basis.

These Community Services efforts were recognized among 20 finalists in the J. C. Penney Golden Rule Award Contest. The Westport Women's Club was awarded a plaque for outstanding work in supplying food to needy families on an emergency basis.

WWC Enterprise Club Formed—A Second Investment Group

At its meetings, the WWC Venture investment group has a speaker or a study of a chapter in their textbook or an analysis of various stocks for purchase. One member, acting as a stock watcher for each of the group's current holdings, gives an update on her particular stock at each meeting.

Due to an unreasonably lengthy waiting list for the WWC Venture Investment group, Betty Woodsum, Venture Chairman, suggested pursuing the idea of forming a second group. She and Dot Citti met with the women who had professed interest, to explain the activities of an investment group. More than adequate response developed a long list of prospective members and twenty-four of them formed a new investment group— the WWC Enterprise Club—in 1982 with Barbara Hart serving as the first president.

Community Services Cited for Performance of Volunteer Services Group

The Volunteer Services group became involved in distributing surplus cheese and butter to families recommended by the Human Services. In an acknowledgement from David Kennedy, director of Human Services, he wrote "It has been nineteen of the Woman's Club members who have made possible, in one town, the distribution of almost six tons of food to some 199 families since July, 1983. Through their hands, 11,777 pounds of cheese, butter, flour, rice, milk, cornmeal and honey have been delivered and distributed." Also, ninety-four families (302 people) were furnished with Thanksgiving and Christmas dinners.

1983–1984—A Brief Return to Golden Age of High-Profile Program Guests

During the early years of WTIA and the WWC, the monthly programs consistently featured high profile speakers presenting timely and often thought-provoking subjects. Many of the speakers at the Club's monthly programs in 1983–1984 were nostalgically of similar quality. The following descriptions of these meetings are edited excerpts from Program Chairman Dee Andrian's reports in *The Bulletin.*

Martha Stewart—A Business Tycoon in the Making

Martha Stewart, author of the national best seller Entertaining and Martha Stewart's Quick Cook was the first guest of our monthly luncheons, beginning September 12, 1983. Mrs. Stewart's career began as one of Connecticut's best-known caterers. And, as we've since seen, Ms. Stewart went on to create a giant business enterprise destined for fame and notoriety.

Julie Belaga—Our Would-be Governor

State Representative Julie Belaga (R–136 District) was the guest at an October 3 luncheon. She reviewed for the Club some of the major legislations enacted during the past year and discussed what she believed would be the important issues facing the state's governing body in the year ahead, including the special session in October on Connecticut's roads and bridges. She also discussed women's role of achieving power in the political arena.

Belaga was elected to the Connecticut House of Representatives in 1976, 1978, 1980 and 1982 and was listed in *Who's Who of American Women.* After unsuccessfully running for governor, Belaga was appointed to several key regional and national governmental posts.

Betty Fisher—Floral Designer for the Kennedy White House

Betty Fisher, professional floral designer at Thurstan House Flowers and Festivities in Westport, was the guest at the November 7th luncheon. Mrs. Fisher demonstrated how easily non-talented individuals can create a bouquet of fresh flowers, an arrangement of dried flowers, a Christmas wreath and other holiday décor.

Having more than 20 years experience in designing and managing florist operations, Mrs. Fisher had designed the floral display arid bouquets for the Miss Connecticut competition of the Miss Universe contest for the previous three years. Also, she created traditional and period pieces for the White House during the Kennedy administration

The Westport Madrigal Singers—International Christmas Caroling

The Westport Madrigal Singers, under the direction of Jeanne Kimball presented a varied program of Christmas and secular music at the Club's luncheon, December 5th. The group of 12 men and women performed Elizabethan madrigals, French chansons, an echo song by Orlando Lassus and a bawdy round for men's voices by Henry Purcell. The Christmas portion of the program included a Bach chorale and unusual carols from France, Spain, Czechoslovakia and England. At the end of the program, the audience was invited to join the singers in a few familiar carols

Claire Gold—Superintendent of Westport Public Schools

Claire S. Gold, Superintendent of Westport Public Schools, was the guest at the January 9th, 1984 Luncheon.

Mrs. Gold reviewed the accomplishments of the system, enumerated some of the curriculum requirements that had occurred in recent years, such as increasing graduation requirements and adding computer courses, introducing foreign languages at an earlier point in the curriculum, etc. At this time, Mrs. Gold held the position of chairman of the Governor's Committee reviewing teacher training programs, and certification requirements in the State of Connecticut. Prior to her role as superintendent, Mrs. Gold was assistant superintendent for Special Education from 1973 to 1977.

Frederick Newman—Writer, Comedian and Television Personality

Frederick Newman, writer, comedian and television personality, was the guest at the February 6th luncheon.

As a comedian, he had performed on such national shows as "The Merv Griffin Show", "PM Magazine", the "David Letterman Show", National Public Radio and the BBC in the United Kingdom. His many voices and imitations could be heard on records, radio shows, cartoons and commercials.

Author of "Mouth Sounds", he would take his audience on a fantastic excursion through the history of sounds and sound making—from cave men to the Bee Gees—with lots of laughter and learning.

Katinka Loeser DeVries—Writer and Poet but "Not Quite Chekhov"

Katinka Loeser DeVries, writer and poet, was the guest at the March luncheon.

Mrs. DeVries was born in Ottumwa, Iowa, raised in Chicago, attended Mt. Holyoke College and graduated from the University of Chicago without significantly high honors (so she claimed), but with the personal pleasure of having been chosen for his writing class by Thornton Wilder, whose final appraisal of her short stories was: "Not quite Chekhov."

Her work appeared in *Poetry* and won that magazine's Young Poet's Prize in 1943. One of the editors making the award was her husband, Peter DeVries.

Mrs. DeVries' poetry first appeared in the New Yorker in 1950, two years after she and her husband and two small children had emigrated to the country town of Westport. Her poems and stories have appeared in the *New Yorker*, and her short fiction has been collected in two earlier books—*The Archers at Home* and *Tomorrow will be Monday*. Of the pieces in "A Thousand Pardons," "Company Manners", and "Taking Care" were cited in *The Best American Short Stories: 1981*.

Colonel John Cottell—Survivor of a Nazi Firing Squad

"It's a miracle that I am alive today," says Colonel John Cottell, who was the guest speaker at the April 2nd luncheon and the survivor of a Nazi firing squad, of Buchenwald, a Spanish concentration camp, and of the Soviet Lubyanka prison,

Colonel Cottell's daring adventures during his 32-year career with British Intelligence have been immortalized in the spy fiction of John LeCarre, including, *The Spy Who Came in from the Cold*, and *Tinker, Tailor, Soldier, Spy*.

GRATITUDE EXPRESSED TO THE BEDFORD FAMILY AND INA BRADLEY—KEY FACTORS IN CLUB'S SUCCESS

Members of the Bedford family pose with the restored portrait of Edward Thomas Bedford, a major benefactor of the Woman's Club

Much of the Club's good fortune was made possible by the Bedford family, and in April 1985 a plaque was hung near the office. The inscription reads as follows:

This plaque is dedicated to the Bedford Family whose early support of the Westport Woman's Club made possible the acquisition of this house and whose continuing assistance substantially benefits the membership and the community. April 1985

A scholarship was awarded in Ina Bradley's name. A plaque recognizing her dedication and service to the Westport Woman's Club was hung in the dining room in June 1985. Her children are still making annual contributions to sustain this scholarship.

Ina Bradley with daughter Deborah, early 1950s

THE CANAL GREEN PROJECT IS COMPLETED

After years of controversy, the housing complex for the elderly had opened on Canal Street. Under the sponsorship of the Garden Department, a new civic improvement project, "The Canal Green Project", was born in 1981. It was chaired by the Garden Department's chairman Lois Lenfest. Lois and her committee working with the town Committee, the Planning and Zoning department, RTM, town Beautification Committee and Eloise Ray Landscape Architect. It was completed and dedicated in June 14, 1985. This was a Garden Department project, helped by Community Services and donations from the Young Woman's League, town of Westport Beautification Committee, Marketing Corporation of America, Bridgeport Hydraulic and installations by the Public Works Department. After most of the work had been completed, the plan had to await the re-routing of the street in front of the project directly across from the elderly housing complex. It provides a pleasant park for the residents to spend leisure time. A Book of Evidence was submitted to the Federated Garden Clubs of Connecticut where the Club won a special second place award for this Community Improvement Program.

1985—A YEAR OF AWARDS FOR THE GARDEN CLUB AND A NEW PATIO BEAUTIFIES THE LANDSCAPE

A very attractive patio, designed by Geiger's Garden Center, was built in April 1983. Upon its completion several flowering shrubs were planted, to beautify the whole area.

The Garden Department added new plantings around the patio. Some memorial contributions were also made by Garden Department members for such plantings and set the stage for more such contributions from the general Club membership. In September, a sundial in memory of past president Rita Keneally, who passed away in July, was placed on the patio. It bears the inscription "Her Heart Was Filled With Sunshine." The gazebo was added in 2000 in memory of Ronnie Kennedy.

ON AN AWARDS WINNING STREAK

Through the efforts and organization of Jean McGibbins and Lillian Weimann, there were many beautiful and diversified entrants in the March 1983 Arts and Crafts Contest, which was held at the March Club Day Luncheon. Twelve of the entrants won Blue Ribbons, and other entrants won lesser ribbons. All twelve winners entered in the District 8 contest in April. The Club won more ribbons at district than any other entering club.

In February 1986, the Woman's Club won five first prizes at the State Convention for their 10 craft entries, three second prizes, and one third prize. They also won a first place for Scholarships, third for Newsletter, Performing Arts and Family Economics, and a Phipps Scholarship recipient. On April 9th at District VIII Day, they received five blue ribbons in Craft, and were awarded first place in the District for their Community Improvement Project—Canal Green.

In May 1986 at the 89th State Convention of Federated Women's Clubs of Connecticut, the Club won four first place awards, three second-place awards, two third-place awards—and in Crafts, continued in their winning ways with three state blue ribbons. A large group marched in the Memorial Day Parade.

HIGH COST OF MEMBERSHIP IN CONNECTICUT FEDERATION OF WOMEN'S CLUBS CHALLENGED.

The perennial issue of the high cost of membership in Connecticut Federation of Women's Clubs was addressed at August 1987 board meeting. Bunny Fontaine, president of Federation, explained why the Westport Woman's Club should remain in the Federation. She cited the benefit of enjoying a 501(c)(3)-tax status available to volunteer organizations. If the WWC were not a member, they would have to apply for a 501(c)(3)-tax status on their own. She also cited automatic insurance coverage up to 100 million dollars for officers of the Club should they be sued. This is available through the Torte Reform Act # 86-388. But the benefits were not enough to justify the cost. At the March 1989 meeting, the board reviewed these and other membership issues and voted to consider leaving the Federation. In April, the Club continued to garner awards at several of the Federation's activities and considered retaining membership if only to support the Federation. In April, President Barbara Culp cited the Federation's value as a "large and strong lobby and locally and nationally and we should be proud to be part of it."

The issue was revisited often in the months that followed. Carla Philcox, president of the Connecticut Federation of Women's Clubs, was invited to speak at the February 1990 meeting to tell the membership about the influence the Federation had on the national level. With 7,000 members in Connecticut, the Federation has significant influence on Connecticut's legislative bodies. She explained the absence of major achievements was due to the Federation's practice of changing projects every two years as the leadership changed.

After the meeting, Johnny Sweeney, the Club's Federation representative, explained how the Federation's activities differ from the WWC, making it difficult to measure projects by their standards. Except for Arts and Crafts, in which the Woman's Club participates and where it has had outstanding recognition over the years, it cannot be compared with any other women's club in the state.

After a discussion on whether the Club should pay the increased membership dues, a motion to withdraw from the Federation was defeated and the Club went on to win more awards at the annual convention than ever before.

THE LEA RUEGG AWARD ENDOWMENT FUND

Lea Ruegg, Carol Panish, and Lea's sister.

The Westport Woman's Club has an endowment fund named in honor of late club member, Lea Ruegg, at the request of her only son, Erhardt, who left WWC the residue of his estate for this purpose.

Lea Ruegg was born in Binghamton, New York to loving parents of modest means. She was the second youngest of five children, one brother and three sisters. Lea moved to Westport in the late 1940s with Erhardt, then two years old. They resided at 35 Prospect Road, where she kept a lovely home and a beautiful garden. Mother and son were very close and together they planted trees and flowers on the property.

Lea joined the Woman's Club in 1976 according to her close friend and club member Carol Panish "mainly to play bridge and to meet more bridge players", which, of course, she did and continued to enjoy until her death in 1983.

When Lea became very ill with cancer, she asked her son to remember the Woman's Club in his will, as he had acquired a considerable trust upon the death of his father. After Lea died, he contacted Carol to inquire further about the Woman's Club. She referred him to club secretary Ruth Kinson, who filled him in on the scope of the Club's activities. In his will, Erhardt Ruegg requested the funds be left to the Club "to be known as *The Lea Ruegg Award Endowment Fund*...I request that a suitable plaque be placed in an appropriate area so that it is prominently displayed in honor of my mother, Lea Ruegg, who was a member of the Westport Woman's Club for many years before her demise."

The legacy amounted to $700,000 with "no strings attached as to how the money must be used." On May 1, 1991 the Community Services Department successfully submitted to the board a proposal for disbursement of yields from the Ruegg Fund investments. Ten percent would be dedicated to an annual college scholarship grant to a Staples student selected by the WWC Scholarship Committee in the name of Lea Ruegg. It was argued that the Club normally granted many small, low-impact scholarships from the Community Services Department and E. B. Fuller Trust funds, ranging from $500 to $1,500 per student. They felt that the Lea Ruegg Award Endowment Fund provided the Woman's Club an opportunity to honor their benefactress by making a significant impact on at least one worthy student's academic prospects each year.

Forty-five percent would be deposited in a reserve account set aside for long-range capital improvements to the Club's building and facilities. Rental income was the prime and adequate source for normal maintenance and repair expenses. But the age of the Clubhouse and its variety of uses created conditions that exceeded this source of funds.

Forty-five percent would be disbursed to Community Services for consolidation with profits from Ways and Means events and the Yankee Doodle Fair for grants to community charities. This would raise the Woman's Club stature to among the top contributors in the community.

In June 1991 a brass plaque identifying *"The Lea Ruegg Room"* was placed over the living room door.

The Westport Woman's Club's extraordinary history of successfully taking on and solving many of the town's community issues began to find fewer and fewer such challenges. While continuing to take on those that remained, the membership found their role evolving from leadership to participation and celebration. In 1997, the board modified its mission statement to reflect the emphasis on fund-raising to support programs and activities managed by other organizations. The Westport Woman's Club was now "a philanthropic organization dedicated to volunteerism and the raising of funds in support of charitable, educational, cultural and public health services in Westport and surrounding towns."

WOMAN'S CLUB BRINGS BACK THE WESTPORT COMMUNITY DIRECTORY

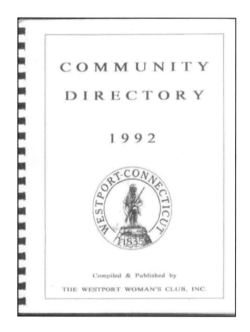

In 1987, the town's Westport/Weston Community Council was disbanded.

Among the many useful and important projects that this group had managed was the well-regarded Westport/Weston Community Directory, which was discontinued upon the dissolution of the Council. This 76-page directory listed alphabetically all the key organizations that served many of the needs of these two communities. Agencies, such as the United Way and the Family Center, sought unsuccessfully to find other volunteer groups to take on the project and to continue to finance, research, publish and market it. The absence of this community resource had an impact on many groups: organizations seeking financial or volunteer assistance; parents researching information on public and private schools or day care; and fund-raising groups attempting to avoid scheduling their events in conflict with others. It was a loss of a convenient, central reference resource by groups such as the local newspapers, the library, the chamber of commerce, school and municipal offices. A significant number of residents, organizations' administrators, and volunteers sorely missed this convenient source of answer to who, what, why, where and when.

In 1991, Eileen Petropoulos, the new Community Services chairman, visited the public service organizations in the community that expressed a need for a centralized reference of services available. She proposed to the WWC board that the Woman's Club revive and update the discontinued Westport Community Directory. The proposal was to expand the scope of WWC services by reaching a larger audience than did the traditional services (loan closet, food closet, scholarship and delivery of government surplus food). Since all of these services were provided to specific target groups in need, Petropoulos felt that the Woman's Club was not adequately recognized by the community-at-large.

The Community Services Department voted to fund this project for its first year, with the assumption that it would generate enough income to become self-supporting for future editions. Any excess funds would be donated to a worthy cause in the name of the WWC. Eileen Petropoulos agreed to chair this new group and Gerry Munce volunteered as vice-chair. Carol Lewis joined the project as editor. Nine additional volunteers completed the staffing of the Community Directory Group,

The Group spent three months canvassing some 500 prospects from those listed in the 1987 directory. Each prospect was called by phone for data that would provide a descriptive text for each listing—a feature that was not included in the original format. Layout, computer entry, proofreading, master sheet preparation, and research spanned a period of nine months and consumed 1,800 volunteer hours. Community Services provided $1,639 for printing expenses and $400 for start-up expenses totaling $2,039. The Directory (500 copies) was ready for sale on April 27, 1992—nine months after it was first proposed.

The Remarkable Book Shop offered to display and sell the directory for WWC. Community Services made three sales mailings to specific target groups, sent sales teams to several local town events, and managed generous publicity in the *Westport News*. They pre-sold 314 books by August 24, 1992. Enough revenue was generated to reserve $2,900 for producing and marketing the 1993 edition, on which work had already begun. The experience gained made the subsequent editions easier and more efficient to produce.

Distribution, pass-along readership, and publicity achieved in the first year created a significant awareness of the directory among town residents and its value as a resource reference impressed its strong sales base of over 300 listed subscribers. The community at-large responded with flattering and supportive phone calls, letters, newspaper coverage and more subscriptions.

The listed services grew to over 600 in the 1993 edition. More sophisticated marketing plans were employed. They included additional distribution points with point-of-sale displays, sales teams at more town events, earlier and more mailings of target group sales letters, more aggressive advance sales, more press and radio publicity, a wider poster distribution area, and paid advertising in the local newspaper.

The WWC was becoming an important source of information on the services available in the community. This group worked long and hard and three successive chairs continued for another two years to build enough circulation to firmly establish the Community Directory and the WWC as a prime resource and service to the town and to create another jewel in the crown of the WWC. But the ongoing task became too formidable and the program was ultimately abandoned.

THE WOMAN'S CLUB HELPS CREATE THE LIBRARY'S EMBANKMENT RIVERWALK AND SAUGATUCK MURAL

The Library Embankment Riverwalk and the installation of the Saugatuck mural in the library were both significant events for the Westport Woman's Club in the fall of 1992. When this idea was first conceived by a group of dedicated beautification volunteers, seed money was needed to pay for mailings explaining the project and to solicit funds. The Community Services Department of the WWC made the first contribution to the start-up expenses in the early stages of these ventures. The Club also purchased a permanent memorial bench installation at the Riverwalk that reads "To all members of the Westport Woman's Club—past, present and future."

AN AILING CLUBHOUSE IN NEED OF ATTENTION

By the fall of 1992, heating the Clubhouse had become too erratic to ignore and WWC's fuel supplier, L. H. Gault, was asked to inspect the system. A serious oil leak was detected on the grounds next to the auditorium steps leading from the patio. Gault discovered a punctured oil pipe—probably due to a tent pole from a wedding rental. Oil-saturated earth mounds had to be removed in an environmentally sound manner. Similar vulnerable ground locations had to be clearly marked to avoid future problems of this sort. Jim Donaher, an executive from Gault, helped arrange the excavation and haulage of the dangerous waste materials and recommended the replacement of the underground tank with two above ground tanks. Donaher graciously committed Gault to provide and install them at no cost.

Leaks were cropping up all over the house and were impacting on the wiring, plaster and floor boards. The age of the pipes and sealing had taken its toll and new plumbing was installed.

Storage space had become scarce and the problem of using a damp basement was temporarily addressed with the installation of dehumidifiers. The re-grading needed to eliminate the water seepage was postponed as too costly.

In April 1995, a portion of the ceiling collapsed in the auditorium during a scheduled event. Fire trucks, EMS and police arrived on the scene. Two people were injured and taken to Norwalk Hospital for treatment and observation. The ceiling had to be replaced in its entirety as the fire inspector had it pulled down the day of its collapse as it was declared "unsafe." The wiring and lighting systems were also replaced after it was found that the wiring could not meet "current code standards."

MEMBERSHIP OPENED TO OUT-OF-TOWNERS

In February 1993, the membership voted overwhelmingly to amend Article III (1) of the Bylaws by replacing the restriction of "any woman in the town of Westport" with "any woman who subscribes to the principles..." effectively eliminating membership restrictions to Westport residents only. This change allowed membership to women from neighboring towns who demonstrated interest in participating in WWC's charitable and fund-raising efforts.

REMEMBERING HARRIET BEECHER STOWE

Westport's two oldest Clubs, the Westport Woman's Club and the Westport Historical Society, joined together for a presentation of historical significance, featuring the famous Connecticut author, Harriet Beecher Stowe, as portrayed by Hartford actress Jean Slade Smith, who had interpreted Mrs. Stowe at several other important celebrations and in a televised documentary.

Mrs. Smith's "one-woman show" took place at the Westport Woman's Club in the afternoon on Sunday, March 14, 1993. The public was invited to attend the presentation and the catered reception that followed.

Although Stowe is the author of many books, she is best remembered for her *Uncle Tom's Cabin,* which was considered a prime influence on the North's entry into the Civil War. Abraham Lincoln described Mrs. Stowe as "the Little Lady who started the big war."

NEW EDITION OF THE CONNECTICUT COOKBOOK PUBLISHED

1993 marked the 85th Yankee Doodle Fair. Fifty years ago, the Westport Woman's Club published a cookbook during World War II. At the 1993 fair a new edition of this cookbook entitled *Feasting in Westport* was published and offered for sale by the Yankee Doodle Fair Committee. A recipe for each section has been selected and included from the 1943 edition with references made to Victory Gardens and also to substitutes for rationed items. One was particularly fascinating: Eggless, Butterless, Milkless Cake.

Feasting in Westport was a collection of recipes gathered from all segments of Westport life, including the arts, entertainment, restaurants, business, founding families, long time residents and new residents. It incorporated a sprinkling of history, a pinch of whimsy, a dollop of art from Westport's local artists and a host of good recipes.

Woman's Club Member Selected as 1994 Memorial Day Parade Grand Marshall

Westport Woman's Club member, U.S. Air Force Captain Jean Plasan, was chosen to represent Westport as its Grand Marshall in the 1994 Memorial Day Parade.

Jean has been among the Club's most active volunteers in support of community health services. She has been and continues to be the Club member the Westport Weston Health District depends on to provide the volunteers needed to stage their annual Flu Clinic and other such events.

Jean Plasan began her outstanding career in serving her country and community when she graduated with her R.N. degree from Grace Hospital in New Haven in December of 1944. In 1945 she was wined, dined and recruited by the Red Cross and thus began her career of active duty. In WWII, Jean joined the Army Nurse Corps as the youngest Second Lieutenant and was stationed at Tinian, the secret Air Force base housing the B-29s that carried the atom bomb to Japan. Her tour in Iwo Jima left her with a vivid image of rows and rows of crosses marking the graves of our young casualties of the invasion. A different image but equally as heart-wrenching and horrifying was the condition of the prisoners of war, the sick, and the injured.

In March of 1946, Jean returned home and worked in the veterans' hospital. She stayed with the Reserves and continued her education, graduating cum laude from the University of Connecticut with a Bachelor of Science degree in public health.

In 1951 Jean Plasan was called up to serve in the Korean War with the Air Force as a First Lieutenant, stationed at Sewards Air Force Base. She was sent to Chaumont, France to care for the fighters, then back to Rhine, Maine. In Rhine, Maine she awarded herself her greatest lifetime souvenir—her husband. Lieutenant Howard Plasan was a special service engineer attached to the Air Force. On October 31, 1965, Captain Jean Plasan retired. For twenty years she served in the Army and Air Force caring for the wounded and the sick. In peacetime she continued to work in the health care industry and today she is a most active member of the Woman's Club Community Service Department.

As Jean marched as Westport's Grand Marshal, perhaps many of her thoughts were for the times and the people she served with and cared for over those twenty years of active duty.

Entering the Computer Age

The Westport Woman's Club had now become a full-time business with a cash flow of $200,000 a year, an endowment of over $1,000,000, and real estate holdings exceeding $700,000. The board members recognized that old-fashioned bookkeeping would no longer do and authorized computerizing the office. In October 1994 they hired Cindy Bulkley, the first computer-literate office employee.

Cindy went on to serve for ten years after succeeding Ruth Kinson, who retired due to illness after serving for 17 years. At the April 1995 Club Day Luncheon, the members celebrated Ruth's many years of dedication to the Club. All past presidents currently living in Westport were present. Letters of appreciation were read from her daughters, friends, and past presidents, who were then living elsewhere. She was awarded a painting by Emily Buck that had hung in her office and was awarded a Life Membership to the WWC.

Comedy

Tragedy

1996 UNVEILING OF JOHN STEUART CURRY'S FRESCOS

In 1934 Westporters had raised $1,000 for materials and supplies and John Steuart Curry donated his time and talent to create *Comedy* and *Tragedy,* which record the history of entertainment in the United States. They are two of very few frescos (a fourteenth-century technique where paint is applied to wet mortar) ever created by an American artist—and we have them here in Westport, located on either side of the auditorium stage at Kings Highway School.

At the 1994 Arts Heritage Awards, Kathleen Curry, the artist's 96-year old widow, expressed the hope that these frescos would be restored by 1997, the hundredth

A Restoration Celebration!

◆

This is your special invitation
to attend the unveiling of the restored
John Steuart Curry Frescos, *Comedy* & *Tragedy*
in the
Kings Highway School Auditorium

Sunday, October 6, 1996 from 4:00 PM to 6:00 PM

Come meet Mrs. Kathleen Curry, our Honorary Chairman
at the reception following the rededication

*The fresco restoration is the joint project of the
John Steuart Curry Restoration Committee and the Westport Woman's Club*

anniversary of Curry's birth. Inspired by her challenge, the John Steuart Curry Restoration Committee was formed to raise the funds to make her wish come true.

At the same time, the Westport Woman's Club was looking for a special project. Since its formation in 1907, Westport artists, including John Steuart Curry, have given of their time and talents to many of the Club's projects. In turn, during the Depression years, the Club organized art shows so local artists could exhibit and sell their paintings.

The Club's Ruegg Committee decided to award a $9,600 grant to restore the frescos as its way of recognizing all the artists who had helped them through the years. The restoration was done by Christy Cunningham-Adams and George Adams during July 1997. This was the first of the ongoing $10,000 awards underwritten by Ruegg Grant.

An impressive New Fund-raiser—the Curio Cottage Thrift Shop

The Curio Cottage Thrift Shop—a very successful new fund-raiser—had its grand opening in the small building next to the Clubhouse on October 6, 1999 with Diane Farrell, Westport's first selectwoman, helping to cut the ribbon.

Chairperson Norma Beck enlisted her committee members, their husbands, their children and grandchildren, along with contributions from local merchants and volunteers from the "Y's Men" to paint the furniture and prepare the facility for the opening celebration.

They created a "fun" facility and people enjoyed browsing, contributing, and purchasing curios, with the added feature of receiving tax donation forms with every donation. Its uniqueness created an instant success. The Curio Cottage grossed $8,000 in its first year of operation.

Norma Beck, who had been chairman of Community Services, originally proposed the concept of a thrift shop as a way of reversing the recent decline in the ability of fund-raisers in general and the Book Barn in particular to produce enough funds to respond adequately to various charities. In 1997–1998, the WWC was able to grant less than 50 percent of funds requested. Characterized as a venue where "buying is giving", the membership approved the renovation of the Book Barn into a thrift shop on May 4, 1998. The name "Curio Cottage" was chosen by Iris Frey and its slogan became "Shop, Donate, Help Others."

"Goodwill" was the only other thrift shop in town and it was felt that a well-promoted WWC thrift shop would improve the visibility of Club's Community

Service organization. Since the Book Barn was located on the grounds outside of the Clubhouse, shoppers would have easy access and a more attractive venue for browsing and making purchases extemporaneously.

The Curio Cottage opened for sales four half-days a week and 882 slots of volunteer help were required yearly, not including the many who scouted tag sales and shops to solicit unsold items. Inventory is all donated with receipt forms given to donors upon request. All sales receipts go to the Club for charitable donations—a listing of which is available to customers.

Norma Beck became its first chairman. A plaque in her honor was placed in the shop and she was named Most Valuable Member in 2001.

THE WESTPORT WOMAN'S CLUB AND THE FEDERATION PART WAYS

At the April 2000 general meeting, the issue of continuing membership in the Federation was brought up. The members asked for and were sent a letter explaining the membership benefits and attached a ballot for choosing to retain or withdraw membership. It was noted that the traditional benefits of membership and

participating in competitions to win awards were no longer a compelling goal for current members. Job relocations had become less frequent and automatic entry into another Woman's Club became less relevant. The members concluded that the dues that had more than doubled since continuing membership was debated in 1987 were no longer justified, and they voted to end their affiliation. The familiar Westport Woman's Club continued to use its seal featuring the Federation's lamp in its center until it was replaced in 2006 by a new logo displaying a sketch of the Clubhouse on Imperial Avenue.

I n the spring of 2001, Lieutenant Governor Jodi Rell was the guest speaker on Club Day to discuss the State of the State and what was going on in Hartford. She concluded her presentation by proclaiming the Westport Woman's Club to be a "Connecticut Treasure." She saluted the Club members as an organization that had demonstrated an extraordinary commitment and contribution in responding to the needs of the people of Connecticut. The only other organization in Westport to have previously received this distinction is EMS (Emergency Medical Services). And, in the final decade of its first centennial, the Westport Woman's Club continued to pursue these noble goals.

Alarmingly, 2000 began apprehensively due to the need to repair or replace many items that had severely impacted on the Clubhouse and property expenses. The upper parking lot had to be re-paved and, in July, the ceiling in the lady's bathroom collapsed. This was the first of several ceiling incidents that included the need to replace the dining room ceiling. After discovering "critters" living above the dropped ceiling and then attempting to remove them, it was discovered that the plaster ceiling above the dropped ceiling was in fragile condition and in danger of falling and taking the dropped ceiling with it. The entire structure had to be repaired. Having experienced several suits regarding the collapse of the ceiling in 1995, it was decided to "bite the bullet." The entire air conditioning and heating system also had to be replaced.

WHERE TO RELOCATE THE SENIOR CENTER AND THE YMCA? WWC—FIRST TARGET

The Club was approached in 2001 regarding appointing a member to serve on the Sub-Committee for the Senior Center due to the possibility that the center would be placed on the commuter parking lot adjacent to the Clubhouse. This would have a debilitating effect on the parking capacity needed for fund-raising events and especially for the Yankee Doodle Fairs. President Winifred Martinek represented the Club on this Committee.

Members of the board attended the Planning and Zoning meeting on this issue as "interested parties." The issue was resolved when it was pointed out that the lower parking lot property had been given to the town with the proviso that the Club would have use of it "in perpetuity" for parking a minimum of 100 cars.

Then, upon attending a meeting of the Downtown Planning Advisors regarding the controversial relocation of the YMCA, Club members were astonished to learn that this group was advocating selection of the lower parking lot for this purpose. 130 members wrote to the Planning and Zoning board protesting this proposal. The board responded by assuring the WWC that this was proposed in error and that the town did not plan to propose moving the YMCA to the lower lot but *was* proposing to move it to the commuter lot.

In 2003, the Senior Center was relocated at another location on Imperial Avenue and the relocation of the YMCA remained a controversial issue. The Woman's Club celebrated this victory by performing an appropriate ditty at a town-wide performance of *Forbidden Westport* to the tune of "O Tannenbaum" using Dorothy Bryce's lyrics: "Oh, parking lot! Oh, parking lot! How could we lose our parking lot?"

WOMAN'S CLUB GIFT BENEFITS NEW SENIOR CENTER

At a ceremony on April 1, 2004 at the new Westport Senior Center, the Westport Woman's Club donated $10,000 to the Friends of the Center for Senior Activities for the recently built fireplace fixture in the main entrance of its neighbor's new home on Imperial Avenue in Westport. The Woman's Club gift was made available through the annual Lea Ruegg Grant, started in 1995, which specifies that the monies be distributed to organizations that would make a continuing difference to the community.

This year's selection of the Senior Center was unanimously approved by the Club's Community Service chairman, Kathleen Goldhawk, and her committee. The choice, Goldhawk reports, was because it mirrors and supports the needs of the town's longtime citizens.

The annual, one-time Ruegg Grants in the past had been awarded to non-profit groups in the arts, educational endeavors, safety programs, new social service programs and health-related issues. Most recently, the recipients have included Westport's Interfaith Housing Association for renovations at Hoskin's Place and the Gillespie Center; the teen social center, Toquet Hall, for the enlargement of the kitchen and its facilities; and the Mercy Learning Center of Bridgeport, which provides literacy instruction and support services to women.

COMMUNITY SERVICES CONTINUE TO SERVE COMMUNITY NEEDS

A new commitment for Community Services in 2004 was to help the Department of Human Services with their "Back to School" program. Club members assisted children by providing equipment needed to go back to school.

The Westport Woman's Club continued to assist the Westport Weston Health District in the annual Flu Clinics, Cholesterol Clinics, and Skin Cancer Clinics.

Community Services Committee members assisted the Westport Weston Health District and the YMCA with the Family Fun Walk by registering participants; handing out pamphlets, water, apples, and free samples; giving directions, and so on.

Members provided sandwiches, salads and desserts for a Canal Park luncheon. The craft group at the Club designed lovely floral arrangements and other gifts to make lovely "treat bags" to send home as a special reminder of the luncheon

In October, WWC assisted with the second annual "Make a Difference Day." Members baked goods to aid "The Youth Ending Hunger" group from Staples High School in their fund-raising. The Club sponsored a drive for donations of good used clothing for the coming winter months and household goods. These were delivered to Christian Community Action in Norwalk.

WWC sent food certificates to needy adults and minors and catered meals for shut-ins for Thanksgiving, Christmas and New Year's Day. In December, members collected toys and gift certificates for the Children's Toy Bank.

In January, when the Westport Warm-Up Fund shifted into high gear, twelve members of the Community Services group phoned every one in the Club directory to help with the mailing. They sent letters to over 7,000 Westport households asking for donations to help low-income families pay their heating bills.

WWC was asked by the American Red Cross to work with the Westport/Weston Health District to assist in Emergency Vaccination Clinics. Members distributed forms, registered people, ran information videos, and did data entry.

The Club's talented Knitters spent 4,402 hours knitting for RSVP and 233 hours knitting for Norwalk Hospital. They knitted hats, mittens, scarves, blankets, children's sweaters, and baby bonnets for RSVP and "preemie" hats for the hospital.

And, as usual, the Medical Loan Closet and the Food Closet provided their highly regarded services directly to people in need and through the Social Services Department at Town Hall.

WWC Considers Joint Venture in a Community Child Identification Program

The March 15, 2004 meeting, started with a presentation by George Underhill, and other members of the Masons of Westport, regarding the program CHIPS (Child Identification Programs) that they sponsor free of charge and invited the WWC to partner with them in an upcoming event at the main firehouse.

The program sought to have all children in the community identified by photo, videotape, fingerprint and tooth print. If a child is reported lost, missing or abducted, these will leave a spit trail for search and rescue dogs. A parent or guardian signs a slip permitting the child's participation. The Woman's Club agreed to participate. The success of this program in Massachusetts helped to get Connecticut's program underway

WWC Asked to Play Key Role in Rehearsal for Emergency Mass Vaccination Clinics

On Friday, May 7, 2004, in the auditorium of the Westport Woman's Club, Monica Wheeler of the Westport Weston Health District gave a brief talk on how the WWC could participate in emergency mass vaccination clinics. Volunteers would help during public health emergencies, such as smallpox outbreaks. They would help distribute and collect forms, run video orientations, do data entry, and provide general information to the public. Two dry run clinics were scheduled in October and November using the scheduled WWHD Flu Shots Clinic as the vehicle for training volunteers. However, a nationwide shortage of flu vaccine canceled these clinics and the dry runs were postponed indefinitely.

Loyal Westport Woman's Club Member and Husband Relate Loyal Citizens' Ordeal as Victims of Injustice in the U.S.A. During WWII.

On October 11, 2004 as part of the town-wide celebration of "Westport Reads," WWC member Vi Takahashi and husband Gene related to a shocked and sympathetic audience at the Westport Public Library their dramatic ordeal as victims of the infamous injustice inflicted upon American citizens of Japanese heritage.

The Takahashis related their story of what happened to a people when they were singled out for "looking like the enemy" and became victims of circumstances over which they had no control. Vi Kosaka and Gene Takahashi were young teenagers living in Seattle, Washington, and El Centro, California, respectively, when Japan attacked Pearl Harbor. The Westporters recounted their experiences when all people of Japanese ancestry on the West Coast were removed and sent to internment camps. Those of Japanese ancestry living away from the West Coast were not interned.

The Takahashis approached the subject from two different perspectives. Vi and her family voluntarily evacuated to Texas to stay with family, while Gene and his family were interned in Poston, Arizona, along with 20,000 other Japanese–Americans.

Vi's father was arrested the night of Pearl Harbor by the FBI and imprisoned in Fort Missoula, Montana. The rest of the family had three days in which to dispose of property and catch the last train out of Seattle before the established deadline or be interned.

SHOW BIZ MUSICALS—SUCCESSFUL FUND-RAISERS

Starting in 2004, third vice-president of Ways and Means Barbara Levy initiated a series of entertaining fund-raisers that involved evening performances and major corporate sponsors.

An Evening with Gershwin was held on February 7, 2004. It was an evening of food, wines, and entertainment. Orin Grossman portrayed George Gershwin, playing many of the Gershwin repertoire, including songs from *Porgy and Bess*. There were Broadway and off-Broadway performers accompanying him. The profits from the event were distributed to Mercy Learning Center and Mid-Fairfield Hospice.

Cabaret Night was held on November 20, 2004. The show starred Leslie Orofino and her trio in Red Hot & Blues. The net proceeds of this exciting event went to Norwalk Hospital, to be applied toward the purchase of Full Field Digital Mammography with Computer Aided Detection. The technology allows a 20 percent improvement in detecting early breast cancer, which can give a better opportunity for less invasive treatment and a successful outcome. The event was sponsored by ICG Financial, LLC.

An Evening With Carol Channing Starring Richard Skipper was held on April 16, 2005. The fabulously entertaining performance by Richard Skipper made it clear why this is an award-winning show. The net proceeds from the event benefited Music and Arts Center for Humanity, Pegasus Therapeutic Riding, and A Better Chance. The Westport Woman's Club thanks the event sponsors Derma Clinic European Day Spa and Newman's Own.

142

Let the Sun Shine In—The Music of the Sixties was performed at the Westport Woman's Club on November 19, 2005. This wonderful and entertaining show, produced by John Franklin and featuring a talented cast of professionals, was a smashing success benefiting the charitable recipients.

I n reading this history of what these extraordinary women accomplished in their first 100 years, one is overwhelmed by the resume of achievement that would be difficult to match by any organization in any field of activity. They healed, comforted, educated, entertained, fed, clothed, lobbied, shared, and elevated lives of so many people with the noblest of motives—to serve their community wherever they found a need. The wonderment is not only in how many extraordinary efforts they made. It's in how often they succeeded. Who were these women who achieved so much?

"A Rare Woman's Club" is how *Life* magazine characterized the Westport Woman's Club in its August 11, 1947 issue in a two-page article stressing its uniqueness among women's clubs. The article included photographs of the Club's officers and the Yankee Doodle Fair and a generous listing of many of the Club's achievements over the years.

ACHIEVERS WITH A SELFLESS COMPASSION AND HUMANITY

Achievers are often thought of as single-minded, uncompromising, stern taskmasters. These women were, indeed, such achievers. But what separates them from all others are the selfless compassion and humanity of their efforts.

No project demonstrates these attributes better than the way a Senior Arts and Crafts Club was created in 1955. President Gladys Schuck and Sophie Bascho, her chairman of the Gerontology Project, demonstrated community service leadership, dedication and compassion at its best in bringing this most heartwarming effort to fruition and bringing hope and cheer to many seniors who despaired in loneliness with no interests to keep them hopeful.

The best way to communicate the passion and dedication these two ladies devoted to this program is to paraphrase Mrs. Schuck's report on the Gerontology Project to the Fairfield County Fall Meeting of the State Federation of Women's Clubs in October 20, 1955, urging all women's clubs to follow the Westport Woman's Club's example:

> *I would like to tell you a little of the background of this project. Before we started, Mrs. Bascho and I visited every group we had heard of both in Connecticut and New York and decided what we would and would not do. So many of these groups looked so desolate—meeting in basements—just sitting around and playing cards—or just sitting. We decided that our group would be an active one with results to show for it. We therefore set out to get a volunteer group of teachers in crafts and*

arts on a trial basis. We started with the following teachers in art, ceramics, rug hooking, textile design, leatherwork and block printing. It was decided to call this project the "Senior Arts and Crafts Club." There is no charge. The Club pays for all materials and refreshments and may I add that we put $500 in our budget for the first year but it has never cost us over $200 a year. It is amazing how much one can do with so little.

The group meets at 1:30 every Friday and they work at their chosen craft until 3:30 when we serve tea, coffee and cake. They usually leave at 4:30. When members first arrive, they are introduced to everyone and asked to do whatever they wish. Sometimes new members might be shy and feel they would not do the work well enough and are afraid to try— so they watch. But before you know it, they join in the work. They have since developed many talents and made beautiful things they never dreamed they were capable of creating.

Our members are solicited through our churches and doctors and everyone else we can think of. Sometimes it is difficult to get older persons to come but once they do, they enjoy it so much that they are regulars after that.

It is one of the most heartwarming things anyone can do. One of our members told me not long ago that she had lived in town over 10 years and this was the first time she had had a friend. They really are a collection of very lonely people. Many times some under 60 request to come—and often they need companionship badly. So we invite them to come to be a hostess and in helping others they help themselves.

I feel that every club could do something for older people. If you do not have a meeting place, provide a project to the shut-ins. Every community has shut-ins. Get their names from your Visiting Nurse, your Doctors and your ministers. Get a committee to call on them. Have parties for them periodically. Bring your magazines and books to them. Send them cards on holidays. Make this a real project.

I believe that if you start this project, it will be the most heartwarming and soul-satisfying work you have done. These people need to feel needed and wanted. You will find that there is always money for anything worthwhile. If you give good, you reflect good and the money will come.

Mrs. Bascho totally dedicated herself to this program every week for seven successful years with steady growth in membership and enthusiasm. In her final report, as she retired from the project she created, she described what she considered "the major event of all its existence…a New England Patchwork Quilt, charming and original in design." Each square was sewn by a different senior woman and carried her signature in testimony to her presence and achievements.

CLUBWOMEN? YES! BUT WHO WERE THEY?

Clearly, many of them were achievers in a variety of fields and found a way to make their mark on their community. Some of them went on to gain elective office:

Sara B. Crawford, after her retirement from the WTIA presidency in 1931, continued to serve six two-year terms (from 1925–1938) as Westport's representative in the General Assembly of the State Legislature, and subsequently (from 1939–1941) as Connecticut's first woman secretary of state.

Judith G. Freedman has been our state senator since 1986. Judith represents the 26th District in the State Senate, which includes the towns of Bethel, New Canaan, Redding, Ridgefield, Weston, Westport, and Wilton. She is a Deputy Republican Leader. Senator Freedman is ranking member of the committee on Higher Education/Workforce Development, which has jurisdiction over all legislation regarding schools of higher education. Senator Freedman is also ranking member of the Government Administration and Elections Committee, which oversees legislation regarding the Ethics Commission, compacts between the state and Indian tribes, constitutional amendments, elections, and campaign finance. Senator Freedman is a member of the Appropriations Committees, which oversees developing the state budget, and the Legislative Management Committee, which oversees the business of the General Assembly. She is a member of the legislature's Internship Committee.

Jo Fuchs Luscombe served as our state representative for five terms from 1987 through 1997. She served five terms as state representative, during which she became assistant minority leader. She is also a former Zoning Board of Appeals chairwoman and most recently served as chairman of Westport's School Building Committee for eight years.

Tammy Pincavage was Westport's second selectman from 1989 to 1993. Also served as president of the Westport Young Woman's League, president of the P.T.A. Council and the Connecticut P.T.A. and president of the Westport Woman's Club. She was appointed by the RTM and Board of Education to serve as vice chairman of the School Westport Building Committee.

Diane Farrell was first elected to the Board of Finance in 1993 and then elected as Westport's First Selectwoman in 1997, serving two terms up to 2005. She introduced a precedent-setting "brown bag lunch" to Westport politics. The luncheons attracted many townspeople who wished to express strongly felt opinions and concerns regarding town issues.

Perhaps the best example of an achieving clubwoman is Mrs. Kenneth (Ina) Bradley, who was among the most active members in the Westport Woman's Club's history. She held key offices for almost a dozen years, culminating as president for two terms (1946–1948 and 1950–1952). She went on to become president of the Federation in 1962 and remained active in the Club until her death in 1995. She wrote an article on "How to be a Clubwoman in One Easy Lesson" for the Club's 50th anniversary. It appeared in the March 7, 1957 issue of the *Westport Town Crier & Herald*. While there is no simple answer to distinguish the achievers from the rest, Mrs. Bradley offers some entertaining distinctions to ponder:

*Portrait of Ina Bradley
by Robert Skemp, 1955*

> *Almost any woman who is or has been deeply entangled in women's clubs and survives with her equilibrium intact must, I am sure, credit it to three blessings, patience, patience, and patience. She learns early in her club "career", that society is divided roughly into two classes when it comes to approbation of clubwomen.*

> *First there is* Group A, *consisting of friends, relatives, neighbors and husband (if any) who are technically in favor of her activities in the community and perhaps even mean it when they praise her efforts (while privately wondering why the dickens she chooses to spend her time that way).*

> *Then there is* Group B, *consisting of friends, relatives, neighbors and husband (if any) who think, frankly, she's an idiot.*

> *Possibly her first awareness of the need for unlimited patience in helping her through is in her association with Group A. She knows that these kindly people who don't fully appreciate her need or urge or desire, serve the community through various and sundry groups and committees, but, loyal to her, they at least go through the motions. She finds in this surface kind of "understanding" a certain condescension*

which irks her somewhat.

Foremost in this group of "technically approving" is, of course, her ever-loving spouse. In this enlightened age he will accept his wife's interest in club life with Spartan resignation. He tries to accept the new doctrine...as preached by family-life counselors and "how-to-be-happy-with-your-wife" magazine articles...that woman is not a domestic slave and must have constructive outlets beyond cooking and dusting.

He does his sweet darnedest to be understanding and to believe that it really is good for him and the youngsters for mamma to be a busy little committee bee. He smiles indulgently and gives the old girl a tender pat on the head when she waxes eloquent, or indignant, about some club matter—and hopes secretly that she'll be through with her meeting in time to have his cocktail ready and a nice dinner in the oven when he gets home from his hard day in the office.

He knows that he is expected, as an intelligent, modern man, not only to accept this liberated, thinking, community leader the little woman has become, but to encourage her. He knows that it is part of the modern social pattern; in fact, he allows himself a moment of sly pride when a commuter pal speaks to him about the wonderful job his wife has. However, in his heart he believes that what she is attempting to do for the community will be accomplished, anyway, as the wheels of progress (or men's committees) turn.

For all his chivalrous support, Mme. Chairman is not fooled. She is on to him and it is here, perhaps as much as anywhere, that she is called upon to fall back on her fund of patience to play the game. She knows that despite their admirable struggle to adjust to the changes in this brave new world, husbands still harbour their woeful inborn belief that woman's place is in the home.

The others in Group A are quite nice about her being a clubwoman. They are generous with their praise of her efforts. They buoy her up and support her and admire her (and are awfully glad that she—not they—has all that work to do).

They believe in better roads and a sounder educational system and more pay for teachers and planting dogwood and installing incinerators and exterminating poison ivy and clothing the poor, and they tell her that women's clubs are simply wonderful and that she is simply wonderful to devote her time to such good work, and they are just as sorry as they can be that they are so busy they can't help her.

She learns to be very patient with these people. They are heavy on praise and light on help. But she realizes that moral support is a fairly good substitute for physical assistance, so she doggedly dials the phone again in her never-ending quest for people to serve on committees, sell tickets, run fashion shows and collect rummage.

149

Then we come to Group B, which consists, chiefly, of those who have conceived their idea of clubwomen through the funny papers (and a few who have soured on women's clubs in toto because of some disappointing personal experience).

Taking their cue from cartoonists, they have fostered the notion that the American Clubwoman is a specie of womanhood commonly believed to be an elephantine, twittering female existing almost entirely on Causes. She has become the pet, the darling, of caricaturists who love to portray her as bosomy, bird-brained, and devoted to the pursuit of such weighty matters as, "Why Has the South African Blaubok Become Extinct—and What Can We as Clubwomen Do About It?"

If she happens not to look like a Helen Hokinson type [New Yorker cartoon shown at right], *they fix her with a mocking eye and say, "What are you doing as president of a woman's club?" And generally there is the unspoken implication that maybe she ought to have her head examined.*

If she happens to look like a model for a cartoonist, no matter how smart, even brilliant, she may be, no matter how hard-working, self-sacrificing, successful, and genuinely helpful to her community, they still think she belongs in the New Yorker and refuse to take her seriously. To them—especially the men—women's clubs are temples of trivia.

Typical is the occasion when, defending women's clubs against the banter of a learned professional friend who took me to task for "wasting time in superficial women's organizations", I spent almost an hour giving him a run-down on some of their achievements. I told him of the tremendous work done by women throughout the country, in slum clearance, better health programs, school improvements, town beautification, help for the poor, the aged and the ill, and important legislation—to mention but a few fields. When I was finished, he said flatly, "I still say all communities would be a lot better off if all the women stayed home and peeled potatoes."

As for the minority in Group B, the disgruntled who have been associated in one capacity or another with a club or clubs where they felt they didn't get a fair shake in the elections or proper recognition or whatever, they are "agin" all women's clubs forevermore. A clubwoman can't win with the Group B-ers. She needs the patience of a saint to cope with them.

And then, of course, there are, within the groups with which she works, all sorts of situations calling for patience of the substance of the Rock of Gibraltar. There are the feuding members, there are the cliques who protest against other segments of the organization as being too cliquey, there is the chairman of one committee who complains that another committee is getting better publicity in the local press, there are the volunteers who give rosy promises of help and then let the chairman down at the last minute, there are the members who vote in meeting in favor of an issue and then go out and hold sidewalk discussions against it, there are members who make federal cases out of such questions as whether the tea sandwiches ought to be round or square, and there are, inevitably, the members who never say a word during a meeting but call the chairman or president at eleven o'clock on a Sunday evening for a long-winded discourse.

Many a busy clubwoman must mutter to herself that quote from Sir Walter Scott, "Patience, cousin, and shuffle the cards." *She may even be allowed to indulge in the occasional wistful thought that maybe she ought to have her head examined.*

A lthough the Club's 100th birthday is August 12, 2007, the official celebration date for celebrating the centennial was set for May 5, 2007. In November 2005, President Barbara Levy appointed a committee of past presidents to serve on the WWC 2007 100th Anniversary Committee. Numerous activities were planned to involve the entire community in their celebrations.

WESTPORT WOMAN'S CLUB PRESENTED A WORLD-PREMIERE PERFORMANCE OF BROADWAY MUSICAL REVUE

As a prelude to the Westport Woman's Club year-long 100th anniversary celebration, the Club presented a world-premiere benefit performance of *Roles Women Play,* a Broadway musical revue. It was held in the auditorium of the Westport clubhouse in October 2006.

The show was created by the team of JIB Productions, Nancy Diamond and Carole Schweid, well known in Fairfield County for the popular lunchtime series "Play With Your Food."

Paralleling the accomplishments of women from 1907 to 2007, a professional group of versatile performers recreated in song, dance and narration the Club's historical achievements: the funding of the town's first concrete sidewalks, the planting of trees along the Post Road, World War II volunteer activities, the annual Yankee Doodle Fair, and many more moments reflecting the moods and times.

Preceding the Friday and Saturday performances were wine and hors d'oeuvres receptions.

*Performers singing around the piano
at a rehearsal for* Roles Women Play

ANNIVERSARY CELEBRATED AT THE INN AT LONGSHORE

The 100th Anniversary Gala took place at the Inn at Longshore in Westport on Saturday, May 5, 2007. The event was a "Black Tie Optional" dinner/dance gala including cocktails, dinner, and dancing to the music of Bob Lasprogato and Uptown Jazz.

The "Anniversary Lady" logo on the invitation was created by Howard Munce. This distinctive lady appeared on all banners, announcements, invitations, and promotional materials throughout the year 2007.

Guess who's turning 100?

On May 5, 2007
The Westport Woman's Club
will be celebrating its
100th Anniversary
with a
Gala Dinner Dance
at the
Inn at Longshore.

Please save the date for
this historic event.

The **Westport Woman's** Club

(203) 227-4240
www.westportwomansclub.org

*The "Anniversary Lady" figure
by Howard Munce*

AN ARRAY OF ACTIVITIES WAS PLANNED TO CREATE PUBLIC AWARENESS AND ENTHUSIASM

WESTPORT
WOMAN'S CLUB
Founded 1907

President Barbara Levy (left) *and past
President Jo Fuchs Luscombe,
Memorial Day Parade, 2006*

Promotion of the 100th anniversary started with President Barbara Levy and past President Jo Fuchs Luscombe displaying a colorful banner at the 2006 Memorial Day parade, proclaiming the Club's imminent 100th birthday.

HISTORICAL SOCIETY EXHIBIT

The Westport Historical Society produced a 100th Anniversary exhibit for the Woman's Club. A members-only opening reception was held on May 27, 2007. The exhibit opened to the public Monday, May 28, Memorial Day, and continued through September 3, 2007. It included photographs and other memorabilia of WWC activities during the first 100 years.

And finally, to coincide with all these centennial celebrations, the WWC authorized Eileen Petropoulos, Club Historian, to prepare this 100-year history book—
A Rare Woman's Club: The First Hundred Years of the Westport Woman's Club, 1907–2007.

WESTPORT, CONNECTICUT

GORDON F. JOSELOFF
First Selectman

PROCLAMATION

WHEREAS: THE WESTPORT WOMAN'S CLUB CELEBRATES ITS 100TH ANNIVERSARY IN 2007; AND

WHEREAS: FOUNDED IN 1907 AS THE WOMAN'S TOWN IMPROVEMENT ASSOCIATION, THE FIRST UNDERTAKING OF THE NON-PROFIT ORGANIZATION WAS TO RAISE FUNDS FOR THE CLEANING OF TOWN STREETS, THE CARE FOR AND PLANTING OF TREES, AND THE INSTALLATION OF PUBLIC SIDEWALKS; AND

WHEREAS: THE YANKEE DOODLE FAIR ALSO CELEBRATES ITS 100TH ANNIVERSARY THIS YEAR PROVIDING THOUSANDS OF FUN-FILLED HOURS FOR THE YOUNG AND THE NOT-SO YOUNG WHILE BEING A MAJOR FUNDRAISING EVENT FOR THE WESTPORT WOMAN'S CLUB; AND

WHEREAS: THE WESTPORT WOMAN'S CLUB FOR 100 YEARS HAS BEEN DEDICATED TO THE PROMOTION OF CHARITABLE, CULTURAL, EDUCATIONAL AND PUBLIC HEALTH SERVICES; AND

WHEREAS: FROM BEAUTIFYING OUR STREETS, PARKS AND BEACHES TO PROVIDING AN EMERGENCY FOOD CLOSET TO STARTING THE SCHOOL HOT LUNCH PROGRAM TO ESTABLISHING THE VISITING NURSE SERVICE, THE CONTRIBUTIONS TO WESTPORT AND ITS CITIZENS BY THE WOMAN'S CLUB HAVE BEEN NUMEROUS; AND

WHEREAS: MEMBERS OF THE WESTPORT WOMAN'S CLUB HAVE VOLUNTEERED UNSELFISHLY THEIR EFFORT, TIME, AND EXPERTISE TO THE BETTERMENT OF WESTPORT AND MANY NONPROFIT ORGANIZATIONS,

NOW THEREFORE, I, GORDON F. JOSELOFF, FIRST SELECTMAN OF THE TOWN OF WESTPORT DO HEREBY PROCLAIM THE MONTH OF JUNE 2007 AS:

WESTPORT WOMAN'S CLUB MONTH

IN WESTPORT, CONNECTICUT, AND EXTEND TO THE MEMBERS OF THE WESTPORT WOMAN'S CLUB OUR COMMUNITY'S APPRECIATION AND THANKS FOR THEIR DEDICATION, EFFORTS AND COMMITMENT TO WESTPORT.

GORDON F. JOSELOFF
FIRST SELECTMAN
DATED THIS 31ST DAY OF MAY 2007

Town Hall 0 Myrtle Avenue • Westport, CT 06880 • (203) 341-1111 • Fax (203) 341-1038
E-mail: selectman@westportct.gov • Website: www.westportct.gov

Now, for the Next 100 Years!

It'll be a hard act to follow. Unresolved community issues are scarcer and institutions to deal with them are more numerous and well financed. The Woman's Club continues to raise funds and support community activities and needs. However, there are fewer new initiatives to pioneer. But there will always be unfortunate citizens whose needs go unattended, emergencies that must be responded to, unresolved civic needs that must be highlighted and lobbied for, and deserving achievements that should be recognized.

These selfless, compassionate clubwomen are still the heart of the Westport Woman's Club. They'll find a way!

Recent WWC Presidents
Back, left to right: *Barbara Levy (current), Ellen Granger,*
Tammy Pincavage, and Winnie Martinek
Front, left to right: *Jo Fuchs Luscombe, Nat Sylander, and*
Barbara Culp. May 2007

APPENDIX A

Officers and Boards of Directors Over the Years

Officers & Boards of Directors 1907-1911

	1907-1908	1908-1909	1909-1910	1910-1911
Officers				
President	Mrs. Wm. Staples	Mrs. Wm. Staples	Mrs. Wm. Staples	Mrs. Wm. Staples
Secretary- Recording	Mrs. I. B. Wakeman	Mrs. I. B. Wakeman	Mrs. I. B. Wakeman	Mrs. I. B. Wakeman
Secretary- Corresponding	Miss Anna Quinlan	Mrs. John Godillot	Mrs. John Godillot	Mrs. John Godillot
Treasurer	Mrs. C. Eloise Thomas	Mrs. C. Eloise Thomas	Mrs. C. Eloise Thomas	Mrs. C. Eloise Thomas
Vice Presidents				
High School	Mrs. F. M. Salmon	Mrs. D. B. Bradley	Mrs. D. B. Bradley	Mrs. D. B. Bradley
Bridge Street District	Mrs. A. U. Smith	Mrs. A. U. Smith	Mrs. A. U. Smith	Mrs. A. U. Smith
Coleytown District	Mrs. Robert Coley	Mrs. Robert Coley	Mrs. Robert Coley	Mrs. Robert Coley
East Saugatuck District	Mrs. W.P. Landers	Miss Katherine Willcox	Mrs. W. P. Landers	Mrs. W. P. Landers
West Saugatuck District	Mrs. W. S, Adams	Mrs. W. S, Adams	Mrs. W. S, Adams	Mrs. W. S, Adams
Greens Farms District	Mrs. E. J. Taylor	Mrs. E. J. Taylor	Mrs. E. J. Taylor	Mrs. E. J. Taylor
East Long Lots District	Mrs. Chas. F. Buckley	Mrs. Chas. F. Buckley	Mrs. Chas. F. Buckley	Mrs. Chas. F. Buckley
West Long Lots District	Miss Lillian Burr	Miss Lillian Burr	Miss Lillian Burr	Miss Lillian Burr
Crosshighway District	Miss Laura Chapman	Mrs. S. M. Foster	Miss Laura Chapman	Miss Laura Chapman
Poplar Plains District	Miss Kate E. Taylor	Miss Kate E. Taylor	Miss Kate E. Taylor	Miss Kate E. Taylor

Officers 1911-1915

	1911-1912	1912-1913	1913-1914	1914-1915
Officers				
President	Mrs. Wm. Staples	Mrs. Wm. Staples	Mrs. Wm. Staples	Mrs. John Godillot
Secretary- Recording	Mrs. I. B. Wakeman	Mrs. I. B. Wakeman	Mrs. I. B. Wakeman	Mrs. Fred B. Hubbell
Secretary- Corresponding	Miss Anna Quinlan	Mrs. John Godillot	Mrs. John Godillot	Mrs. K. Mackenzie
Treasurer	Mrs. C. Eloise Thomas	Mrs. C. Eloise Thomas	Mrs. C. Eloise Thomas	Mrs. Kate Taylor Mrs. E. C. Bridge
Vice Presidents				
High School	Mrs. F. M. Salmon	Mrs. F. M. Salmon	Mrs. F. M. Salmon	Mrs. F. M. Salmon
Bridge Street District	Mrs. A. U. Smith	Mrs. Arnold Schlaet	Mrs. A. U. Smith	Mrs. A. U. Smith
Coleytown District	Mrs. Robert Coley	Mrs. Robert Coley	Mrs. Robert Coley	Mrs. Robert Coley
East Saugatuck District	Mrs. W.P. Landers	Mrs. W.P. Landers	Mrs. W.P. Landers	Mrs. W.P. Landers
West Saugatuck District	Mrs. W. S, Adams	Mrs. Charlotte Nash	Mrs. T. C. Stearns	Mrs. W. S. Adams
Greens Farms District	Mrs. E. J. Taylor	Mrs. E. J. Taylor	Mrs. E. J. Taylor	Mrs. E. J. Taylor
East Long Lots District	Mrs. Chas. F. Buckley	Mrs. Chas. F. Buckley	Mrs. Chas. F. Buckley	Mrs. Chas. F. Buckley
West Long Lots District	Miss Lillian Burr	Miss Lillian Burr	Miss Lillian Burr	Miss Lillian Burr
Crosshighway District	Miss Laura Chapman	Mrs. F. B. Hubbell	Miss Laura Chapman	Miss Laura Chapman
Poplar Plains District	Miss Kate E. Taylor	Miss Kate E. Taylor	Miss Kate E. Taylor	Miss Kate E. Taylor

Officers 1915-1919				
	1915-1916	1916-1917	1917-1918	1918-1919
Officers				
President	Mrs. John F. Godillot	Mrs. Wm. Staples	Miss Edith Wheeler	Miss Edith Wheeler
Secretary- Recording	Mrs. Fred B. Hubbell	Mrs. I. B. Wakeman	Mrs. I. B. Wakeman	Mrs. I. B. Wakeman
Secretary- Corresponding	Mrs. K. Mackenzie	Mrs. K. Mackenzie	Mrs. K. Mackenzie	Mrs. K. Mackenzie
Treasurer	Mrs. C. Eloise Thomas	Mrs. C. Eloise Thomas	Mrs. C. Eloise Thomas	Mrs. C. Eloise Thomas
Vice Presidents				
High School	Mrs. F. M. Salmon	Mrs. F. M. Salmon	Mrs. F. M. Salmon	Mrs. F. M. Salmon
Bridge Street District	Mrs. A. U. Smith	Mrs. A. U. Smith	Mrs. A. U. Smith	Mrs. A. U. Smith
Coleytown District	Mrs. Robert Coley	Mrs. Robert Coley	Mrs. Robert Coley	Mrs. Robert Coley
East Saugatuck District	Mrs. W.P. Landers	Mrs. W.P. Landers	Mrs. W.P. Landers	Mrs. W.P. Landers
West Saugatuck District	Mrs. W. S, Adams	Mrs. W. S, Adams	Mrs. W. S. Adams	Mrs. W. S. Adams
Greens Farms District	Mrs. E. J. Taylor	Mrs. E. J. Taylor	Mrs. E. J. Taylor	Mrs. E. J. Taylor
East Long Lots District	Mrs. Chas. F. Buckley	Mrs. Chas. F. Buckley	Mrs. Chas. F. Buckley	Mrs. Chas. F. Buckley
West Long Lots District	Miss Lillian Burr	Miss Lillian Burr	Miss Lillian Burr	Miss Lillian Burr
Crosshighway District	Miss Laura Chapman	Miss Laura Chapman	Mrs. George Wright	Miss Laura Chapman
Poplar Plains District	Miss Kate E. Taylor	Miss Kate E. Taylor	Miss Kate E. Taylor	Miss Kate E. Taylor

Officers 1919-1923				
	1919-1920	1920-1921	1921-1922	1922-1923
Officers				
President	Mrs. John Crawford	Mrs. John Crawford	Mrs. John Crawford	Mrs. John Crawford
1st VP				Mrs. R Sherwood
2nd VP				
3rd VP				Mrs. O. Van Sant
Secretary- Recording	Mrs. Edward C. Nash	Mrs. William Coley	Mrs. William Coley	Mrs. Alice C. Rauber
Secretary- Corresponding	Mrs. K. Mackenzie	Miss Josephinr Godillo	Miss Josephinr Godillot	Miss Josephinr Godillot
Treasurer	Mrs. C. Eloise Thomas	Mrs. C. Eloise Thomas	Mrs. C. Eloise Thomas	Mrs. C. Eloise Thomas
Vice Presidents				
High School	Mrs. F. M. Salmon	Mrs. F. M. Salmon	Mrs. L. Mazzanovich	Mrs. F. M. Salmon
Bridge Street District	Mrs. A. U. Smith	Mrs. A. U. Smith	Mrs. B. Wakeman	Mrs. Arnold Schlaet
Coleytown District	Mrs. Robert Coley	Mrs. Robert Coley	Mrs. Robert Coley	Mrs. Robert Coley
East Saugatuck District	Mrs. W.P. Landers	Mrs. W.P. Landers	Mrs. W.P. Landers	Mrs. W.P. Landers
West Saugatuck District	Mrs. W. S, Adams	Mrs. John A. Thayer	Mrs. W. S. Adams	Mrs. W. S. Adams
Greens Farms District	Mrs. E. J. Taylor	Mrs. E. J. Taylor	Mrs. E. J. Taylor	Mrs. E. J. Taylor
East Long Lots District	Mrs. Chas. F. Buckley	Miss Charlena Guild	Mrs. Chas. F. Buckley	Mrs. Chas. F. Buckley
West Long Lots District	Miss Lillian Burr	Miss Lillian Burr	Miss Lillian Burr	Miss Lillian Burr
Crosshighway District	Miss Laura Chapman	Miss Laura Chapman	Mrs. George Wright	Miss Laura Chapman
Poplar Plains District	Miss Kate E. Taylor	Miss Alice C. Rauber	Miss Kate E. Taylor	Miss Kate E. Taylor

Officers & Boards of Directors 1923-1927				
	1923-1924	1924-1925	1925-1926	1926-1927
Officers				
President	Mrs. J. Crawford	Mrs. W. A. Peck	Mrs. B. Eager, Sr.	Mrs. C. P. Harris
1st VP	Mrs. R. Sherwood	Mrs. A. D. Keys	Mrs. C. P. Harris	Mrs. W. A. Peck
2nd VP	Mrs. H. R. Steeves	Mrs. C. P. Harris	Mrs. E. C. Nash	Mrs. W. R. Munson
3rd VP	Mrs. O. B. Van Sant	Mrs. O. B. Van Sant	Mrs. O. B. Van Sant	Mrs. H. M. Brown
Secretary- Recording	Miss Alice C. Rauber	Miss Alice C. Rauber	Miss Martha Taylor	Miss Elizabeth Baldwin
Secretary- Correspondence	Mrs. H. O. Beers	Miss Frances Allen	Miss Frances Allen	Miss Esther Raymond

158

Officers & Boards of Directors 1927-1931

	1927-1928	1928-1929	1929-1930	1930-1931
Officers				
President	Mrs. C. G. Child	Mrs. C. G. Child	Mrs. J. Crawford	Mrs. J. Crawford
1st VP	Mrs. W. A. Peck	Mrs. J. Crawford	Mrs. W. A. Peck	Mrs. S. B. Hoyt
2nd VP	Mrs. S. B. Hoyt	Mrs. E. F. McKenna	Mrs. D. A. Shambaugh	Mrs. D. A. Shambaugh
3rd VP	Mrs. A. M. Minnick	Mrs. C. P. Harris	Mrs. C. P. Harris	Mrs. E. J. Taylor
Secretary- Recording	Mrs. W. B. Kellog	Mrs. W. B. Kellog	Mrs. E. St. John	Mrs. E. W. Andersen
Secretary- Correspondence	Mrs. H. W. Withington			
Treasurer	Mrs. L. Sniffen	Mrs. L. Sniffen	Mrs. L. Sniffen	
Directors				
Finance				Mrs. H. Booth
Membership				Mrs. P. Mathewson

Officers & Boards of Directors 1931-1935

	1931-1932	1932-1933	1933-1934	1934-1935
Officers				
President	Mrs. S. C. Carlton	Mrs. H. J. Millard	Mrs. R. T. Baldwin	Mrs. R. T. Baldwin
1st VP	Mrs. W. A. Peck	Mrs. H. A. Jennings	Mrs. M. C. Hill	
2nd VP	Mrs. H. Steinkraus	Mrs. H. Steinkraus	Mrs. H. Lillibridge	
3rd VP	Mrs. H. A. Jennings	Mrs. D. W. Nye	Mrs. H. M. Ayres	
Secretary	Mrs. E. W. Anderson	Mrs. J. M. Nesbitt	Mrs. A. S. Uhler	
Treasurer	Mrs. L. Sniffen	Mrs. L. Sniffen	Mrs. L. Sniffen	
Committee Chairmen				
Advisory Board	Mrs. W.G. Staples / Mrs. J. Crawford	Mrs. W. G. Staples	Mrs. W. G. Staples	
Bedford House	Mrs. D. A. Shambaugh	Mrs. J. W. Underwood	Mrs. H. Lillibridge	
Publicity		Mrs. F. B. Converse	Mrs. J. Crawford	
Public Health	Mrs. A. C. Rauber	Mrs. A. C. Rauber	Mrs. H. J. Millard	
Membership	Mrs. P. Mathewson	Mrs. H. J. Millard / Mrs. W. A. Peck	Mrs. J. Nesbit	
Program	Mrs. H. Booth	Mrs. S. Dyke / Mrs. H. A. Wake	Mrs. H. A. Wake	
Scholarship Awards		Mrs. C. P. Harris / Mrs. L. Sniffen	Mrs. C. F. Harris / Mrs. E. E. Jennings	
Y-Cooperative	Mrs. G. M. Darby	Mrs. G. M. Darby	Mrs.	
Saugatuck Playground		Mrs. O. B. VanSant		

Officers & Boards of Directors 1935-1939

	1935-1936	1936-1937	1937-1938	1938-1939
Officers				
President	Mrs. R. T. Baldwin	Mrs. A. F. Myers	Mrs. R. P. Myers	Mrs. B. J. Paladini
1st VP	Mrs. M. A. Cobb	Mrs. E. F. Oates	Mrs. H. A, Wake	Mrs. H. A. Wake
2nd VP	Mrs. L. R. Gustavson	Mrs. H. A, Wake	Mrs. K. Hay	Mrs. H. W. Sternberg
3rd VP	Mrs. H. A, Wake	Mrs. K. Hay	Mrs. H. T. Wood	Mrs. R. T. Baldwin
Secretary	Mrs. K. Hay	Mrs. R. P. Buell	Mrs. F. Robertson	Mrs. J. M. Batschy
Treasurer	Mrs. L. Sniffen	Mrs. L. Sniffen	Mrs. L. Sniffen	Mrs. L. Sniffen
Directors & Committee Chairmen				
Bedford House	Mrs. J. W. Fenton	Mrs. J. W. Fenton	Mrs. J. W. Fenton	Mrs. R. S. Palmer
Civics & Legislation	Mrs. J. Crawford			Mrs. E. W. Boughton
Fine Arts				
Art		Mrs. I. Sametz	Mrs. I. Sametz	Mrs. I. Sametz
Drama				Mrs. D. Plessett
Music				Mrs. L. Sokoloff
Garden				Mrs. R. C. Witmer
Junior		Mrs. J. Roche	Mrs. C. Buhler	Mrs. R. C. Beck
Membership	Mrs. G. Lewis	Mrs. H. H. Pell, Jr.	Mrs. R. C. Witmer	Mrs. R. C. Witmer
Program	Mrs. A. F. Myers	Mrs. R. T. Baldwin	Mrs. A. F. Myers	Mrs. J. W. Fenton
Publicity	Mrs. A. Evans	Mrs. R. T. Baldwin	Mrs. R. T. Baldwin	Mrs. A. R. Dodd
Public Health	Mrs. L. Sniffen	Mrs. E. W. Beard	Mrs. H. T. Wood	Mrs. H. T. Wood
Scholarship	Mrs. C. P. Harris	Mrs. C. P. Harris	Mrs. C. P. Harris	Mrs. C. P, Harris
Woman's Exchange	Mrs. L. H. Gamble	Mrs. J. C. Lee, Jr.	Mrs. J. C. Lee, Jr.	Mrs. E. Woolson
Thrift Shop	Mrs. L. H. Gamble	Mrs. J. C. Lee, Jr.	Mrs. J. C. Lee, Jr.	Mrs. W. Burnham
Athletic	Mrs. L. R. Gustavson			

Officers & Boards of Directors 1939-1943

	1939-1940	1940-1941	1941-1942	1942-1943
Officers				
President	Mrs. B. J. Paladini	Mrs. R. C. Witmer	Mrs. R. C. Witmer	Mrs. R. C. Witmer
1st VP	Mrs. H. A. Wake	Mrs. H. W. Sternberg	Mrs. H. W. Sternberg	Mrs. J. B. Warnock
2nd VP	Mrs. H. W. Sternberg	Mrs. A. R. Dodd	Mrs. A. R. Dodd	Mrs. R. Dustman
3rd VP	Mrs. R. T. Baldwin	Mrs. R. T. Baldwin	Mrs. R. T. Baldwin, Sr.	Mrs. C. I. Christie
Secretary	Mrs. J. M. Batchy	Mrs. C. W. Vogt	Mrs. J. B. Warnock	Mrs. J. K. Bradley
Director	Mrs. R. P. Buell	Mrs. B. J. Paladini		
Treasurer	Mrs. L. Sniffen	Mrs. R. Seitz	Mrs. R. Seitz	Mrs. J. D, Hitch
Committee & Department Chairmen				
Bedford House	Mrs. R. S. Palmer	Mrs. R. S. Palmer	Mrs. P. Darling	C. S. Scott
Civics & Legislation	Mrs. E. W. Boughton	Mrs. A. Corbin Mrs. J. A. Thompson	Mrs. R. A. Stephenson	Mrs. O. Wintraub Dr. L. M. Phillips
Federation		Mrs. J. W. Fenton	Mrs. I. Sametz	Mrs. L. Clark
Fine Arts				
Art	Mrs. O. M. Stanfield	Mrs. S L. Conn	Mrs. H. Ramsey	Mrs. L. Rounds
Drama	Mrs. D. Plessett	Mrs. J. E. Knox	Mrs. J. K. Bradley	Mrs. J. E. Knox
Literature	Mrs. B. A. Griffiths	Mrs. B. A. Griffiths	Mrs. B. A. Griffiths	Mrs. J. J. Dunne
Music		Mrs. R. Dustman	Mrs. R. Dustman	
Garden	Mrs. H. B. Molony	Mrs. C. I. Christie	Mrs. C. I. Christie	Mrs. P. C. McAbee
Hospitality	Mrs. R. Seitz	Mrs. H. Gray	Mrs. G. Baker	Mrs. C. J. Child
Junior	Mrs. E. M. Reynolds	Mrs. T. Finnegan	Mrs. R. Bailey, Jr. Mrs. D. Gray	Mrs. E. F. Boyd, Jr. Mrs. R. T. Baldwin
Membership	Mrs. H. W. Sternberg	Mrs. A. R. Dodd	Mrs. A. R. Dodd	Mrs. R. Dustman
Publicity	Mrs. M. Dunn	Mrs. W. H. Perun	Mrs. R. G. Thew	Mrs. J. M. Mullin
Program	Mrs. J. W. Fenton	Mrs. H. Wake	Mrs. F. Charles	Mrs. F. Charles
Public Health	Mrs. H. T. Wood	Mrs. M. Newburger	Mrs. M. Newburger	Mrs. M. Newburger
Scholarship	Mrs. C. P. Harris	Mrs. C. P. Harris	Mrs. C. P. Harris	Mrs. W. B. Kellog
Ways & Means	Mrs. R. C. Witmer	Mrs. R. T. Baldwin	Mrs. R. T. Baldwin	Mrs. C. L. Christie
Woman's Exchange	Mrs. W. M. Simpson	Mrs. W. Simpson	Mrs. W. Simpson	Mrs. H. Sutphen
Thrift Shop	Mrs. B. Chapman		Mrs. W. Simpson	Mrs. H. Sutphen

Officers & Boards of Directors 1943 - 1947

	1943-1944	1944-1945	1945-1946	1946-1947
Officers				
President	Mrs. R. C. Witmer	Mrs. J. B. Warnock	Mrs. J. B. Warnock	Mrs. K. Bradley
1st VP	Mrs. J. B. Warnock	Mrs. K. Bradley	Mrs. K. Bradley	Mrs. C. O. Raushkolt
2nd VP	Mrs. R. Dustman	Mrs. L. B. Clark	Mrs. L. B. Clark	Mrs. O. Wintrab
3rd VP	Mrs. L. B. Clark	Mrs. I. Sametz	Mrs. I. Sametz	Mrs. R. T. Baldwin
Secretary	Mrs. K. Bradley	Mrs. O. Wintrab	Mrs. O. Wintrab	Mrs. G. C. Mullen
Corresponding Secretary	Mrs. R. T. Baldwin	Mrs. C. W. Janson	Mrs. C. W. Janson	Mrs. C. W. Janson
Treasurer	Mrs. J. W. Storey	Mrs. J. W. Storey	Mrs. J. W. Storey	Mrs. J. W. Storey
Committee & Department Chairmen				
Bedford House	Mrs. T. R. Olive	Mrs. T. R. Olive	Mrs. B. V. Brooks	Mrs. S. B. Smith
Building		Mrs. H. Wake	Mrs. H. Wake	Mrs. H. Wake
Civics & Legislation	Dr. L, M. Phillips	Mrs. R. T. Baldwin, S	Mrs. K. Griffin	Mrs. K. Griffin
Clothing Relief				Mrs. R. L. Lambdin
Cookbook	Mrs. V. N. Dorr Mrs. H. J. Fry		Mrs. R. C.Witmer	Mrs. L. R. Stewart
Federation	Mrs. H. Wake	Mrs. J. Crawford	Mrs. J. Crawford	Mrs. H. Long
Fine Arts				
Art	Mrs. L. S. Rounds	Mrs. L K. Holden	Mrs. R. G. Thew	Mrs. R. G. Thew
Drama	Mrs. J. E. Knox	Mrs. J. E. Knox	Mrs. P. Morgan	Mrs. E. D. Howard
Literature	Mrs. J. J. Dunne	Mrs. J. J. Dunne	Mrs. J. J. Dunne	Mrs. B. A. Griffiths
Music	Mrs. J. W. Stokes	Mrs. J. W. Stokes	Mrs. J. B. McMahon	Mrs. A. T. Scully
Garden	Mrs. P. C. McAbee	Mrs. C. O. Raushkolt	Mrs. C. O. Raushkol	Mrs. K. Greiner
Hospitality	Mrs. H. Sternberg	Mrs. C. W. Vogt	Mrs. I. B. Hazelton	Mrs. F. Boos
Junior	Mrs. W. Rousseau	Mrs. J. W. Vasst, Jr.	Mrs. R. T. Baldwin, Jr.	Mrs. G. Peabody, Jr. Mrs. H. Wake
Membership	Mrs. R. J. Dustman	Mrs. L. B. Clark	Mrs. L. B. Clark	Mrs. O. Wintraub
Publicity	Mrs. J. B. Warnock	Mrs. D. S. Muni	Mrs. J. K. Bradley	Mrs. W. B. Eager, Jr.
Program	Mrs. F. Charles	Mrs. H. Sternberg	Mrs. D. H. Parker	Mrs. J. E. Knox
Public Health	Mrs. J. D. Hitch, Jr.	Mrs. J. D. Hitch, Jr.	Mrs. G. C. Mullen	Mrs. J. B. Warnock
Scholarships	Mrs. W. B. Kellog Mrs. L. S. Rounds Mrs. J. D. Hitch, Jr.	Mrs. R. Sherwood Mrs. L. K. Holden	Mrs. F. R. Sherwood Mrs. R. G. Thew	Mrs. J. W. Storey Mrs. R. G. Thew
Ways & Means	Mrs. L. B. Clark	Mrs. I. Sametz	Mrs. I. Sametz	Mrs. R. T. Baldwin
Woman's Exchange	Mrs. H. A. Sutphen	Mrs. L. R. Stewart	Mrs. W. H. Perdun	Mrs. W. H. Perdun
Thrift Shop	Mrs. H. A. Sutphen	Mrs. L. R. Stewart	Mrs. W. H. Perdun	Mrs. W. H. Perdun

Officers & Boards of Directors 1947-1951				
	1947-1948	1948-1949	1949-1950	1950-1951
Officers				
President	Mrs. J. K. Bradley	Mrs. F. H. Appleton	Mrs. T. Veltfort	Mrs. J. K. Bradley
Execurive VP	Mrs. C. O. Rauschkolb	Mrs. T. Veltfort		Mrs. W. B. Eager
1stVP	Mrs. O Wintrab	Mrs. F. R. Sierwood	Mrs. F. R. Sierwood	Mrs. C. Shongood, Jr.
2nd VP	Mrs. R. T. Baldwin	Mrs. G. Baker		Mrs. G. Ingham
3rd VP			Mrs. G. R. Trafton	Mrs. R. T. Baldwin
4th VP			Mrs.	Mrs. G. R. Trafton
Secretary	Mrs. G. C. Mullen	Mrs. G. G. Pitts	Mrs. C. R. Chisholm	Mrs. G. G. Pitts
Treasurer	Mrs. J. W. Storey	Mrs. C. H. Schuck,Jr.	Mrs. C. H. Schuck,Jr.	Mrs. C. H. Schuck,Jr.
ExecutiveSecretary	Miss Frances Allen	Miss Frances Allen		
Committee & Department Chairmen				
Bedford House	Mrs. S. B. Smith			Mrs. C. Shongood, Jr.
Building	Mrs. H. Wake		Mrs. R. T. Baldwin	
Civics & Legislation	Mrs. K. B. Griffin	Mrs. J. B. Warnock	Mrs. L. Jerman	Mrs. L. Jerman
Clothing Relief	Mrs. R. L. Lamdin	Mrs. R. L. Lamdin	Mrs. R. L. Lamdin	Mrs. R. L. Lambdin
Cook Book	Mrs. L. S. Rounds	Mrs. L. S. Rounds	Mrs.	Mrs.
Entertainment	Mrs. R. Seitz	Mrs. G. Johnson	Mrs. E. Andersen Mrs. J. Lovejoy	Mrs.
Federation	Mrs. H. J. Long	Mrs. C. O. Rauschkolb	Mrs. C. O. Rauschkolb	Mrs. L. P. Pack
Finance				Mrs. R. C. Witmer
Fine Arts				Mrs.
Art	Mrs. R. G. Thew	Mrs. S. Holden	Mrs. J. Hastings	Mrs. F. Clay
Drama	Mrs. D. L. Poor	Mrs. D. L. Poor	Mrs. C. K. Panish	Mrs. C. K. Panish
Literature	Mrs. B. A. Griffiths	Mrs. B. A. Griffiths	Mrs. B. A. Griffiths	Mrs. B. A. Griffiths
Music	Mrs. D. Case	Mrs. D. Case	Mrs.	Mrs.
Garden	Mrs. K. Greiner	Mrs. A. Bernhard	Mrs. A. Bernhard	Mrs. R. C. Beck
Hospitality	Mrs. T. G. Walker	Mrs. I. B. Sproat	Mrs.	Mrs. I. E. Sproat
Junior	Mrs. W. B. Eager, Jr. Mrs. H. Wake	Mrs. J. M. Lupton Mrs. R, C. Beck	Mrs. S. Betts Mrs. G. Pitts	Mrs. J. B. Nunez Mrs. G. C. Mullen
Membership	Mrs. O. Wintrab	Mrs. F. R. Sherwood		Mrs. K. J. Griffin
Publicity	Mrs. J. B. Warnock	Mrs. R. T. Baldwin	Mrs. C. Shongood	Mrs. R. G. Thew
Program	Mrs. J. E Knox	Mrs. H. Sternberg	Mrs. H. C. Hazelton	Mrs. P. C. McAbee
Public Health	Mrs. E. E. Reynolds	Mrs. G. Ingham	G. Ingham	Mrs. G. Ingham
Scholarship	Mrs. J. W. Storey Mrs. R. G. Thew	Mrs. L. Dolge Mrs. G. Thew Mrs D. Chase	Mrs. Dolge Mrs. G. Ingham	Mrs. L. Dolge
Ways & Means	Mrs. R. T. Baldwin	Mrs. G. Baker	Mrs. G. R. Trafton	Mrs. G. R. Trafton
Woman's Exchange	Mrs. T. Kugeman	Mrs. R. Conn	Mrs. R. Conn	Mrs. R Bury
Thrift Shop	Mrs. T. Kugeman	Mrs. R. Conn	Mrs. R. Conn	Mrs. R Bury
Yankee Doodle Fair			Mrs. R. T. Baldwin	

Officers & Boards of Directors 1951-1955				
	1951-1952	1952-1953	1953-1954	1954-1955
Officers				
President	Mrs. J. K. Bradley	Mrs. C. H. Schuck, Jr.	Mrs. C. H. Schuck, Jr.	Mrs. C. H. Schuck, Jr.
Executive VP	Mrs. W. B. Eager, Jr.			
1st VP	Mrs. C. Shongood, Jr.	Mrs. R. L. Conn.	Mrs. Robins Conn	Mrs. R. L. Conn.
2nd VP	Mrs. G. Ingham	Mrs. L. Dolge	Mrs. L. Dolge	Mrs. L. Dolge
3rd VP	Mrs. R. T. Baldwin	P. Schuyler	Mrs. Philip Schuyler	Mrs. M. Lue
4th VP	Mrs. R. Trafton		Mrs. Merald Lue	
Secretary	Mrs. T. G. Walker	Mrs. L. Conaty	Mrs. Leo Conaty	Mrs. L. Conaty
Treasurer	Mrs. C. H. Schuck, Jr.	Mrs. M. Lue	Mrs. D. S. Rodgers	Mrs. D. S. Rodgers
Committee & Department Chairmen				
House	Mrs. C. Shongood, Jar.	Mrs. W. V. Lawson	Mrs. R. L. Conn	Mrs. R. L. Conn
Civics & Legislation	Mrs. L. Jerman		Mrs. O. Wintrab	Mrs. C. Speaks Mrs. B, Lefcourt
Clothing Relief	Mrs. R. L. Lamdin	Mrs. R L. Lambdin	Mrs. R. L. Lambdin	Mrs. R. L. Lamdin
Federation	Mrs. P. Pack			Mrs. R. T. Baldwin
Finance	Mrs. R. C, Witmer	Mrs. O. Wintrab	Mrs. D. L. Poor	Mrs. D. L. Poor
Fine Arts				
Art	Mrs. F. Clay	Mrs. R. G. Thew	Mrs. R. G. Thew	Mrs. R. G. Thew
Drama	Mrs. C. K. Panish	Mrs. D. L. Poor		Mrs. J. F. Odell
Literature	Mrs. B. A. Griffiths			Mrs. B. A. Griffiths
Music		Mrs. J. Edgar	Mrs. R.Trafton	Mrs. D. Case
Garden	Mrs. R Beck	Mrs. M. F. Kirtley, Jr.	Mrs. M. Kurtley, Jr.	Mrs. W. V. Lawson
Hospitality	Mrs. I. Sproat			Mrs. W. F. Grabill
Juniors	Mrs. J. B. Nunez	Mrs. E. G. Courcier Mrs. R. Dodge	Mrs. E. G. Courcier	Mrs. R. Trafton
Membership	Mrs. K. B. Griffin	Mrs. D. Harrison	Mrs. D. E. Harrison	Mrs. D. Harrison
Parliamentarian		Mrs. G. R. Trafton		
Publicity	Mrs. R. G. Thew	Mrs. D. S. Rogers	Mrs. M. Lue	Mrs. M. Lue
Program	Mrs. P. C. McAbee	Mrs. E. C. Nash	Mrs. C. S. Schuck, Jr.	Mrs. C. S. Schuck, Jr.
Public Health	Mrs. G. E. Ingham	Mrs. J.K. Joyner	Mrs. Cornelia E Joyner	Mrs. J. K. Joyner
Scholarship	Mrs. L. Dolge	Mrs. L. Dolge	Mrs. Lloyd Dolge	Mrs. L. Dolge
Ways & Means	Mrs. G. R. Trafton			
Woman's Exchange Thrift Shop	Mrs. R. Bury	Mrs. R. Bury	Mrs. A. Lockwood	Mrs. A. Lockwood

Officers & Boards of Directors 1955-1959

	1955-1956	1956-1957	1957-1958	1958-1959
Officers				
President	Mrs. C. H. Schuck, J	Mrs. M. Lue	Mrs. M. Lue	Mrs. M. Lue
1st VP	Mrs. R. L. Conn	Mrs. L. Dolge	Mrs. L. Dolge	Mrs. G. W. Patch
2nd VP	Mrs. L. Dolge	Mrs. F. Kidd, Jr.	Mrs. F. Kidd, Jr.	Mrs. J. M. Rencken, J
3rd VP	Mrs. M. Lue	Mrs. E. B. Schryver	Mrs. E. B. Shryver	Mrs. T. Driscoll
Secretary	Mrs. L. J. Conaty	Mrs. W. F. Grabill	Mrs. J. A. Rencken, J	Mrs. E H. Moss
Treasurer	Mrs. D. S. Rodgers	Mrs. S. Dawson	Mrs. W. F. Grabill	Mrs. L. Dolge
Committee & Department Chairmen				
Bulletin		Mrs. L. J. A. Villalon	Mrs. L. J. A. Villalon	Mrs. F. Thomas
			Mrs. D. Mikhael	
Clothing Relief		Mrs. R. Lambdin	Mrs. R. I. Lamdin	Mrs. R. I. Lamdin
Clubhouse & Rentals		Mrs. E Shook	Mrs. E. Shook	Mrs. H. Kephart
Federation		Mrs. C. Shongood	Mrs. G. W. Patch	Mrs. J. F. Hysler
Finance	Mrs. D. Poor	Mrs. T. Driscoll	Mrs, T, Driscoll	Mrs. A. V. Lockwood
Fine Arts				
Art		Mrs. W. Brackett	Mrs. Thew/Clay, Jr.	Mrs. Thew/Clay, Jr.
Drama			Mrs. D. L. Poor	
Literature			Mrs. J. K. Joyner	
Music		Mrs. D. Case	Mrs. D. Case	Mrs. D. Case
Garden		Mrs. H. Kephart	Mrs. H. Kephart	Mrs. S. A. Kiss
Grounds		Mrs. F. L. Kidd	Mrs. F. L. Kidd, Jr.	Mrs. F. N. Merriam
Junior		Mrs. G. V. Land		
Membership		Mrs. B. V. Brooks	Mrs. B. V. Brooks	Mrs. C. Rowlands
		Mrs. G. W. Patch	Mrs. G. W. Patch	Mrs. F. R. Thomas
Public Relations		Mrs. A. Hannes	Mrs. D. L. Poor	Mrs. D. L. Poor
Program		Mrs. A. Tigner	Mrs. S. A. Kiss	Mrs. E. L. Townsend
Public Health		Mrs. J. K/ Joyner	Mrs. J. K. Joyner	Mrs. J. M. Rencken
Rules		Mrs. L. Dolge	Mrs. L. Dolge	Mrs. L. Dolge
Scholarship		Mrs. E. Schryver	Mrs. E. Schryver	Mrs. E. Schryver
Social Affairs				Mrs. C. K. Panish
Woman's Exchange Thrift Shop		Mrs. J. M. Rencken	Mrs. J. A. Rencken,	Mrs. D. S. Rodgers
Member-at-Large	Mrs. P. N. Schuyler	Mrs. E. B. Schryver	Mrs. A. V. Lockwood	Mrs. E. B. Schryver
	Mrs. H. Magee		Mrs. E. Shook	Mrs. C. Rowlands
Yankee Doodle Fair		Mrs. T. Driscoll	Mrs. T. Driscoll	

Officers & Boards of Directors 1959-1963				
	1959-1960	1960-1961	1961-1962	1962-1963
Officers				
President	Mrs. R. Destino	Mrs. G. Patch	Mrs. G. Patch	Mrs. G. Patch
1st VP	Mrs. T. Driscoll	Mrs. T. Driscoll	Mrs. P. Michel	Mrs. P. Michel
2nd VP	Mrs. F. N. Merriam	Mrs. H. P. Croft	Mrs. T. Driscoll	Mrs. T. Driscoll
3rd VP	Mrs. G. Patch	Mrs. P. Michel	Mrs. H. P. Croft	Mrs. H. P. Croft
Secretary	Mrs. G. Erickson	Mrs. G. Erickson	Mrs. W. Paine	Mrs. W. Paine
Treasurer	Mrs. L. Dolge	Mrs. L. Dolge	Mrs. L. Dolge	Mrs. L. Dolge
Committee & Department Chairmen				
Clothing Relief	Mrs. R. L. Lambdin	Mrs. R. L. Lambdin		
Clubhouse & Rentals	Mrs. F. N. Merriam	Mrs. F. N. Merriam	Mrs. T. Cens	
Federation	Mrs. S. A. Kiss	Mrs. S. A. Kiss		
Finance	Mrs. M. F. Davitt	Mrs. M. F. Davitt		
Fine Arts				
Art	Mrs. T, Driscoll	Mrs. T, Driscoll	Mrs. D. Reilly	Mrs. W. Neff
Literature	Mrs. F, L, Griffiths	Mrs. F, L, Griffiths	Mrs. B, A, Griffith	Mrs. B, A, Griffiths
Music	Mrs. C. W. Gemeck	Mrs. R.L.Lambdin		
Garden	Mrs. A. L. Omohun	Mrs. W, Kirchner	Mrs. W, Kirchner	Mrs. W, Kirchner
Grounds	Mrs. H. Kephart	Mrs. H. Kephart	Mrs. H. Kephart	Mrs. H. Kephart
Hospitality	Mrs. A. G. Copeland	Mrs. E. Nolan, Jr.	Mrs. W. Wiisanen	Mrs. W. Wiisanen
Membership	Mrs. R. E. Clark	Mrs. R. E. Clark	Mrs. H. P. Croft	Mrs. H. P. Croft
Publicity	Mrs. J. Cole	Mrs. J. Cole		Mrs. P. Bassford
Program	Mrs. A. Morell	Mrs. A. Morell	Mrs. P. Michel	Mrs. P. Michel
Public Health	Mrs. L. Dolge	Mrs. T. Driscoll	Mrs. T. Driscoll	Mrs. T. Driscoll
Rules	Mrs. D. Mikhael / Mrs. F. N. Meriam	Mrs. R. H. Shirey	Mrs. R. H. Shirey	Mrs. R. H. Shirey
Thrift Shop	Mrs. C. W. Vogt	Mrs. C. W. Vogt	Mrs. H. C. O'Shea	Mrs. H. C. O'Shea

Officers & Boards of Directors 1963-1967

	1963-1964	1964-1965	1965-1966	1966-1967
Officers				
President	Mrs. E. Nolan, Jr.	Mrs. E. Nolan, Jr.	Mrs. D. Schnack	Mrs. D. Schnack
1st VP	Mrs. D. Schnack	Mrs. D. Schnack	Mrs. V. R. Chase	Mrs. V. R. Chase
2nd VP	Mrs. C. Olmstead	Mrs. C. Olmstead	Mrs. C. E. Kendall	Mrs. W. E. Burt
3rd VP	Mrs. T, Cens	Mrs. T, Cens	Mrs. W. E. Burt	Mrs. F. N. Merriam
Secretary	Mrs. F. Rubman	Mrs. F. Rubman	Mrs. K. H. Roll	Mrs. J. Cuneo
Treasurer	Mrs. J. A. Ulrich	Mrs. A. J. Dion	Mrs. A. J. Dion	Mrs. A. J. Dion
Members at Large & Committee Chairmen				
Bridge	Mrs. J. Beecher	Mrs. J. Beecher	Mrs. R. Destino	Mrs. R.Destino Mrs. C. Panish
Bulletin	Mrs. J. B, Beecher	Mrs. J. B, Beecher	Mrs. A. Kaye	Mrs. D. Hunn
Department Advisory			Mrs. K. A. Gardner	Mrs. F. N. Merriam
Federation	Mrs. G. W. Patch		Mrs. F. N. Merriam	
Finance	Mrs. R.Destino	Mrs. R.Destino	Mrs. E. Burt	Mrs. E. Burt
Art Classics				
Art	Mrs. W. Neff	Mrs. W. Neff		
Drama		Mrs. D. Hunn		Mrs. D. Hunn
Literature	Mrs. F. L. Griffiths Mrs. J. Powers	Mrs. K. H. Roll	Carol Jones	
Garden	Mrs. F. W. Spooner	Mrs. F. W. Spooner	Mrs. J. F. Carrot, 2nd Mrs. L. A. Russ	Mrs. J. H. Bailey
Grounds	Mrs. U. H. Brockway, 3d. Mrs. W. Kirchner	Mrs. U. H. Brockway, 3d. Mrs. W. Kirchner		
Hospitality	Mrs. E. Morris Stadum Mrs. J. E. Newman	Mrs. E. Morris Stadum Mrs. J. E. Newman	Mrs. A. Booth	Mrs. J. L. Senior
House			Mrs. D. E. Bowers	Mrs. C. Lunny
Membership	Mrs. K. A. Gardner	Mrs. K. A. Gardner	Mrs. R. L. Cobb	Mrs. R. L. Cobb
Publicity	Mrs. A. L. Omohundro	Mrs. A. L. Omohundro	Mrs. W. J. Gog	Mrs. W. Kirchner
Program	Mrs. R. Healy	Mrs. R. Healy	Mrs. H. Baldwin	Mrs. H. Baldwin
Public Service	Mrs. J. Beecher			
Rentals	Mrs. T, Cens	Mrs. D. D. Schnack Mrs. G. W.Patgh	Mrs. V. R. Chase	Mrs. V. R. Chase
Scholarship	Mrs. R. H. Shirey	Mrs. R. H. Shirey		
Social Affairs	Mrs. O. W. Ehrhorn	Mrs. O. W. Ehrhorn	Marge Walker	
Social Services			Mrs. C. E. Kendall	Mrs. R. H. Shirey
Thrift Shop	Mrs. H. H. O'Shea	Mrs. C. H. Schuck		Mrs. C. H. Schuck
Ways & Means	Mrs. G. H. Schuck	Mrs. C. H. Schuck	Mrs. R. Kennett	Mrs. A. Booth
Yankee Doodle Fair	Mrs. T. Cens			

166

Officers & Boards of Directors 1967-1971

	1967-1968	1968-1969	1969-1970	1970-1971
Officers				
President	Betty Chase	Rita Keneally	Rita Keneally	Myrtle Cuneo
1st VP	Pat Senior	Jacky Booth	Myrtle Cuneo	Marjorie McRo)
2nd VP	Jacky Booth	Myrtle Cuneo	Elsie Ball	LaVerne Beeche
3rd VP	Yette Alford	Solveig Lunny	Solveig Lunny	Solveig Lunny
Secretary	Myrtle Cuneo	Joan Clark	Jean Thomas	Jean Thomas
Treasurer	Rita Keneaally	Elsie Ball	Carol Panish	Esther Shirey
Members at Large & Committee Chairmen				
Department Advisory	Jean Roll		Myrtle Cuneo	Joyce Kaye
Federation				
Finance	Elsie Ball	Betty Zajac	Elsie Ball	LaVerne Beeche
House	Solveig Lunny		Peggy Sampson	Peggy Sampson
Parliamentarian				
Garden	Betty Woodsum		Lois Lenfest	
Membership	Helen Delaney	MaryAl;ice Clary	Cathy Kirchner	Frances Peters
Program	Pat Senior	Ronnie Bailey	LaVerrne Beecher	Rita Keneaally
Publicity	Yette Alford	Catherine Fisher	Florence Israel	Bea Kelly
Rentals	Nancy McQuilli	Nancy McQuillin	Solveig Lunny	Solveig Lunny
Social Services	Esther Shirey	LaVerrne Beecher	Jean Haven	Arlene Dion
Ways & Means	Jacky Booth		Ann Ducey	Marjorie McRo)
Thrift Shop	Gladys Schuck	Gladys Schuck	Gladys Schuck	
Yankee Doodle Fair				

Officers & Boards of Directors 1971-1975

	1971-1972	1972-1973	1973-1974	1974-1975
Officers				
President	Myrtle R. Cuneo	Jacky Booth	Jacky Booth	Joan Croarkin
1st VP	Jacky Booth	Joan Croarkin	Joan Croarkin	Frances Peters
2nd VP	Solveig Lunny	Solveig Lunny	Frances Peters	Lois Schneider
3rd VP	LaVerne Beecher	Dorothy Dale	Dorothy Dale	Jackie Cafarelli
Secretary	Lois Schneider	Doris Courtney	Ruth Harwood	Ruth Harwood
Treasurer	Esther Shirey	Sue Haman	Sue Haman	Evelyn Hynd
Executive Secretary			Alice Ouelette	Alice Ouelette
Members at Large				
Community Services	Marguerite Filson	Betty Dunbar	Betty Dunbar	Lois Schneider
Department Advisory	Solveig Lunny	Solveig Lunny		Marie Taylor
Federation	Myrtle R. Cuneo	Ann Bradley	Ann Bradley	Jacky Booth
Finance	LaVerne Beecher	Dorothy Dale		Jackie Cafarelli
House	Pat Hibbard	Ruth Gallo	Bobbie Clark	Sue Tichenor
Membership	Frances Peters	Mona McKiernan	Mona McKiernan	Dorothea Citti
Program	Rita Keneally	Adele Collins	Adele Collins	Mona McKiernan
Publicity	Eelyn Hynd	Eelyn Hynd	Jan Waite	Irene Naughton
Rentals	Jerry Lord	Jerry Lord	Charlotte Brenner	Charlotte Brenner
Social Affairs		Cam Lamb	Cam Lamb	Margaret Bailey
Ways & Means	Joan Croarkin	Joan Croarkin	Frances Peters	Frances Peters

Officers & Boards of Directors 1975-1979

	1975-1976	1976-1977	1977-1978	1978-1979
Officers				
President	Joan Croarkin	Dorothea Citti	Dorothea Citti	Kathleen Roach
1st VP	Mona McKiernan	Charmian Bowsher	Dorothy Gambaccir	Dorothy Gambaccir
2nd VP	Lois Schneider	Dorothy Gambaccir	Eleen Cummins	Phyllis Hillebrand
3rd VP	Jackie Cafarelli	Mary Cummins	Maryn Killough	Adele Collins
Secretary	Ruth Harwood	Bobbie Clark	Bobbie Clark	Charmian Bowsher
Treasurer	Evelyn Hynd	Phyllis Hillebrand	Phyllis Hillebrand	Pat Limburg
Executive Secretary	Alice Ouelette	Ruth Kinson	Ruth Kinson	Ruth Kinson
Directors				
Community Services	Lois Schneider	Dorothy Gambaccir	Dorothy Gambaccir	Barbara D'Agostino
Department Advisory	Marie Taylor	Mona McKiernan	Mona McKiernan	Dorothy Gambaccir
Federation	Jacky Booth	Joan Gorski	Carol Weitz	Weitz
Finance	Jackie Cafarelli	Eleen Cummins	Eleen Cummins	Phyllis Hillebrand
House	Sue Tichenor	Adele Hollingswort	Adele Hollingswort	Marilyn Freeman
Parliamentarian				
Grounds		Harriet Bryniczka	Harriet Bryniczka	Jill Adelman
Membership	Dorothea Citti		Cynnie Moll	
Program	Mona McKiernan	Maryn Killough	Maryn Killough	Estelle Ormand
Publicity	Irene Naughton	Joan May	Joan My	Elisabeth Shippam
Rentals	Charmian Bowsher	Charmian Bowsher	Kathleen Roach	Marilyn Killough
Ways & Means	Kathleen Roach	Kathleen Roach	Jerry Davies	Adele Collins
Yankee Doodle Fair				

Officers & Boards of Directors 1979-1983

	1979-1980	1980-1981	1981-1982	1982-1983
Officers				
President	Kathleen Roach	Adele Collins	Mona McKiernan	Mona McKiernan
1st VP	Phyllis Hillebrand	Mona McKiernan	Pat Limburg	Charmian Bowsher
2nd VP	Marilyn Killough	Pat Limburg	Jo Anne Siebrasse	Beth McCarthy
3rd VP	Irene Naughton	Vera Holms	Beth McCarthy	Vivian Johnson
Secretary	Charmian Bowsher	Marilyn Freeman	Betty LaBonte	Donna Russell
Treasurer	Pat Limburg	Charmian Bowsher	Charmian Bowsher	Patricia Limburg
Executive Secretary	Ruth Kinson	Ruth Kinson	Ruth Kinson	Ruth Kinson
Directors				
Community Services	Vera Holmes		Aggie Sibley	Aggie Sibley
Department Advisory	Dorothea Citti	Donna Lint	Donna Lint	Jo Anne Siebrasse
Federation	Barbara Van Orden	Barbara Van Orden	Phyllis Hillebrand	Phyllis Hillebrand
Finance	Phyllis Hillebrand		Pat Limburg	Charmian Bowsher
House	Marilyn Freeman	Marilyn Killough		Beth McCarthy
Parliamentarian				
Grounds	Jill Adelman	Harriet Sherman	Harriet Sherman	Ina Deecken
Membership		Phyllis Hillebrand	Clara Sandner	Clara Sendner
Program	Jacky Booth	Jacky Booth	Eileen Ellis	Eileen Ellis
Publicity	Mamie Hannaway	Mary Jean Boston	Martha Conant	Martha Conant
Rentals	Marilyn Killough	Jo Anne Siebrasse	Jo Anne Siebrasse	Vivian Johnson
Ways & Means	Carol Weitz		Barbara Culp	Barbara Culp
Directors at Large	Adele Collins	Eileen Dullmeyer	BettyJackel	Claire Angle
	Beth McCarthy	Beth McCarthy	Vivian Johnson	Wanda Koskoska
	Mona McKiernan	Mary Retelle	MaryRetelle	Vivian Ohlhorst
Yankee Doodle Fair				

Officers & Boards of Directors 1983-1987				
	1983-1984	1984-1985	1985-1986	1986-1987
Officers				
President	Mona McKiernan	Charmian Bowsher	Charmian Bowsher	Adele Collins
1st VP	Charmian Bowsher	Patricia Limburg	Adele Collins	Barbara Culp
2nd VP	Vivian Johnson	Jo Anne Siebrasse	Patricia Limburg	Betty McGrath
3rd VP	Dee Andrian	Dee Andrian	Jo Anne Siebrasse	Janie Hazel
Secretary	Tanya Simonton	Mary Ellen Wittneb	Connie Lynch	Lola Gerhardt
Treasurer	Patricia Limburg	Vivian Johnson	Vivian Johnson	Marie Taylor
Directors				
Community Services	Nancy Dennis	Nancy Dennis	Edith Earl	Edith Earl
Department Advisory	Jo Anne Siebrasse	Patricia Limburg	Patricia Limburg	Betty McGrath
Federation	Lis Shippam	Lillian Weimann	Lillian Weimann	Pat Limburg
Finance	Charmian Bowsher	Jo Anne Siebrasse	Jo Anne Siebrasse	Janie Hazel
House	Mary Wilson	Clara Sandner	Adele Collins	Barbara Culp
Parliamentarian				
Grounds	Ina Deecken	Elaine Rusk	Elaine Rusk	Mary Jo Robison
Membership	Martha Conant	Martha Conant	Barabar Vigars	Barbara Vigars
Program	Dee Andrian	Dee Andrian	Beatrice Kelly	Beatrice Kelly
Publicity	Aggie Sibley	Aggie Sibley	Debby May	Debby May
Rentals	Vivian Johnson	Betty McGrath	Betty McGrath	Cele Greene
Ways & Means				
Directors at Large	Clair Angle	Lola Gehrhardt	Lola Gehrhardt	Beth McCarthy
	Marie Boersma	Edella Johnson	Beth McCarthy	Joyce Roessler
	Heinke Ashton	Marie Taylor	Marie Taylor	Pat Wettach
Executive Secretary	Ruth Kinson	Ruth Kinson	Ruth Kinson	Ruth Kinson
Yankee Doodle Fair		Vivian Johnson Joyce Roessler	Joyce Roessler	

Officers & Directors 1987-1991				
	1987-1988	1988-1989	1989-1990	1990-1991
Officers				
President	Barbara Culp	Barbara Culp	Vivian Johnson	Vivian Johnson
1st VP	Vivian Johnson	Vivian Johnson	Ginnie Cardozo	Eileen Petropoulos
2nd VP	Betty McGrath	Lola Gehrhardt	Beverlee Kohnken	Joan Croarkin
3rd VP	Barbara Hart	Barbara Hart	Judy Chable	Jo Anne Siebrasse
Secretary	Lola Gerhardt		Pat Wettach	Pat Wettach
Treasurer	Marie Taylor	Lynn Ogren	Lynn Ogren	Shirley McGhee
Executive Secretary	Ruth Kinson	Ruth Kinson	Ruth Kinson	Ruth Kinson
Directors				
Community Services	Ginny Cardozo	Ginny Cardozo	Eileen Petropoulos	Eileen Petropoulos
Department Advisory	Betty McGrath	Lola Gehrhardt	Connie Herlihy	Mary Lee Clayton
Federation	Pat Limburg	Johnny Sweeny	Johnny Sweeny	Laurel Hoffman
Finance	Barbara Hart	Barbara Hart	Ginnie Cardozo	Joan Croarkin
House		Vivian Johnson	Judie Chable	Margaret Howard-Goldsmith
Parliamentarian				
Grounds	Mary Jo Robins(	Pat Logemann	Jo Anne Siebrasse	Jo Anne Siebrasse
Membership	Carolyn Brink	Carolyn Brink	Bea Kelly	Deirdre Bugbee
Program	Deirdre Bugbee	Deirdre Bugbee	Helen Luedke	Helen Luedke
Publicity	Beverlee Kohnke	Barbara Vigars	Barbara Vigars	Nancy Brown
Rentals	Cele Greene	Beverlee Kohnke	Beverlee Kohnken	Gerry Pellegrino
Ways & Means				
Directors at Large	Judy Chable	Judy Chable	Barbara Hart	Jackie Muse
	Helen Luedke	Helen Luedke	Jo An Kingsley	Cheryl Stoebe
	Pat Wettach	Cele Greene	Vi Takahashi	Vi Takahashi
Yankee Doodle Fair	Joan Ruehle	Mary Jo Nugent	Vivian Johnson	Frenchie Everitt

Officers & Boards of Directors 1991-1995				
	1991-1992	1992-1993	1993-1994	1994-1995
Officers				
President	Helen Luedke	Deirdre Bugbee	Deirdre Bugbee	Carol Wright
1st VP	Deirdre Bugbee	Joan Croarkin	Carol Wright	Anne Jacques
2nd VP	Alice Kosiba	Alice Kosiba	Anne Jacques	Susan Wood
3rd VP	Jackie Muse	Marie Taylor	Shirley McGhee	Pat Everson
Secretary	Eileen Petropoulos	Eileen Petropoulos	Marjorie Allen	Marjorie Allen
Treasurer	Shirlee McGhee	Shirley McGhee	Alice Koshiba	Alice Koshiba
Executive Secretary	Ruth Kinson	Ruth Kinson	Ruth Kinson	Ruth Kinson
Directors				
Community Services	Vi Takashaki	Vi Takashaki	Jo Anne Siebrasse	Jo Anne Siebrasse
Department Advisory	Joan Croarkin	Joan Croarkin	Anne Jacques	Anne Jacques
Federation	Laurel Hoffmann	Barbara Culp	Barabare Culp	Jacky Booth
Finance	Alice Koshiba	Alice Kosiba	Shirley McGhee	Pat Everson
House	Margarite Howard-Goldsmith	Carol Wright	Carol Wright	Elizabeth Peloso
Parliamentarian		Laurel Hoffmann	Laurel Hoffmann	
Grounds	Lucille Christian	Lucille Christian	Grace Booth	Grace Booth
Membership	Deirdre Bugbee	Marilyn Payne	Marilyn Paine	Tammy Pincavage
Program	Aggie Sibley	Aggie Sibley	Margaret LeBedis	Margaret Lebedis
Publicity	Nancy Brown	Rosalie Puglia	Roalie Puglia	Ann Rossell
Rentals	Marie Taylor	Marie Taylor	Susan Wood	Susan Wood
Ways & Means	Jackie Muse			
Directors at Large	Mary Fisher	Grace Booth	Jacky Booth	Norma Beck
	Ashby Cassidy	Shirley Reynolds	Lucille Christian	Sandra Feder
		Joan White	Ronnie Kennedy	Mila Grieb
Yankee Doodle Fair	Mary Lee Clayton	Carol Mata	Pat Coulson	Mary Fisher

Officers & Boards of Directors 1995-1999

	1995-1996	1996-1997	1997-1998	1998-1999
Officers				
President	Marliyn Paine	Tammy Pincavage	Tammy Pincavage	Ellen Granger
1st VP	Tammy Pincavage	Carol Lewis	Harriet Benson	Marie Nilson
2nd VP	Harriet Benson	Joyce Netherton	Joyce Netherton	Joyce Netherton
3rd VP	Pat Everson	Barbara Sanderson	Barbara Sanderson	Jeannette Tewey
Secretary	Pat Coulson	Patricia Wettach	Patricia Wettach	Helen Doxtator
Treasurer	Sue Cushman	Patricia Everson	Winnie Martinek	Winnie Martinek
Executive Secretary		Cindy Bulkley	Cindy Bulkley	Cindy Bulkley
Directors				
Community Services	Carol Wright	Norma Beck	Norma Beck	Inge VanGelder
Department Advisory	Tammy Pincavage	Carol Lewis		Maria Nilson
Federation	Pat Limburg	Jacky Booth	Jacky Booth	Ann Rossell
Finance	Pat Everson	Joyce Netherton		Joyce Netherton
House	Dianne Swetonic	Dianne Swetonic	Marilyn Paine Helen Luedke	Helen Luedke
Parliamentarian	Winnie Martinek	Winnie Martinek	Helen Luedke	Barbara Wagner
Grounds	Fran Johnson	Harriett Gartner	Harriet Gartner	Harriet Berson
Membership	Norma Beck	Jeannette Tewey	Pat Coulson	Deirdre Bugbee
Program	Ann Jacques	Ann Rossell	Ann Rossell	Lois Harner
Publicity	Ann Rossell	Jeri Skinner	Lois Harner	Mikki Bunting
Rentals	Harriet Benson	Harriet Benson	Linda Debo	Linda Debo
Ways & Means	Sandra Feeder Ginny Ferrara Mila A.Grieb	Barbara Sanderson Maria Underwood Ellen Granger	Ellen Granger Jeanette Tewey	Marion Potter Victoria Forrest
Curio Cottage				Norma Beck Karen Eikhoff
Yankee Doodle Fair	Carol Mata		Barbara Sanderson	

Officers & Boards of Directors 1999-2003

	1999-2000	2000-2001	2001-2002	2002-2003
Officers				
President	Ellen Granger	Winnie Martinek	Nat Sylander	Nat Sylander
1st VP	Jeanette Tewey	Linda Debo	Linda Amos	Pat Jensen
2nd VP	Nat Sylander	Nat Sylander	Winnie Martinek	Winnie Martinek
3rd VP		Marion Potter	Jean Simons	Jean Simons
Secretary	Helen Doxtator	Inge VanGelder	Inge VanGelder	Jo Fuchs Luscombe
Treasurer	Sonja Friedman	Pat Jensen	Pat Jensen	Joyce Netherton
Executive Secretary	Cindy Bulkley	Cindy Bulkley	Cindy Bulkley	Cindy Bulkley
Directors				
Community Services	Inge VanGelder	Barbara Wagner	Barbara Wagner	Kathy Goldhawk
Department Advisory	Jeanette Tewey	Nat Sylander	Linda Amos	Pat Jensen
Federation	Barbara Culp Jacky Booth			
Finance	Nat Sylander		Winnie Martinek	Winnie Martinek
House	Linda Amos	Linda Amos	Linda Volckmann	Linda Volckmann
Parliamentary Advisor	Joyce Netherton	JoAnne Siebrasse	JoAnne Siebrasse	Sandra Hagmann-Blinn
Grounds	Linda Debo	June Ahlgren	Fay Farquhar	Fay Farquhar
Membership	Bobbie Herman Ronnie Kennedy	Doris Stevens	Wendy McKeon	Wendy McKeon
Program	Lois Harner	Jo Luscombe	Jo Luscombe	Ann Rossell
Communications	Barbara Wagner	Ann Rossell	Ann Rossell	Helene Crawford
Rentals	Linda Volckmann	Linda Volckmann	Arlene Wolfe	Arlene Wolfe
Ways & Means		Marion Potter	Inge VanGelder	Jean Simons
Curio Cottage		Kathi Mitchell	Kathi Mitchell	Linda Amos
Yankee Doodle Fair		Winnie Martinek Nat Sylander	Nat Sylander	Ellen Granger Linda Amos

Officers & Board of Directors 2003-2007

	2003-2004	2004-2005	2005-2006	2006-2007
Officers				
President	Jo Fuchs Luscombe	Jo Fuchs Luscombe	Barbara Levy	Barbara Levy
1st VP	Pat Jensen	Jean Simmons	Leah Scherzer	Leah Scherzer
2nd VP	Carol Goetz	Linda Clair	Linda Clair	Barbara Szefc
3rd VP	Barbara Levy	Barbara Levy	By Committee	
Secretary	Joan Desfosses	Rose Jordan	Rose Jordan	Josephine Laska
Treasurer	Joyce Netherton	Joyce Netherton	Barbara Szefc	Linda Clair
Executive Secretary	Cindy Bulkley	Eileen Solomito	Eileen Solomito	Eileen Solomito
Directors				
Community Services	Kathy Goldhawk	Inge Van Gelder	Audrey Rabinowitz	Audrey Rabinowitz
Department Advisory	Pat Jensen			
Finance	Carol Goetz			
House	Fay Farquhar	By Committee	Fay Farquhar Linda Amos	Fay Farquhar Linda Amos
Parliamentary Advisor	Vi Takahashi	Jean Golden	Jean Golden	Jane Plotkin
Grounds	Arlene Wolfe	Arlene Wolfe	Catherine Smith	Catherine Smith
Membership	Linda Debo	Linda Debo	Wendy McKeon	Wendy McKeon
Program	Jean Simmons	Pat Coulson	Betty McGrath Barbara Raffel	Betty McGrath Barbara Raffel
Communications	Ann Rossell	Ann Rossell	Ann Rossell	Ann Rossell
Historian				Eileen Petropoulos
Rentals	Catherine Smith	Catherine Smith	Maryann Razzano	Maryann Razzano Diana Zaslow
Ways & Means		Barabara Levy		
Curio Cottage	Johnny Sweeny	Johnny Sweeny	Sally Shauer	Sally Shauer
Yankee Doodle Fair	Winnie Martinek	Zita Casey	Zita Casey	Dorothy Curran Mary Lee Clayton

INDEX

Index

1

100th Anniversary Committee, 152

A

A Midsummer Night's Dream, 48
A Rare Woman's Club, 1, 3, 4, 13, 61, 62, 63, 144, 153
A Woodland Festival, 20
Adams Academy, 109, 117
Adams, George, 136
Adams, Mrs. W. S., 19
Agramonte, Jules, 35
Alcoholics Anonymous, 88
Alger, Mrs., 29
All-American City, 79
Allen, Frances, 42, 115
Allen, Miss, 104, 106, 115
Allen, Miss Frances, 42
Alphabet Fair, 27
American Cancer Society, 88
American Red Cross, 29, 30, 91, 140
An Evening with Gershwin, 142
Anderson, Karl, 29, 35, 84
Anderson, Mr. Karl, 29
Anderson, Percy, 35
Andrian, Dee, 123
Annual Fashion Show, 56
Arms, John Taylor, 35
Army Engineers, 86
Ashe, Edmund, 35
Aspetuck Valley Health District Office, 91
Athenian Oath, 41, 111

B

Bailey, Dr., 44
Baker, Mrs. John, 51
Balcom, Lowell, 35
Balcom, Sophie, 35
Baldwin, Herbert, 104
Baldwin, Herbert E., 50
Baldwin, Mrs. Robert T., 45, 50
Baldwin, Roger, 54
Baldwin's, Mrs., 53
Barlow, Perr, 35

Bascho, Sophie, 84, 144
Battle of Compo Hill, 116
Battle of Compo in 1777, 82
Beach Commission, 50, 89
Beach Pavilion, 26
Beck, Norma, 136, 137
Bedford Fund, 34, 59, 68, 69, 70, 106
Bedford House, 33, 34, 35, 39, 41, 44, 45, 46, 48, 49, 52, 53, 54, 60, 61, 68, 69, 91, 94, 111
Bedford Junior High School, 57, 60, 80, 81
Bedford Mr. Frederick T., 68, 106
Bedford, E. T., 33, 39
Bedford, Mary A., 106
Beers Roadside Market, 44
Belaga, Julie, 123
Benson, Leslie L., 35
Big Top Circus, 57
Bigley, Stuart, 71, 72
Billboard Committee, 43
Birchwood Country Club, 39
Board of Education, 24, 64, 84, 89, 146
Book Barn, 136, 137
Booth, Jacky, 108, 119
Booth, Mrs. Jacky, 108
Born Yesterday, 77
Bowling, 111
Boy Project, 47
Boy Scouts, 49, 60, 83
Boyd, Edward, 35
Boyd, Virginia P., 80
Boyer, Ralph, 35
Boyer, Rebecca, 35
Brabner, Mr. George, Jr., 82
Bradley, Ann, 117
Bradley, Mrs., 58, 59, 61, 67, 69, 70, 79, 95, 148
Bradley, Mrs. D. B., 19
Bradley, Mrs. Ina, 103, 111
Bradley, Mrs. J. Kenneth, 92, 94
Bridge, 28, 30, 40, 67, 106, 109, 111
Bridgeport Hydraulic, 126
brown bag lunch, 147
Brown, Samuel E., 35
Brush, Jerome, 35
Bryan, William Jennings, 54
Bryce, Dorothy, 139
Bryniczka, Harriet, 116
Buck, Mrs. Charles, 27
Buell, Mrs., 53
Bulkley, Cindy, 134

Bundles for America, 55, 60, 61, 66
Bundles for Britain, 61
Bunny, Fontaine,, 127
Burr, Mr. Algernon T., 39
Butcher, Sarah Payne, 72

C

Canal Green, 17, 118, 126, 127
Canal Street, 107, 118, 126
Carlton, Mrs. Schuyler, 45
Chamber of Commerce, 33, 43, 73
Chase, Betty, 103, 109
Chase, Mrs. Betty, 103
Child, 43, 51, 87, 91, 98, 107, 140
Child Identification Program, 140
Christian Community Action, 140
Chubby Lane's restaurant, 113
Citti, Dorothea, 118
Citti, Dot, 119, 122
Clean-Up Westport, 108
Clisbee, George, 35
Clothing Bank, 61
Clothing Relief Committee, 55, 65
Coley, Merrick H., 26
Coley, Mrs., 20
Coley, Robert H., 26
Collins, Adele, 119
Columbia University, 94
Comedy and Tragedy, 135
Community Services Committee, 65, 116, 140
Compo Beach, 26, 27, 38, 39, 48, 50, 63, 90, 115
Compo Fire Engine Company, 37
Compo Reading Club, 19
Conant, Homer, 35
Conn, Suzanne, 22, 56
Connecticut Agricultural College, 30
Connecticut Braille Association, 72, 101, 109, 115
Connecticut Children's Aid, 65
Connecticut Council of National Defense, 30
Connecticut Defense Council, 60
Connecticut State Federation of Women's Clubs, 26, 117
Conservation Committee, 29, 108, 113, 115
Consumer League of Connecticut, 33
Cool, Howard, 69
Cottell, Colonel John, 125
Couard, Alexander P., 35
Country Fair, 22, 38, 48, 56
Crawford, Mrs. John, 32, 43, 47
Crawford, Sara B., 51, 72, 146
Croarkin, Joan, 119
Crossman, Clarke, 98
Crossman, Clarke W., 95
Culp, Barbara, 13, 127, 155
Cuneo, John R., 116
Cuneo, Mrs. Myrtle, 103

Cuneo, Myrtle, 103, 110, 116, 119
Cunningham-Adams, Christy, 136
Curio Cottage, 136, 137
Curry, John Steuart, 35, 135, 136

D

Daniels, Gibson, 70
Darrow, Clarence, 54
Davis, Henry B., 39
Dead Man's Brook, 23, 110, 117
dental clinic, 17, 33, 42, 45, 64, 88, 90, 91, 95, 96, 97
Destino, Jo, 102, 119
Destino, Mrs. Jo, 102
Diamond, Nancy, 152
DiBlanda, Dr. H. A., 95
diphtheria, 42, 90, 93
Dirty Work at the Crossroads, 76
Dixie Lunch, 44
Dodd, Mrs. Allan, 53
Dolce, Dr. James A., 95
Dolge, Ruth, 76, 119
Donaher, Jim, 132
Dorne, Albert, 105
Dorr, Mrs., 66
Downtown Planning Advisors, 138
Dr. Ruland's Pond, 38
Drama Department, 59, 67, 75

E

Eager, Miss, 42, 43
Eckstein, Ernest, 116
Ecology Workshop, 107, 108
Edwards, Doug, 81
Elliot, Irwin, 87
Ely, Kerr, 39
Emergency Food Distribution Program, 17
Emergency Medical Services, 121, 138
Evaluation Committee, 102
Executive Board, 51, 53, 67, 77, 103

F

Fairfield Furniture store, 22
Fanning, Miss, 42, 90
Farrell, Diane, 136, 147
Fashion Show, 48, 49, 55, 56, 109
Fashionata, 106
Fashions by the Clock, 49
Feasting in Westport, 133
Festa Della Luna, 38
Fine Arts Theater, 37
Fine Arts Theatre, 57
First National Store, 61
Fisher, Betty, 123

Flower Carnival, 27
Food Closet, 115, 119, 122, 131, 140
Food Conservation Committee, 29
Food Pledge Card Campaign, 30
Forbidden Westport, 139
Forty-niners, 57
Franklin, John, 143
Frazer, Mrs.Aurora, 106
Free Milk, 98, 107
Freedman, Judith G., 146
Frey, Iris, 136
Friendly Town Project, 52
Fry, Mrs., 66
Fuller, Emily B., 38, 39, 78, 106
Fuller, Howell F., 92

G

G.I. Pin-Up Baby Contest, 57
Garden Department, 27, 70, 72, 88, 107, 108, 113,
    114, 115, 116, 117, 118, 119, 121, 126
Gault, 30, 132
General Federation of Women's Clubs, 59
General Putnam Inn, 49, 57
Gerontology Project, 84, 144
Gillespie Center, 139
Gillette, Dr., 92, 93
Gillette, Dr. C. W., 92, 93, 95
Girl Scouts, 49, 60, 83
Glynn, Thomas, 23
Godillot, Mrs. John F., 19, 30
Gold, Claire, 124
Goldhawk, Kathleen, 139
Good Neighbor Week, 84
Grace Salmon Park, 115
Grace, W. R., 121
Grahn John,, 105
Granger, Ellen, 155
Greaves, Russell, 114, 117
Greening of the Post Road, 9, 17, 112, 113, 114
Greens Farms School, 40, 49
Greenwich Birth-Control Clinic, 50
Grossman, Orin, 142

H

Hall-Brooke Sanitarium, 88
Hannes, Art, 81
Harley, Ruth, 117
Harper & Brothers, 66
Harrar, William, 77
Harris, Miss, 19, 20, 38, 43
Harris, Mrs. Channing, 19, 20
Hart, Barbara, 122
Headley, Nan, 116
Helping Hands Fund, 84
Heneage, Jackie, 118

Heneage, Jacqueline, 117
High Light, 33, 38
High Lights, 33
Home Defense Committee, 55, 59, 60
Home Economics Committee, 29
Hoskins, Ted, 121
Houdini, Mr. Harry, 30
Human Resources Services, 121, 122
Human Services, 122, 139
Hunt Club, 39
Hurlbutt School, 82

I

I Love Lucy, 81
Inn at National Hall, 22
International Circus, 48

J

J. B. Lowery, Jr., 34
Janson, Dr. C. William, 92
Jesup (Westport Public) Library, 21
JIB Productions, 152
John F. Godillot's place, 23
John Hancock Mutual Life Insurance Company, 73
Jones, William, 71
Junior Woman's Club, 51, 52, 54, 72, 79, 83
Junior Woman's League, 52, 72
Junior Years, 72

K

Kelly, Bea, 116
Kemper, Mr. C. B., 23
Kemper, Selectman, 24
Keneally, Mrs. Rita, 103
Keneally, Rita, 103, 110, 116, 119, 126
Kennedy David,, 121, 122
Kennedy, Ronnie, 126
Kimball, Jeanne, 123
Kinson, Ruth, 128, 135
Kiss, Mrs. Stephen, 111
Klein, Woody, 15
Knitters, 140
Knox, Velma, 75
Kolb, Ursula, 117
Korean War, 134

L

Ladies Home Journal, 28
Ladies, I Address You Privately, 75
LaGuardia, Mayor and Mrs., 49
Lambdin, Lillian, 65
Landers, Mrs., 20
Lea Ruegg Award Endowment Fund, 128

League of Women Voters, 33, 43, 86, 97
Lenfest, Lois, 118, 126
Let the Sun Shine In, 143
Levitt Pavilion, 116, 119
Levy, Barbara, 11, 142, 152, 153, 155
Lewis, Carol, 131
Lewis, F, E., 29
Leyden Rita,, 117
Library Trustees, 89
Lichtenauer, Mr., 37
Life magazine, 13, 24, 61, 62, 63, 64, 65, 70, 144
Little League baseball, 84
Loan Closet, 65, 72, 88, 98, 107, 109, 119, 140
Lodge, Francesca, 22
Loeser DeVries, Katinka, 124
Longshore Country Club, 82, 104, 106, 109
Look magazine, 79
Lue, Marjorie, 86
Lue, Ms., 79, 82, 86
Luscombe, Jo Fuchs, 146, 153, 155

M

MacCalmont, Dr. R., 97
Maddock, Mr., 27
Make a Difference Day, 140
Mahar, Susan, 15
Mansfield State Training School, 107
Mare, Bosco Al, 38
Marketing Corporation of America, 126
Marks, Morris, 68
Martinek, Winnie, 155
Masons of Westport, 140
Mayne, Marne, 116
McClinton, Thurman, 71
McGibbins, Jean, 126
McGilvray, Mrs., 102
McKiernan, Mona, 119
Me Pink 'at, 75
Medical Loan Closet, 140
Mercy Learning Center, 139, 142
Merritt, Mr., 44
Metropolitan Opera Guild, 84
Meyers, Mrs., 53
Michel, Mrs. Philip, 103
Mid-Fairfield Child Guidance Center, 107
Mid-Fairfield County Youth Museum, 107
Mid-Fairfield Hospice, 142
Millard, Mrs. Herbert, 45
Minuteman statue, 82
Mother Goose Lane, 48
Mulkley, Mrs. Chas., 20
Munce, Gerry, 13, 131
Munce, Howard, 13, 18, 153
Munson, Dr. William R., 60
Murgetroyd, Munroe, 76

N

Nash Pavilion, 38
Nash, Mr. E. C., 29
National Council of Garden Clubs, Inc., 114
National Council of Jewish Women, 88, 101
National Council of State Garden Clubs, 72
National Hall, 21, 22
Navaho Indians, 65
Nelbach, Philip E., 94
New England Patchwork Quilt, 85, 145
Newman, Frederick, 124
Newman, Paul, 37
Night Fall, 75
Nike missile site, 86
Nolan, Iris, 103
Norwalk Community College, 107
Norwalk Hospital, 49, 52, 65, 73, 78, 88, 91, 107, 119, 132, 140, 142
Norwalk Hospital School of Nursing, 73
Norwalk Hour, 58

O

O'Dwyer, Edward, 109
Ogden, Miss Anne, 71
Old Methodist Church, 22
Open Door Inn, 49
Operation Feed a Friend, 122
Oscar Howard, 39

P

P.M. Club, 52
Paine, Ruth, 102
Panish, Carol, 13, 128
Parcel Packing Mamas, 65
Parker, Emerson F., 94
Patch, Helen, 102
PATE (People and Their Environment), 108
Pearl Harbor, 55, 141, 142
Periwinkle Players, 49
Petropoulos, Eileen, 11, 13, 130, 131, 153
Phantasy Tableau, 37
Phil Donahue Show, 121
Philcox, Carla, 127
Pincavage, Tammy, 146, 155
Pink House, 46
Plasan, Jean, 134
Plasan, Lieutenant Howard, 134
polio vaccine tests, 94
Potts, Eve, 15
Prism '76, 116
Pritchard, Mrs. R., 91
Public Health Nurse, 34, 42
Public Works Department, 126
Purcell, Henry, 124

Q

Quinn, Julia Farnum, 106

R

Rainbow Carnival, 27
Rally 'Round the Flag, Boys, 37
Randolf, Bryan, 76
Ray, Eloise, 70, 112, 113, 114, 117, 118, 126
Ray, Mrs. Eloise, 70, 112
Raymond, Allen, 33
Real Estate Board, 43
Rehber, J. C., 39
Rell, Jodi, 138
Remarkable Book Shop, 131
Rempl, Esther Veronica, 92
Renaissance, 107
Ritar, Miss, 32
Roach, Kathy, 118
Roadside Conservation Association, 108, 113
Roadside Conservation Committee, 113, 115
roadside planting program, 89
Roles Women Play, 152
Rooney, Kay, 115
Rosenau, Mrs. Hazel, 95
RSVP, 140
Ruegg Grant, 136, 139
Ruegg, Lea, 128, 129, 139
Ruland, Dr., 37, 38
Rusk, Elaine, 113, 114

S

Salmon , Mrs. F. M., 19, 20
Salmon, Grace, 71, 115
Salmon, Mrs., 21, 23
Salmon, Mrs. F. M., 19, 20
Salute to Westport Artists, 57, 74
Saturday Evening Post, 18
Saugatuck Congregational Church, 39, 69, 70, 121
Saugatuck Elementary, 30, 61
Saugatuck mural, 132
Saugatuck Playground, 45
Saugatuck Station, 43
Save the Children, 107, 121
Save the Children Federation, 107
Schlaet , Mrs. Arnold, 19, 38
Schlaet, Mr. and Mrs. Arnold, 38
Schlaet, Mrs. Arnold, 19
Schnack , Mrs. Carol, 103
Scholarship Committee, 128
School Study Council, 89
Schuck, Gladys, 84, 86, 144
Schuck, Ms., 79, 81, 84, 85, 86, 144
Schweid, Carole, 152
Scopes, John T., 54

Seiden, William, 119
Senior Arts and Crafts Club, 85, 144, 145
Sevareid, Eric, 86
Seventh Annual Fair, 27
Shakespeare Students Program, 107
Shelton, Alice, 82
Sherry, John, 71
Sherwood Island, 50
Shops of New York Fair, 27
Show Boat and Plantation Party, 48
Silvermine College, 107
Sing Out Sweet Land, 76
Sioux Indians, 65
Sister Kenny Foundation, 94
Smith, Jean Slade, 133
Smith, Miss Helen, 38
Smith, Mrs. Wm. H., 19
Society of Friends, 71
Southern New England Telephone Company, 46
Speaks, Mrs., 86
Special War Services Committee, 60, 61
St. Luke's Church, 116
Standing Rules, 67, 102
Staples High School, 30, 38, 39, 74, 119, 121, 140
Staples, Mrs., 19, 20, 21, 23, 26, 28, 30
Staples, Mrs. William G., 20
State Convention of Federated Women's Clubs, 127
State Federation of Women's Clubs, 26, 59, 110, 117, 144
State Legislature, 51, 73, 146
State Senate, 146
Stewart, Margot, 66
Stewart, Martha, 123
Stowe, Harriet Beecher, 133
Student Aid Fund, 107
Sweeney, Johnny, 127
Sylander, Nat, 155

T

Takahashi, Gene, 141
Takahashi, Vi, 141
Taylor, William L., 37
Thayer Art Award, 74
Thayer, Mrs. John Adams, 74, 106
The Bulletin, 53, 123
The Connecticut Cook Book, 64
The Historical Society, 15, 18, 82
The Metropolitan Life Insurance Company, 73
The New Connecticut Cook Book, 65
The Old Westport Hotel, 48
The Town Crier of Westport, 22, 39
The Westport Garden Club, 113
The Witch, 76
The Woman's Town Improvement Association, 23, 35

Thomas, Miss C. E., 28, 42
Thomas, Miss L.V.M., 19
Thomas, Miss Lizzie, 23
Thomas, Norman, 54
Tiffin for Sniffin', 87
Toquet Hall, 20, 139
Town Crier, 13, 22, 29, 39, 56, 57, 58, 59, 77, 79,
    82, 86, 88, 93, 98, 99, 100, 103, 105, 148
Traffic Control and Regulation Committee, 89
Trafton, Mrs. George R., 70
Treadwell Henry R., 68
Trinity Church, 21, 71, 83
Tuberculosis Seals Campaign, 73

U

Underhill, George, 140
Unitarian Church of Fairfield County, 71
United Fund of Westport, 107
University of Bridgeport, 73

V

Van Hook Bean, Caroline, 35
Vanderbilt, Amy, 87
Victory Review of '42, 76
Village Mart, 38, 46
Visiting Homemaker Service, 17, 88, 101, 107
Visiting Nurse Committee, 42, 90

W

Wagner, Addie, 120
Wake, Hereward, 48, 53, 95
Wake, Mrs. Hereward, 48, 53
Wakeman , Selectmen Lewis B., 26
Wakeman, Florence A., 22
Wakeman, Mrs., 26
Wakeman, Mrs. Isaac, 19
War Savings Stamps, 57
Warnock, Helen, 67, 73
Warnock, Mrs. Helen, 67
Watts House, 68
Watts, Sidney, 68, 117
Wayside Stand Committee, 44
Weimann, Lillian, 126
Weiskopf, Bob, 81
Well Baby Conference, 44, 91
Well Child, 87, 98, 107
Westport Beautification Committee, 112, 113, 126
Westport Community Directory, 130, 131
Westport Community Theatre, 77, 78
Westport Country Playhouse, 76
Westport Emergency Unemployment Relief
    Committee, 46
Westport Garden Club, 72, 113, 115
Westport Hardware, 84

Westport Junior Woman's League, 52
Westport Loan Closet, 65
Westport Madrigal Singers, 123
Westport New England Motor Hotel, 105
Westport News, 13, 119, 131
Westport Players, 71, 75, 76, 77, 78, 79
Westport Public Library, 20, 116, 141
Westport Senior Center, 139
Westport Theatre Guild, 76
Westport Town Crier, 13, 29, 59, 79, 86, 98, 99,
    103, 148
Westport Unemployment Relief Committee, 46
Westport Warm-Up Fund, 140
Westport Weston Health District, 13, 90, 97, 134,
    139, 141
Westport Woman's Club, 1, 3, 4, 5, 11, 13, 17, 18,
    19, 21, 24, 44, 47, 50, 53, 54, 60, 61, 64, 65, 67,
    68, 70, 75, 77, 79, 82, 83, 84, 87, 90, 91, 92, 93,
    98, 99, 101, 103, 105, 106, 111, 113, 114, 115,
    116, 117, 118, 119, 120, 121, 125, 127, 128,
    130, 132, 133, 134, 136, 137, 138, 139, 141,
    142, 143, 144, 146, 148, 152, 153, 155
Westport Woman's Club Dental Clinic, 45
Westport Woman's Club Newsletter, 53
Westport Woman's Club Players, 75
Westport Woman's Exchange, Incorporated, 47
Westport Woman's Shop, Incorporated, 47
Westport Youth Ecology Workshop, 107
Westporter-Herald, 24, 37, 43, 48, 53, 56, 59, 77
Westportettes, 76
Wheeler, Miss Edith, 19, 31
Wheeler, Monica, 141
White House, 123
White Iris, 75
Wilcox, Miss, 29
Willis, Lorin W., 58
Willow Brook Cemetery, 30
Wilson, President, 30
Winifred Martinek, 138
Wintraub, Mrs., 86
Wisconsin Federation of Women's Clubs, 92
Woodsum, Betty, 122
Woodward, Joanne, 37
World War II, 43, 47, 55, 65, 67, 133, 152
WPA Marionette Unit, 49
Wright, George, 39, 83
WTIA, 9, 17, 20, 21, 23, 24, 25, 26, 27, 28, 29, 30,
    32, 33, 34, 35, 37, 38, 39, 40, 41, 42, 43, 44, 45,
    46, 47, 48, 49, 50, 51, 53, 90, 91, 99, 122, 146
WTIA News Letter, 53
WWC Enterprise Club, 122
WWC Venture investment group, 122

Y

Yankee Doodle Charity Ball, 80, 82

Yankee Doodle Fair, 11, 18, 21, 22, 35, 56, 57, 59, 62, 64, 67, 74, 77, 80, 81, 82, 85, 86, 88, 99, 104, 105, 118, 129, 133, 138, 144, 152
Yankee Doodle Goes to Paris, 81
Ye Village Mart, 38
YMCA, 33, 34, 35, 39, 48, 52, 54, 67, 74, 83, 91, 107, 119, 138, 139, 140
Young Woman's League, 102, 104, 113, 115, 117, 126, 146

Young Women's Beauty and Popularity Contest, 49
Youth Ending Hunger, 140

Z

Zoning Board of Appeals, 89, 104, 146
Zoning Commission, 89, 118